Performativity and Belonging

Edited by
Vikki Bell

SAGE Publications
London · Thousand Oaks · New Delhi

Performativity and Belonging is simultaneously published as Volume 16, Number 2 of *Theory, Culture & Society*

First published 1999

Published in association with *Theory, Culture & Society*, Nottingham Trent University

SAGE Publications Ltd
6 Bonhill Street
London EC2A 4PU

SAGE Publications Inc
2455 Teller Road
Thousand Oaks, California 91320

SAGE Publications India Pvt Ltd
32, M-Block Market
Greater Kailash - I
New Delhi 110 048

British Library Cataloguing in Publication data

A catalogue record for this book is available from the British Library

ISBN 0 7619 6522 X
ISBN 0 7619 6523 8 (pbk)

Library of Congress catalog record available

Typeset by Type Study, Scarborough, UK
Printed in Great Britain by The Alden Press, Oxford

Contents

Theory, Culture & Society

Theory, Culture & Society caters for the resurgence of interest in culture within contemporary social science and the humanities. Building on the heritage of classical social theory, the book series examines ways in which this tradition has been reshaped by a new generation of theorists. It also publishes theoretically informed analyses of everyday life, popular culture, and new intellectual movements.

THE TCS CENTRE
The Theory, Culture & Society book series, the journals *Theory, Culture & Society* and *Body & Society*, and related conference, seminar and postgraduate programmes operate from the TCS Centre at Nottingham Trent University. For further details of the TCS Centre's activities please contact:

Centre Administrator
The TCS Centre, Room 175
Faculty of Humanities
Nottingham Trent University
Clifton Lane, Nottingham, NG11 8NS, UK
e-mail: tcs@ntu.ac.uk
web: http//tcs@ntu.ac.uk

Recent volumes include:

Culture as Praxis
Zygmunt Bauman

Radical Converatism and the Future of Politics
Göran Dahl

Spaces of Culture
City, Nation, World
Mike Featherstone and Scott Lash

Love and Eroticism
edited by Mike Featherstone

Polar Inertia
Paul Virilio

Feminist Imagination
Vikki Bell

Performativity and Belonging

An Introduction

Vikki Bell

JUST AS Western philosophy has been unable to shake itself free of the question of Being, so sociology, with its shorter history, has retained its initial preoccupation with the dual questions of social stratification and social reproduction. The beauty of the term 'belonging' is that it affords those of us who were never sure which discipline we were meant to reside within, the opportunity to address both philosophical and sociological concerns. The term enables an escape from the long shadow cast by Heideggerian formulations without completely losing philosophical questions in the consideration of identity. The concern with dwelling in the world can take a more Foucauldian turn as part of the question: what makes us who we are within a particular social complex? How are we to understand ourselves, our politics, our desires and our passions as produced within this historical present? Thus, the concern is with the ways in which technologies, discursive deployments and power/knowledge networks produce the lines of allegiance and fracture in the various orders of things within which people and objects move. Moreover, as Elspeth Probyn has highlighted (1996), the term 'belonging' allows an affective dimension – not just be-ing, but longing. The yearning implied within the term will also concern us here: what is identity without that affect implied more strongly by the term identification? And how is identity related to theories of 'the subject' or the more sociological notion of 'agency'? Coupled with the term 'performativity', a term arising within linguistic theory but so powerfully introduced into feminist theory through the work of Judith Butler, one begins to see the premise from which this collection of articles arises. Reaching back to the philosophy of Nietzsche, but drawing explicitly on Foucault and linguistic theorists, Butler's thought problematizes the task of investigating belonging by turning attention to the production of selves as effects. The articles

■ *Theory, Culture & Society* 1999 (SAGE, London, Thousand Oaks and New Delhi),
Vol. 16(2): 1–10
[0263-2764(199904)16:2;1–10;008251]

presented here take as their shared ground, therefore, the need to locate oneself, philosophically and politically, within the radical critique of essentializing modes of thinking difference, investigating performativity in various contexts. An emphasis on performativity, however, does not mean an assumption of fluid, forever changing identities. Indeed, taking the temporal performative nature of identities as a theoretical premise means that more than ever, one needs to question how identities continue to be produced, embodied and performed, effectively, passionately and with social and political consequence. In the world, moreover, their appearance keeps the theorist on her toes; forms and modes of subjectivization, identity and affiliation are always complex, often suprising, and politically unpredictable.

Disrespecting disciplinary boundaries, this special issue ambitiously brings together philosophical, sociological and anthropological modes of questioning. My intention was to make explicit the links that are evident in certain approaches to these questions. I am pleased to present to the *Theory, Culture & Society* audience the conversations that have been going on within the work of scholars influenced by the work of both Judith Butler and Paul Gilroy, and to include here interviews with each of these writers, the latter in conversation with anthropologist Arjun Appadurai. While Butler and Gilroy have often met, their mutual respect and their resonances (as well as their differences) are left largely implicit in their written work. In the interview published here, Gilroy says, partly tongue-in-cheek and partly very seriously indeed, that there are reasons why he has not been 'out' about that resonance:

> There are tactical limits to how much I'm prepared to be 'out' about my own radically deconstructive aspirations, with regard to race and its observance, but at the same time, I draw great inspiration from the rigour with which she has made that argument about gender, bodies and discourse in ways that always open it to the question of race.

The hope is that by putting these theories 'to work' the persuasiveness of their shared theoretical directions will be illustrated and tested, without stretching the plausibility of the connections.

The conversation between Appadurai and Gilroy was recorded on the occasion of their first meeting, which I was delighted to facilitate (an occasion dreamed up a few months earlier by Arjun and myself as we walked in the Lake District in north-west England, having escaped for a few hours from a conference at Lancaster University). They were knowledgeable, of course, about each other's writing, and the suspicions I tried to pursue concerning the similarity of their concerns and impulses were I think borne out.

The theoretical perspectives and concepts raised by these articles and interviews are numerous and complex. I want to take several themes as routes into the collection in order to give some sense of the array and the sophistication of the interventions that the articles represent.

Belonging

Let us begin with this question of belonging. It is worth reiterating that the collection begins from a position which insists that one does not simply or ontologically 'belong' to the world or to any group within it. Belonging is an achievement at several levels of abstraction. Butler's work has been vastly influential in arguing that even the notion that one belongs to a sex or gender can be problematized, not merely because of cultural and historical variation, but because gender, to cut a long story short, is an effect performatively produced. Gender is, she has written, 'a construction that conceals its genesis, the tacit collective agreement to perform, produce and sustain discrete and polar genders as cultural fictions is obscured by the credibility of those productions' (1990: 140). Identity is the effect of performance, and not vice versa. The articles in this special issue push this form of argument further, exploring the ways in which forms of self-identification are sustained through complex incorporations. Anne-Marie Fortier, for example, suggests the effects of forms of performative belonging can work to maintain religious affect and community, in her case in relation to an Italian émigré community in London, such that the question of belonging necessarily incorporates the issue of how common histories, experiences and places are created, imagined and sustained. Similarly, the work of Jonathan and Daniel Boyarin, discussed here in my contribution, argues in relation to Judaism, that one's Judaism is not a constant in either an essential or performative sense, but that religious and ethnic affiliation can be performed to a greater or lesser extent depending on the context within which 'the Jew' finds him or herself. This is argued not just in the sense of the possibilities of 'passing' as or as not, but also in terms of the places and communities within which one finds oneself and the sense of belonging elicited or desired.

The 'citational' nature of identity, a term that has become more central in Butler's thought (see the interview presented here), is embraced in the work of the Boyarins and of Fortier in the sense that the performativity of belonging 'cites' the norms that constitute or make present the 'community' or group as such. The repetition, sometimes ritualistic repetition, of these normalized codes makes material the belongings they purport to simply describe. As Fortier writes, the highly ritualized movements that one performs in Catholic Mass are the incorporation of norms, a 'stylized repetition of acts' that cultivate the sign and the sense of belonging. Moreover, she suggests that since it was in her study, performed within a non-Catholic country, the communal activity of Mass produces an attachment of the group to the site of its performance. Through embodied movements, the citation operates to recall and reconnect with places elsewhere that, through those very movements, are re-membered; at the same time, a site of diasporic belonging is created.

Religious affiliation is also the subject of Chetan Bhatt's contribution here, that illustrates how highly negotiated the 'belonging' presented and promoted within contemporary Hinducentric movements is. Bhatt highlights the ways in which these movements are not conservative in the sense of making themselves 'of the past' – indeed, the belonging imagined within their discourse is one that will be enriched fully only in a future civilization – but they are examples of politicized counter-movements that incorporate within them highly problematic redeployed versions of history. In particular, the histories of people's movements across space, and the manner of their meeting with others becomes paramount, and as they inform contemporary Hindu nationalism, they necessarily append questions of blood, land, nature and culture. Bhatt traces the complexities of the citation and redeployment of cultural and historical fact by way of an example of how contemporary concepts of racism and anti-racism struggle to speak of a situation in which political discourse and movements assimilate aspects that radicals have applauded, such as anti-colonialism, alongside those that in their appeal to natural hierarchies, to notions of aryanism and racialized imagining of 'the future', resonate with proto-fascism.

Bhatt makes reference to Gilroy's work in his piece, in particular an article that appeared in *New Formations* (1996), that gives an insight into Gilroy's recent work on thinking the dangers of embracing certain counter-movements without questioning their parameters. The interview with Gilroy here, also suggests such a direction of thought, where he states that his sympathies were with the Fanon who wrote baldly, at the end of *Black Skin, White Masks*: 'I will not make myself a man of the past'; but more than this, that versions of political hope and imaginings of the future, need to be kept under careful scrutiny as well. He argues:

> . . . to be bound to the past is to become hostage to patterns of political work in our communities which are strongly authoritarian in character. I've become very interested in how a future-oriented political language can or cannot break with those patterns of authoritarian irrationalism. That has become a central issue for me. Black Protestantism has elements of looking forward, but it's always been limited by its eschatology, it always says 'well, you know those utopian questions are for another, better world'. When the authoritarian nationalism of the early twentieth century comes along and makes that utopian aspiration into a worldly thing – you have a very strange result – people like Garvey turning around and saying 'we were the first fascists, I was the one that Hitler and Mussolini stole their act from'. He goes to Germany in 1928 and looks at Hitler and says: 'I did this before'.

One of the impulses of Gilroy's work is to consider the boundaries of modes of identifications that are available in our contemporary present, and to enquire as to the histories of their constitutive assumptions around difference, leaving open the question as to whether these can be neatly divided into, say, the racist and the progressive. As a corollary, he highlights modes and sites of incorporation that produce but that may also redeploy those histories, a theme which is taken up by many of the authors in this issue.

Differences and their Differences

As Mariam Fraser reminds us, through Butler, the problem of difference is not that which emerges between one identity and another: we have to reach beyond a model that regards people and struggles as neatly divided. Difference is sustained and produced on several levels and in complex ways, both within and beyond 'the subject'. Butler speaks in the interview here about the way in which her work, initially focused most overtly on gender and sexuality, has begun to explicitly address questions of 'race' as well, and how she is reaching for an adequate way of theorizing and analysing these variables:

> For me, it's not so much a double consciousness – gender and race as the two axes, as if they're determined only in relation to one another, I think that's a mistake – but I think the unmarked character of the one very often becomes the condition of the articulation of the other. Then the question is how to sustain an analysis that is able to shift perspectives sequentially in such a way that no one reading is actually adequate without the other. I'm not sure that what I want is a synthetic reading. I think what I want is a set of sequential readings that expose the partiality of each constitutive reading.

The point is not to find similarities, but, she argues, is about how one site of the construction of difference can act as the 'unmarked background' for another. Gilroy and Bhatt both gesture in this direction when they note the masculinism of the forms of political and religious discourses under consideration; the patrilinearity of blood tropes, in which the mother disappears from the narrative, for example, can confer a racialized identity on the speaking subject that simultaneously operates to fashion a gendered mode of distinction. Fortier's analyses of the performativity of ethnic affiliation, moreover, emphasizes the ways in which the performance of gender is central to the reaffirmations that, especially on religious and ritualized occasions, are made within the community she spent time with. The first communion, for example, involves a highly gendered ritual. The procession in honour of Our Lady of Carmel, she argues, is a moment of cultural re-processing – that is, it is not simply an authentic continuation of an Italian tradition, but is a diasporic moment in which traditions are sites for multiple memories – that symbolically foregrounds women's bodies in the figure of the Madonna.

The argument presented in my contribution to the issue attempts to begin from such a stance, but also to consider how tempting it is to regard gender and ethnicity as operating as aspects of subjectivities that can be analysed according to the same cultural and psychic processes. Rather than assume that this is the case, I reach for some level of conceptual abstraction that would enable a conversation on such a topic to begin. The concepts I chose are mimesis and cultural survival. Both are terms that arise in Butler's work in relation to gender, but that I trace through the former to a history of thinking about anti-Semitism, in order to highlight the import of the latter. Drawing on the work of Jonathan Boyarin and Daniel Boyarin, I argue that thinking gender in terms of cultural survival brings it on to the terrain by which one might more commonly speak of 'non-hegemonic' identities, and that such a manoeuvre enables one to think about the simultaneity of ethnicity and gender difference without assuming their equivalence to operate at the level of psychic processes of incorporation.

Mariam Fraser's contribution complements such a line of enquiry insofar as she addresses the tendency to list identities or analytic variables of identity – 'race', gender, sexuality – and to regard the identity politics around each as discrete. Such a stance can no longer suffice. However, Fraser's article is concerned about attempts to create a theory of identity and a mode of politics that can operate universally. She builds her position by considering the differing temporal and spatial assumptions that operate when thinking of these terms in relation to embodiment, representation and political possibilities. In particular, sexuality has a fraught relationship to 'the visual' that queer politics variously attempts to disrupt, making what is assigned to invisibility and the temporal highly visible as a political strategy. Drawing on Bourdieu's notions of habitus and distinction, and their use in the work of Beverley Skeggs, Fraser's argument is that progressive politics in one arena may very well not translate to other 'variables' especially insofar as politically progressive strategies are thought to involve practices of resignification. Class identities are not invisible – they are also about representation – but, she argues, distinctions of class are unlikely to operate in the same way that queer politics argues sexuality does with regard to issues of recognition. While identities are certainly not discrete, political strategies may struggle to grapple with what recognition might mean for different positionalities.

Politics of Visuality

If Butler's work has been premised in part upon linguistic theories of performativity, it has become widely discussed in terms of the politics of visuality. In the interview presented here, Butler responds to the question about the relation between 'textual' and 'the visual' by arguing that her motivation would be to question the ease with which the visual is understood as 'read' in the same way that texts are within a Derridean framework. Referring to the video that captured police officers beating Rodney King in Los Angeles, she argues:

> I do think that there is a performativity to the gaze that is not simply the transposition of a textual model onto a visual one; that when we see Rodney King, when we see that video we are also reading and we are also constituting, and that the reading is a certain conjuring and a certain construction. How do we describe that? It seems to me that that is a modality of performativity, that it is racialization, that the kind of visual reading practice that goes into the viewing of the video is part of what I would mean by racialization, and part of what I would understand as the performativity of what it is 'to *race* something' or to be 'raced' by it. So I suppose that I'm interested in the modalities of performativity that take it out of its purely textualist context.

The notion of performativity has encouraged many writers within cultural studies in particular, to consider the constitutive moments and modes of identity. Placing Butler in the same realm as Fanon, especially the Fanon of 'Algeria Unveiled', for example, opens space for discussion of modes and schemas of categorization that operate to differentiate through visual cues. Much of Fanon's work was concerned with what Butler is terming racialization. The gaze is of course, in Butler as in Fanon, an historical deployment that does not innocently respond to visual cues, but that operates as part of a wider *dispositif* that enables cues to be seen as such. Lines of light and lines of knowledge that are entangled, as Deleuze (1992) has argued, with lines of power and subjectification. Vision and knowledge are not simply causally related, in either direction, but are entangled with each other in the schemas and complexities of specific histories and specific events.

Sara Ahmed's contribution begins by sounding a note of caution in response to those who might leave the analysis of visuality at the point at which 'subversions' take place. Celebration of moments of passing or 'crossing boundaries' may mistake analytic illumination for political triumph; whereas, she suggests, it is also the case that 'instability and crisis can enable the *stabilization* of relations of power'. Ahmed argues that although 'passing', as a phenomenon may prompt a questioning and may 'demonstrate that there are no absolute criteria for making decisions about identity, property and belonging', there is a need to ask: to what extent can that questioning be understood as proving something intrinsically transgressive in passing? Ahmed interrogates the notion of passing, arguing that passing is a mobile encounter that is not to be collapsed into a becoming, since the one does not become the other: there are two identities mobilized, 'that which one "already has" and the identity one takes on'. In each encounter, one has to consider how self identity and the passer's identification by others operate before and within the encounter, such that any discontinuity felt or 'revealed' is understood in relation to the movements that are taking place. Whether there is a transgressive moment depends in part, she suggests, on the reconfiguring of economies of identity. Ahmed's argument warns that moments of resignification can be incorporated into the economies of desire and privilege that existed prior to the encounter.

Fraser discusses some similar issues, but her concern with the politics of visuality focuses on the ways in which the 'making visible' of certain identities – especially in relation to gay liberation – may challenge a heterosexual matrix, while simultaneously fostering a form of complicity with a commercial capitalism that appeals to differentiated identities as 'markets'. Modes of making 'visible' have to be placed within a critical framework, that treats them as forms of knowledge-making, rather than as simply political uncoverings, which they may or may not be. The changing commercial conditions, as well as the changing technologies by which we 'see' difference, for example, change the task for comprehension and intervention. Gilroy considers new technologies an important aspect of the political present, to be linked with what one might call technologies of existence that inform self-knowledge as well as knowledge of 'others'. Thus one needs to be turned to:

> . . . the value of the technological intermediation of our corporeality and the possibility of turning some of that in a more political way to our understanding of embodied difference. . . . [This involves] thinking a lot about the history of optics and visuality, about the visualization and observation of racial difference over a long period of time.

Embodiment

Much of what I have drawn attention to thus far has concerned embodiment. The production of the effect of identity, the effect (and affect) of various modes of affiliation, is an embodied process. But how is the body implicated within the historical complex? How is the incorporation to be understood? Many of the articles mentioned are necessarily about embodiment, through considerations of mimesis or passing or specific sites of embodied practices, looking variously at the processes of incorporation, at questions of technologies and at the issues of the circumscribed or constitutive limitations of such processes. Through her focus on the terms 'subject, psyche, agency' Lois McNay addresses the issue of embodiment, in part by highlighting Butler's recent reference in *Excitable Speech* (1997) to Bourdieu's arguments. The performative power of the illocutionary act rests upon prior conventions such that the 'moment' of performativity is 'a condensed historicity', in Butler's words, that 'exceeds itself in past and future directions, an effect of past and future invocations that constitute and escape the instance of utterance'. McNay argues that the radical historicity of symbolic structures (again I think of Fanon here – 'and above all historicity' – describing the visual politics of the historico-epidermal schema) is central to understanding the notion of resignification in Butler. However, McNay argues, to seek out a notion of political agency at this point is to be disappointed. Converging with Ahmed's position, McNay questions resignification as inherently subversive, seeing in Butler an underestimation of the 'systematic recuperation of seemingly radical gestures'. Her direction is different from Ahmed's, as she turns to the theorization of the psyche in Butler in order to argue that it is there is a crucial possibility of non-correspondence between hegemonic norms and symbolic identification that although figured in predominantly negative terms of constraint in Butler, can equally be emphasized as creative. Both innovation and sedimentation, McNay argues, through Ricoeur, are important in the process of thinking these questions, and especially in reaching for her socio-theoretical aim, which is to able to speak of the performative constitution of the subject in relation to social and historical changes.

Moya Lloyd's contribution connects with McNay's concerns at several points, as she engages in a critical exploration of Butler's terms 'performance' and 'performativity'. The ambiguity in their distinction one from the other, an ambiguity that results from the fact that both are embodied renderings of the same norms and conventions, can be clarified, Lloyd argues, neither by reference to excess, seen as present in the first and absent in the second, nor by a form of voluntarism where the actor's will is understood as present in the first but absent in the second. Rejecting both these readings, Lloyd emphasizes that the crucial task for the political theorist is to critically attend to the 'space within which performance occurs, the others involved in or implicated by the production, and how they receive and interpret what they see'.

Probyn's contribution takes a rather different approach to the question of embodiment, posing her questions on the level of changing ethical regimes, and focusing on food, and food/sex, drawing the discussion of incorporation onto the site of 'corporeal ethics'. Decentring 'sex' as a privileged site of thinking identity and ethics, Probyn turns attention to notions of food preparation as forms of sociality, with all the connotations that that has in terms of differentiating between as well as bringing together, but more than this, as forms of self-constitutive ritually embodied practice. Food and cooking, as practices of the care of the self and sites of social connection, may offer a route to thinking corporeal ethics in such a way as to stress that the 'delicacy and restraint' that go into cookery might well serve well in thinking an ethics of existence.

Routes

Probyn's wider project has a strong Deleuzean debt, and here she evokes the image of the rhizome to introduce the sense in which she is following the idea of the 'alimentary-sexual' regime. The link she makes with Arjun Appadurai's writings on food emphasizes that although there is something that makes food universal, the routes that food moves through means that it cannot be understood without its specific cultural and social contexts. The Deleuze–Appadurai connection is one that he himself makes in the interview presented here, where he responds to a question about the shared concern he has with Gilroy in routes and movement by stressing the complexities of global movements and argues that understandings of spatiality have to be able to capture those complexities. The rhizome has been an important analogy here, conveying as it does an image of movement that can come to temporary rest in new places while maintaining ongoing connections elsewhere. Appadurai adds to it a second Deleuzean notion, that of the fold, to describe his notion of implosion, formulated in part as a reaction to the implicit celebration of globalization in theoretical work. He explains:

> [What] I'm struggling with especially in relation to the work I'm doing on violence – and I can only draw on geological ideas here – is the way that smaller spaces are being deformed by the pressure of the others. That pressure makes certain kinds of cities not just violent but violent in certain ways. What I want to talk about is the folding in of national violence, partition and so on, into cities in very concrete ways, so that that in Bombay, for example, one street 'is' Pakistan, to put it crudely. You have to see that both

> spaces and subjectivities have been deformed in the technical sense, because things are folded in, so the implosion idea is trying to catch that phenomenon without falling into the use of metaphors that are too biological or too organic . . . language is limited.

The concern that Appadurai expresses here is, again, one that is at its most broad, about 'belonging'. In the cultural anthropologist's hands, this is also necessarily a question that is tied to spatiality. Attention to where connections are, however rhizomatically, made, and attention to which spaces these connections are made 'across', in different ways unites several of the articles here. The spaces of the city that are resignified and reshaped according to the forms of belonging that are performed and permitted there is relevant to Fortier's concern with the constitution of diasporic belongings around certain sites, as it is to Fraser's concerns with the making visible of identities, such as the visibility that has been made more possible for gay people within certain areas and public spaces in cities, or to Bhatt's attention to political and religious discourses of belonging and their retracings of the relationship between belonging and place.

The articles collected here represent some of the most innovative directions of thought in this area. They represent a concern with advancing theoretical and conceptual issues through testing the integrity of their theoretical analyses around specific questions or examples. They represent a politics that is ever vigilant against those ways of posing the relation between places and identities that have too readily sought to locate that relation between people and places, or people and their bodies, or people and history. They represent the scholarship that is demanded in order to make an intervention in the modes of thought available for tackling the complexity of the appearance of identities in our contemporary world.

References

Butler, J. (1990) *Gender Trouble*. London: Routledge.

Butler, J. (1997) *Excitable Speech: A Politics of the Performative*. New York: Routledge.

Deleuze, G. (1992) 'What is a Dispositif?', in T. Armstrong (ed.) *Michel Foucault: Philosopher*. Hemel Hempstead: Harvester Wheatsheaf.

Fanon, F. (1986) *Black Skin, White Masks*. London: Pluto Press. (First published 1952.)

Fanon, F. (1989) 'Algeria Unveiled', in F. Fanon *Studies in a Dying Colonialism*. London: Earthscan.

Gilroy, P. (1996) 'Revolutionary Conservatism and the Tyrannies of Unanimism', *New Formations* 28: 65–84.

Probyn, E. (1996) *Outside Belongings*. London: Routledge.

Vikki Bell is a lecturer in the Department of Sociology, Goldsmiths College, University of London.

Revisiting Bodies and Pleasures

Judith Butler

I BELIEVE IT is fair to say that lesbian and gay studies in the United States became entranced with Foucault's writing in the late 1980s, which is not to say that his work did not profoundly affect lesbian and gay anthropology and social theory before that time. But it was interesting to see how various scholars were drawn to similar passages in Foucault at this historical juncture, and how they came to incorporate his views into positions that were at once academic and activist.

I remember that heady moment at the end of the first volume of *The History of Sexuality* (1978: 157) in which Foucault claims that 'the rallying point for the counterattack against the deployment of sexuality ought not to be sex-desire, but bodies and pleasures'. For a brief but impressive linguistic moment, Foucault held out the possibility that we might cease to think of sexuality as a specific attribute of sexed persons, that it could not be reducible to the question of his or her 'desire', and that overcoming the epistemic constraint that mandated thinking of sexuality as emanating from sexed persons in the form of desire might constitute an emancipation, as it were, beyond emancipation. The phrase, 'bodies and pleasures' held out the possibility of unmarked bodies, bodies that were no longer thought or experienced in terms of sexual difference, and pleasures that were diffuse, possibly nameless, intense and intensifying, pleasures that took the entire body as the surface and depth of its operation.

The turn from 'sex-desire' to 'bodies and pleasures' promised for some a turn away from both feminism and psychoanalysis, from the insistence that sexuality be thought of in terms of sexual difference, and that sexual difference be thought of as a function of oedipally induced differentiations, and that desire be understood as structured by lack in relation to a sexually differentiated Other. The insistence on sexual difference appeared to be

■ *Theory, Culture & Society* 1999 (SAGE, London, Thousand Oaks and New Delhi),
Vol. 16(2): 11–20
[0263-2764(199904)16:2;11–20;008252]

linked to a heterosexualizing of desire, especially when both the meaning and aim of desire are derived from a symbolic law of desire elevated to the status of the immutable.

It might make sense to return to this passage, and the ones in which Foucault takes his distance from it, in order to understand something of the allure of 'bodies and pleasures' as a conjectured site of resistance as well as the specific kinds of disappointments to which it invariably gives rise. And here I would suggest that the problem is not exclusively a speculative one, for a wide array of political disagreements can be understood in light of the controversies that have emerged over this proposed change in the conceptualization of sexuality.

'Sex-desire' designates a regulated connection between the concepts of sex and desire, an instance of which is the way in which sex has been understood causally to induce desire, and desire to follow from sex, and both to be in the service of a vast exemplification of heterosexual necessity at a level that crosses biology and culture. The nexus of 'sex-desire' has also meant, for Foucault, the production of a desire for sex, where sex is not simply a biological facticity or set of acts, but a category sedimented with ideality, a speculative ideal, as he puts it. Bodies and pleasures appear to overcome this problem of sex, and with that problem, sexual difference itself. For Foucault, the regulatory operation of 'sex' operates as an abstract monolith that regulates bodies in uniform ways; sexual difference is, of necessity, secondary to sex.

Foucault's insistence that we move to bodies and pleasures, and away from sex-desire, thus risks from the start an eradication of both sexual difference and homosexuality. Unwittingly, it constricts our vocabulary through a move that appears to prioritize bodies and pleasures over sex-desire, and which makes sexual difference and homosexuality strangely unspeakable within this frame. Same-sex desire: that belongs to the older regime; sexually differentiated desire; that, too, seems to belong to the regulatory apparatus from which we are asked to break. Toward the end of my remarks, I would like to suggest that I think this break might be read as a repudiation, and that the distance Foucault takes from this very break is one that begins to recognize the costs of separating an analysis of bodies and pleasures from the analysis of sex and desire. I want to suggest that the romance of this break, of this separation, continues to haunt lesbian and gay studies as well as the more recently inaugurated queer studies. The latter has sought to establish an autonomous methodology based on a set of acts and pleasures imagined as shared. Sometimes the opposition is between sex–desire, a strange conjunction that assumes the latter is in some way derived from the former, and bodies and pleasures, other times bodies and pleasures are understood as acts, and what they are opposed to is identity. Indeed, queer activist groups in the United States now have buttons with slogans on them: acts, not identities. Queer theorist Eve Sedgwick suggests that it may be that individuals who practice similar sorts of sex acts have more in common with one another than those who happen to be of the same gender. In this way, sexual alliances that cut across gender appear to take the place of gender-based solidarities, and queer activism, though indebted to feminism, takes its distance from feminism through this formulation that Foucault in part inspired.

Indeed, there are those who would claim, and have claimed, that sexuality can and ought to be thought in separation from the problem of gender, that sexuality is organized by powers that cannot be subsumed under the category of gender. And some of these also hold that gender is primarily to be understood as identity, but it may be important to note that there are positions within feminism that take gender to be an analytic category, indeed, a theoretical point of departure that assumes a differential relation of bodies to power, that are not, strictly speaking, reducible to identitarian positions. The effort to separate the study of sexuality from the study of gender has been an important move to make, even if it is finally untenable, considering those many feminist and anti-feminist frameworks that understood sexuality to be synonymous with heterosexual relations, and with forms of masculine domination that are said to pervade their structure. What Foucault permitted in many ways was a conceptualization of sexuality that insisted that the power with which it is coextensive is, in fact, not the same as relations of domination, and he also insisted that the point of departure for the thinking of sexuality was not the sexual subject, and certainly not a gendered subject, or any subject who enters into desire through the matrix of sexual difference, a thesis that pervades those forms of feminist theorizing inspired by the Lacanian premise, even sometimes those forms of feminist theory that are most vehemently opposed to Lacan.

How then are we to read the move from sex-desire to bodies and pleasures that constituted the theoretically and politically animating conclusion of the first volume of the *History of Sexuality*? And what do we make of the distance that Foucault ultimately takes from this most thrilling of his political rallying calls? Foucault's reference to bodies and pleasures comes to us as an injunction, an injunction to pleasure, a prescription, one that is clear about what we ought and ought not to do. ('The rallying point for the counterattack against the deployment of sexuality *ought not to be* sex-desire, *but* bodies and pleasures.') So there is a certain qualifying of pleasure that takes place through the very injunction to pursue it. And this seems to follow only because mandatory pleasure is not always the most pleasurable kind. 'Sex-desire' designates a nexus of concepts that have come to dominate thinking on sexuality, he tells us, one which he earlier characterizes not simply as the desire for sex, the desire to have it, but the desire for 'sex' as speculative currency, as the value-laden concept that holds out the promise of the unfolding of truth, the truth of our ostensible selves. Bodies and pleasures, on the other hand, seem to be introduced as a new nexus, one that stands for the possibility of resistance. That resistance, we all probably remember, is characterized in the following way:

> It is the agency of sex that we must break away from, if we aim – through a tactical reversal of the various mechanisms of sexuality – to counter the grips

> of power with the claims of bodies, pleasures, and knowledges, in their multiplicity and their possibility of resistance. (1978: 157)

The 'agency of sex' – is that from which we must break away, and yet, this breaking away, what kind of agency does it introduce in return? This act of aiming, tactically, to reverse the various mechanisms of sexuality, this agency is not to be understood as the agency of sex, nor is it, strictly speaking, the agency of sexuality, for, in the first instance, we are speaking of a speculative fiction, and in the second, a regulatory discourse. These bodies, these pleasures, where do they come from, and in what does their agency consist, if they are the agency that counters the regime of sex-desire? That regime supposes that one might explain desire through reference to sex, that one might figure desire as emanating magically from sex itself, its consummate moment, as it were. And that regime attributes agency to sex: sex initiates the unfolding of ourselves, remains the causal condition of desire, is linked to the disclosure and conferral of truth on the self that is displayed in and through our various thoughts and deeds. To counter this 'agency of sex' would mean to break the nexus of sex-desire, but from where does this break emerge? Is it a break that is performed by a subject? It is a break in the subject as it were, a certain constituting hiatus on which the subject nevertheless draws? And who are the 'we' who are said to exercise this agency against the agency of sex? What are the resources that counter the regulation of sexuality if they are not in some sense *derived* from the discursive resources of normative regulation? For Foucault, it sometimes appears that the body exceeds its discursive construction at every instant (*instance*), posing a limit to discursive construction precisely at the surface of its application. In other words, the body that is constructed according to the norms exercised in discourse is precisely that which is never fully captured by an instance of construction and which, therefore, remains as that which is yet to be constructed, an indefinite future of construction, as it were, that eludes every moment of its instantiation.

But in this view, is the body idealized as a principle of necessary and permanent disruption? Does it thereby become the name for something which eludes the control of every nomination, a name, as it were, that functions without the referential conceit of nominalism?

To counter the agency of sex, then, requires a different order of agency, but also a different register through which agency is to be thought. And if the body is in some sense the surface for any discursive inscription as well as the site of resistance to any such inscription, is it the body that constitutes the site of resistance, that different order of agency, one that counters the agency of sex. This move to bodies comes late in Foucault's text, and at first it appears to sit uneasily with the historical demand that he also makes in this text, namely, to enquire precisely, into how this 'agency of sex' was established, and at what cost.

The agency of sex emerges only through an action of suppression. What is excised, suppressed, rendered invisible such that the connection called 'sex-desire' can emerge as if it were a natural teleology? The cost if instating this notion of 'sex' is precisely bodies and pleasures: 'bodies and pleasures' is the name given for what is remaindered in the construction of 'sex-desire'. And although 'bodies and pleasures' is the name given for what is remaindered, it is a name that does not precisely construct what it names, for what it names is the limit to construction itself; what 'the body' names is a certain limit to nominalism.

At the level of sexuality as a regulatory discourse – for which 'sex' is the central, organizing idealization – the nexus of 'sex-desire' is a production, but a production with a cost. This production coincides with the advent of a certain late modernity, one which produces in its wake prefigurations of another order, one that counters the regime of sexuality and that we are tempted to call 'bodies and pleasures'. 'Bodies and pleasures' thus signals a time that might free us from our own time, a time before and/or beyond the regulatory power of sexuality, the postulated site of our resistance to modernity in its prolonged and persistent state. Foucault's text vacillates on the question: to which history do these bodies and pleasures belong? Do they belong to *a story of a prehistory* that modernity tells itself? Were there once bodies and pleasures that were subsequently suppressed by the regulatory discourse on sex? Or ought we to think of this early and pre-modern history as one that does not, chronologically speaking, precede this late modernity, but rather one which is *produced* as part of the narrative that a modernist tells him or herself? If this arcadian prehistory to the regulation of sex, in which disordered and non-gendered pleasures abound, is part of a modernist narrative, is it also characteristic of a modern narrative to tell the story of its own emergence through postulating an idealized pleasure as what that emergence has foreclosed. Is Foucault not affirmed as a modernist in his effort to circumscribe the time of sexuality as the time of modernity, and to imagine recourse to what precedes and exceeds the bounds of this regulatory regime? Is the pre-modern prior to modernity for Foucault, or is it perhaps modernity's utopian future, one imagined through the instrument of genealogy. 'Genealogy' is not the history of events, but the enquiry into the conditions of the emergence (*Entstehung*) of what is called history, a moment of emergence that is not finally distinguishable from fabrication, that produces on this occasion a time that is called the pre- and early modern.

But how does this historiographical excursus relate to the problem of the proposed break with 'sex-desire'? How is the pursuit of the tactical reversal of sexuality in the name of bodies and pleasures possible, and what might it consist in? This break is not supposed to be a simple dialectical opposition, one that is absorbed back into the terms that it opposes. On the contrary, we are to separate the two at all costs and find an agency that is *not* the agency of sex, find another order of agency such that we might inaugurate another time of sexuality, one that cannot be called 'sexuality' or can only be called 'sexuality' through a catachresis. This will be an order that breaks with the regulatory discourse that constrains the thinking of sexuality, one that calls for a new order of nomination or, indeed, a counter-nominative move within nomination. 'Bodies and pleasures' will be the names given to the time that inaugurates the break with the discursive regime of sexuality; these are bodies and pleasures that run counter to or disrupt the regulatory apparatus of sex-desire, of the teleological link between sex and desire, that break with the investment of truth in sex (which is not the same as affirming the falsity in sex, which would only be a further confirmation of the regime of truth in the service of which sex performs); these will be bodies and pleasures in an extra-moral sense.

But what are these bodies and pleasures, and can they be given an ontological determination? Do they exist somewhere, and can they receive the question of ontology? Is it that some set of bodies and pleasures, some organization of bodies and pleasures emerges to counter the regulatory production of sex, or is it rather that the force of this countering is what is called 'bodies and pleasures', and that bodies and pleasures are not the source of this resistance, but simply the name that that resistance assumes?

Foucault identifies bodies and pleasures as a 'rallying point', a strategic and discursive site, and he sets up an opposition that suggests that the difference between bodies and pleasures and the regime of sex that they oppose is an absolute one. 'The rallying point for the counterattack against the deployment of sexuality ought *not* to be sex-desire, *but* bodies and pleasures'. These are not moments in which Foucault is describing a history of sexuality in any ordinary sense; they are moments in which he seeks to inaugurate an authoritative historiography, one in which an historical period whose geography and whose geopolitical boundaries are rarely explained, is *produced* through *the staging* of a break.

How is the pre-modern to be understood in such a genealogical way? Is it produced through a line that is drawn, one in which an historiographical desire to delineate a regime and to inaugurate a break with a contemporary regime culminates precisely in the production of the pre-modern as an historical object? Some scholars within lesbian and gay studies understand the pre-modern to be precisely the historical occasion in which to trace the emergence of sexuality as regulatory regime, and hope to find there the historical and conceptual resources for resistance to the modern regime of sexuality. While there is no doubt that such historical work is crucial for showing how the specific mechanisms of 'sexuality' in the modern sense emerged, there remain some questions to ask about the romance with the pre-modern. When, for instance, we draw the line between the pre-modern and the modern, and identify the modern as the suppression of a prior resistance, or identify the pre-modern as the source of resistance for the future, do we not produce the pre-modern as the imaginary of the modern, as it were, the site of a lost pleasure, and do we not also imagine that the pre-modern will return to us as the postmodern, the break-up of the current regime, the proleptic return of a prior and lost happiness. Is resistance attributed to a time that we have in part produced by drawing the line between the modern and the pre-modern when and where we do?

Not sex-desire, *but* bodies and pleasures: a strange binarism at the end of a book that puts into question binary opposition at every turn. Thus, the very 'sex-desire' that bodies and pleasures are said to refute is precisely what bodies and pleasures must *presuppose*. And 'sex-desire' must be presupposed in order for 'bodies and pleasures' to become the name for an historical time of sexuality that is decisively beyond sexuality in its regulatory sense; is this anti-regulatory deployment of bodies and pleasure one whose very status as an opposition is dependent upon reinstating what it seeks to counter? At the moment in which Foucault writes the distinction between the pre-modern and the modern, to which time does he belong? The very act by which they are differentiated, the act of Foucault's writing itself, is it the pre-modern re-emerging as the sign of late modernity, is it the modern in its characteristic postulation of an abundant and lost past of pleasure? How are we to understand the time in which the option emerges, in which the binary itself is articulated and articulable? What is the time in which the option is written? How is the former time constituted precisely through the line that is drawn between the 'then' and the 'now', the line that is then regarded as a decisive break?

Finally, then, is there a way to make this line less distinct, and to ask whether the regime of 'sex-desire' does not *invariably* return in the midst of the new time of bodies and pleasures, or announce that it has never quite been overcome? Does the regime of 'sex-desire' not become the 'unconscious' of the time of bodies and pleasures, the spectre of alterity, that which the new time is not and, hence, that to which the new time is tied through the very labor of negation. Does it not follow that the de-shackling of regulatory sexuality through bodily pleasure turns out to be a shackling of a new and different order?

Foucault himself came to recognize that he could not sustain the exuberance for such a break with the past and I would suggest here that queer theory might similarly seek to reflect on its own exuberance. On the one hand, the intellectual force of the critique of heterosexual presumption in the thinking of bodies and sexuality has been enormously important and successful in the United States and England, and it has on occasion borrowed precisely a utopianism from Foucault that Foucault himself came to suspect. The possibility of imagining a life of bodies and pleasure beyond the regulatory force of 'sex' remains an ideal for many who work within queer theory, and yet it has been remarked of late, especially by Biddy Martin and others, that it is not precisely possible to free sexuality from gender even as it remains methodologically crucial to refuse the reduction of sexuality to gender. I join in speaking this cautionary note not because I believe that there is a law of 'sex' to which all Foucauldian permutations of power must finally succumb. I do not. But I do think that the fantasy of transcending gender in the name of sexuality, when and where it is installed as a heuristic for sexuality studies, keeps us from asking certain crucial questions about the formation of sexuality across genders, about how identification works within lesbian and gay sexuality, how it is implicated in heterosexual desire, how heterosexual identifications are implicated as well in homosexual desire, how normative gender does not always line up with normative sexuality, and how cross-gendered identification is not the aberration, but the very condition of gender norms. These questions all assume that there is no easy formula for understanding the relation between sexuality and gender, but they do suggest that a set of volatile and animating relations persist between them. Thus, it would make no sense to divide and oppose bodies and pleasure, on the one hand, and 'sex-desire' on the other, if the normativity of the latter continues to haunt and structure the lived modalities of the former. Indeed, if we claim that 'sex-desire' and the intense teleological and heterosexual normativity that it brings with it is vanquished by the politics based on the rallying point of 'bodies and pleasures', we deprive ourselves of the critical tools we need in order to read the trace and phantom of heteronormativity in the midst of our imagined transcendence. This is where a certain kind of exuberant utopianism works in the service of maintaining a compulsory ignorance, and where the break between the past and present keeps us from being able to see the trace of the past as it re-emerges in the very contours of an imagined future.

Recent objections from feminists who are not usually allied with one another to this utopian strain within queer studies is an interesting sign. I know that in some quarters of French intellectual life the very term 'feminism' is associated with an anti-intellectual ideology, and that it may be difficult to persuade those who hold such views that these debates, between queer studies and feminist studies, are intellectually sound, significant and even urgent. The critique that I offer is also part of the very intellectual enterprises that I engage. They revolve around the question of whether there can be an emancipatory vision after the critique of emancipation, and whether it can or ought to be based on a break with the past that compels the return of what it has repressed, and a disruption of that vision from precisely what it sought to repudiate. Within some quarters in queer studies, the future is imagined as a time in which pleasure is released from the regulatory power of sex, and where any and all talk of gender is always already dismissed through recourse to the anachronism of 'sex-desire'. Is it that one has broken with sex-desire in order to turn to pleasure, or is it rather that one wants to experience and re-experience the *pleasure of the break itself*, the pleasure of continually breaking with that past, a pleasure that can only be sustained if the past does not vanish through the act by which it is renounced. If then, symptomatically, the pleasure of this utopian break is derived in part from the disavowal and repudiation of sex and, correspondingly, with sexual difference, then feminism remains the disparaged object with which no queer theoretical pleasure can be sustained.

In the opening pages of the second volume of *The History of Sexuality* (1985: 5), we read of a different sort of break. Foucault breaks with this very moment of breakage outlined at the end of the first volume. He explains that he sought in the first volume to understand how sexuality, as an experience, came into being in the 19th century, one which he calls Western, but which we ought to redefine as more narrowly European at the end of the 19th century; he asks, how did this historically constituted experience become the basis on which individuals came to recognize themselves as subjects of a 'sexuality'?

In the second volume, he realizes that the question he sought to pose presupposes a prior question: how did the subject come to recognize him or herself as a subject of desire, how did becoming a subject take place only through becoming a subject of desire? Such questions lead Foucault to the realization that the subject of desire demanded a *separate history*, one that could not be told under the rubric of 'bodies and pleasures'. He could not ask, what is the experience of sexuality such that individuals come to recognize themselves as a subject of sexuality without *first* asking, what is the genealogy of the subject such that the subject might understand itself as a desiring being? Desire becomes the phenomenological register of sexuality, the one in which sexuality comes to appear to the subject as the subject's own. To deny the sphere of desire, or to call for its replacement, is precisely to eradicate the phenomenological ground of sexuality itself.

But this question of Foucault's raises another: who is it who is able to recognize him or herself as a subject of sexuality, and how are the means of recognition controlled, dispersed and regulated such that only a certain kind of subject is recognizable through them? One might very well be the bearer of a sexuality in such a way that one's very status as a subject is destroyed by bearing that sexuality. When and where did women come to see themselves as subjects of sexuality, when and if they did, and at what cost was such a recognition achieved? And is it clear that lesbians and gays now recognize themselves as a subject of sexuality, or is there not the possibility that one is so fully sexualized, so fully determined in and as the sexuality that one is, that no possibility for acquiring the status of a subject of sexuality exists? How do we understand the process of discursive construction or, indeed, of interpellation, that casts one as a sexual being as the precondition of becoming a subject of sexuality, one whose subject-status initiates agency into the chain of subjection?

I would suggest that these questions concerning the differential distribution of the means of sexual recognition are questions that remain to be posed, and that these questions suggest that we have not left the realm of 'sex-desire' even as we may well develop a critical relation to it. To the extent that sexuality remains structured by norms that presume natural heterosexual teleology, they also persist in posing the problem of asymmetrical gender norms, and so keep the problem of the gender differential central to the analysis of sexuality and power, a better coupling, I would suggest, than bodies and pleasures. If the subject who recognizes him or herself is a sexed subject, it does not follow that 'sex' is always and only a moment of naturalization and idealization, a regime that governs men and women in the same way throughout time. By claiming that the subject of desire is sexed, I do not mean that the subject is simply 'marked' by sex, or sexed from the start, but, rather, to insist that this sexing is part of the very temporality of sexual regulation; that to become a woman or a man takes time, and that the process is never fully complete, since no teleology is ever finally realized. And it means, within the normative heterosexual frame, to submit to an operation of power that works through control and constraint, but where that constraint is also productive, crafting sexuality and desire, and excessive, confounding the very norms by which it is enabled.

In this sense, power, understood as productive, is productive only on the condition of prior constraint, its juridical form, and so whatever form that power takes in relation to sexuality has to be thought in relation to the constraining power by which it is *enabled*. This is, by the way, one place where the convergence of the Foucauldian and psychoanalysis becomes possible to think, despite the allergic reactions that each camp has toward the other. Only on the condition of a prior constraint is sex instituted and established over time, which is why sex is not a given, although it most often appears to be.

To cite the cadence of Foucault, then, I offer a final word of caution: if we think we might say no to sex and desire in the rush to embrace bodies and pleasures, or say no to modernity and its regulatory shackles in an effort to rehabilitate a utopia of the past, then I think we miss the chance to understand how the analysis of sexuality is pervasively structured by sexual difference. We also lose the chance to understand how pleasures are staged through the workings of a desire that is the desire of a subject, and how a subject is both constituted by power and a nodal point in the rearticulation and transformation of power. The desire of the subject is not transparent: it does not give us the truth of the self from which it emerges. Its opacity, however, is the mark of the constraints by which our pleasures are produced, afflicted, enhanced and proliferated. And pleasure might then be understood once again in relation to pain, and both in relation to desire and the problem of recognition; in other words, a return to Spinoza that cautions against moving into any future without a certain ineradicable sense of ambivalence.

References

Foucault, Michel (1978) *The History of Sexuality: Volume I, An Introduction*. New York: Random House.

Foucault, Michel (1985) *The Use of Pleasure: The History of Sexuality, Volume II*, trans. R. Hurley. New York: Pantheon.

Sedgwick, Eve Kosofsky (1991) *Epistemology of the Closet*. New York: Routledge.

Judith Butler is Maxine Elliot Professor in the Departments of Rhetoric and Comparative Literature at the University of California at Berkeley. She is the author of *Subjects of Desire* (Columbia University Press, 1987), *Gender Trouble* (Routledge, 1990), *Bodies That Matter* (Routledge, 1993), *The Psychic Life of Power* (Stanford University Press, 1997), *Excitable Speech* (Routledge, 1997), as well as numerous articles and contributions on philosophy, feminist and queer theory. She is currently finishing a manuscript on Antigone and the politics of kinship.

Historical Memory, Global Movements and Violence
Paul Gilroy and Arjun Appadurai in Conversation

Vikki Bell

THIS INTERVIEW was conducted in order to give an opportunity for these two thinkers, who stem from different disciplines, but whose work meets at certain crucial junctures, to present a discussion to a wider audience about the themes and issues that were currently motivating them in their work. Paul Gilroy's work is well known as a central reference point within the contemporary analysis of 'race' and racism. At its most broad, he has a reputation for thinking throughout his writings about the historical constitution of race and the mobility of forms of racism over time and space. Arjun Appadurai's work emanates from the discipline of anthropology, and he has a specific and on-going interest in South East Asia Studies. He has been influential in the exploration of new modes of conceptualizing the remit and processes of forming anthropological knowledge. While both authors share certain key concerns, their interconnections are not explicit in their writings. This interview, conducted in London during Arjun Appadurai's visit in 1997, was an opportunity to bring these two authors together to discuss the themes and connections which they are both exploring in different ways, but in ways that have similar theoretical and political impulses. In particular, I wanted to ask them about the themes that I think animate the critical edge of cultural studies: the politics of memory, the theorization of movement and new conceptualizations of spatiality, the critique of authenticity and modes of theorizing embodiment,

■ *Theory, Culture & Society* 1999 (SAGE, London, Thousand Oaks and New Delhi), Vol. 16(2): 21–40
[0263-2764(199904)16:2;21–40;008253]

and concurrent directions in their present work, especially around the notions of extreme actions, of war and violence.

VB: I wanted to ask first of all as an initial question about the fact that both of you have written within the context of 'home' disciplines – anthropology in your case, Arjun, and sociology or cultural studies in yours, Paul – but both of you I think have been very critical of the traditions that you have inherited. In your case, Arjun, I was interested in the way in which the very concept of place in anthropology is something that you have written about, critiquing the tendency for certain places to become 'show cases' for certain ideas, as well as critiquing concepts of temporality that anthropology works with. Paul, in your case, I think you've been critical of sociological modes of categorization, particularly in relation to 'race' as an explanatory concept, and of central sociological ideas of method. So, what I wanted to ask you both is how you feel your work resides within those disciplines, how you see it critiquing whilst remaining within them, and how you see your audience responding to your work?

PG: It seems to me that sociology lacks its own version of the very interesting self-critical conversation that was forced on anthropology for obvious reasons at a much earlier point. Although sociology has been kind to me, much of the time I don't think of sociologists as being people who would be interested in the things that I have wanted to talk and write about. This seems borne out by the fact that I haven't had a lot of sociological responses to what I've done. I suppose what I'm most interested in doing is prompting a disciplinary crisis in sociological thinking, something like the reflexivity that followed the impact of Talal Asad's work in anthropology some years ago now and has been consolidated by writers like James Clifford, Renato Rosaldo and the rest. These are people who applied the tools of literary criticism to anthropological writings, who put anthropology back into colonial history and who saw the production of anthropological knowledge in the context of a wider system of political and cultural relations in which the academy negotiated the needs and priorities of governments, artists and intermediate institutions like museums. I'm interested in feeding a disciplinary crisis like that. I think there are all sorts of reasons why sociologists in this country in particular haven't really been comfortable in confronting the imperial and colonial dynamics that have constituted and refined their discipline, or even been prepared, with quite the same enthusiasm as literary scholars have, to seek for the kind of repressions and elisions and lapses of memory that have characterized the configuration of sociological modernity. So I wanted to provoke some of that, and that is an ongoing project.

I know that one of the issues you want to raise later on is the current state of the sociology of globalization. That seems a good example of how partial and selective – on some occasions almost trivial – sociological writing has been. Once the light does come on, the problems that appear get reduced to the simplest and most easily assimilable forms: markets, states, cultures are essentially what they always were. The concepts aren't being re-worked, re-thought. People want to put up a signal that says 'business as usual'. It's that business as usual signal that I want to interrupt.

AA: In my own case, the relationship to anthropology is slightly more deliberate perhaps. First of all I should say that I teach in the US context, which is peculiar. Anthropology comes not so much with the 'business as usual' sign, but with a crisis bulb on all the time. So the problem becomes 'What's the crisis, what's the *real* crisis?' whether it's the reflexivity business, or the impact of Said, or the impact of cultural studies. Everything precipitates crisis. Moreover, because the space of anthropology in the US simultaneously hosts issues in natural science as well as issues which are entirely sociological, you inevitably have a kind of crowding and have times when consensus is weak but departmental and university institutional realities force people to have a common position. The question is the relationship of these crises, some of which are institutional, not trivial but not exactly conceptual, and others of which are conceptual and which may be interesting, historical and productive. So my interest has been to try to use the things I have engaged with over time – India first of all and most of all – as well as other concerns such as globalization and colonialism – to try to identify which of those crises are the productive and interesting ones. My subjects have emerged at that intersection between the locations I know best and to which I'm committed, and what I imagine to be this panoply of crises of which some are more consequential than others. I do think it's been helpful to have some of idea of a disciplinary history or a canon of some kind. I'm fully aware that these vary depending where you are, but in my location there is a history of a field, and there is a picture of its best actors, and its distinctions and so on. All of these are contestable, of course, but it's identifying, opening up and resisting those narratives that has been helpful for me. I can imagine it would be very different if I were in sociology or psychology, I might have a more loose relationship like that which I sense from Paul, but in the case of anthropology, it has been helpful for me to be able to say, 'Well you think this is the issue ... but it's really this.'

PG: Let me clarify lest I sound too ungenerous to the very tolerant responses of some sociologists to the things I've said. I wasn't trained as a sociologist and I didn't think of myself as a sociologist until I became a sort of domesticated foe of sociology. It was through trying to critique the complicity of too much sociological thinking that reduced critical political questions to policy questions and showing where academic sociology was entirely comfortable with reproducing, for example, a number of pathological assumptions about the way that black culture and social life were constructed, that I got drawn on to sociological ground. I would have to admit that people have been very tolerant of my interventions in their field, perhaps too tolerant. I think it is very different from anthropology. It's important given that the audience for this conversation is wider, to mark out some of the very specific problems that mark the development of *British* sociology, because I think Arjun is right to point to the different character of sociology in the American academy where the line between political science and sociology is sometimes the most difficult one to draw and a great deal of energy is invested in that, and where questions of social policy have a different flavour altogether because of the absence of the Welfare State institutions that have always guided a great deal of sociological thinking in this country. So I'd want to be careful to confine what I say about sociology to a particular moment. And yet I think the reification of race and culture is still very strong, in spite of the easy victories that were achieved, not by me but by others who shared the critique of sociological rationality around race. I think the easy resort to reified notions of race and culture is still to be found in the present. The complex history and experience of migrants and settlers to this country is still represented continually in pathological terms. So there is still an endless amount of that work to be done. And what causes me a great deal of sadness is to see the failure of the generational group to which I belonged as a graduate student. We have not been able to reproduce ourselves in the academy, and there are all kinds of reasons for that, but I'd say that teaching at Goldsmiths, the brightest and the cleverest black students who I would have thought would have a great deal to contribute to the intellectual life of the discipline aren't always open to that possibility. That is a very interesting thing, to see that that interruption hasn't been sustained.

VB: You were saying Arjun that sometimes you took the debates within anthropology as a way to bring people back, as it were, to anthropology; that you used the interventions from other disciplines and the sense of perpetual 'crises' to bring the focus back on to the question 'What is important about what we anthropologists, specifically, are doing?' I thought that the piece that you wrote about the past, this is quite an old piece of yours now, but it's one I really like – 'The Past as a Scarce Resource' in the journal *Man* – is a piece where you do just that, where you seem to be arguing against an emerging attachment to the idea that the past is infinitely malleable, by addressing it in relation to your own area of anthropological knowledge. If I could use that as a way to pose my second question, I wanted to ask you both about ideas of the past, or more specifically, about the place of memory, remembering the past, because I think it is a question that you both work upon. I wondered, Arjun, if you would say something about how remembering is performed? And Paul, for you also, memory is a very strong theme in *The Black Atlantic*, the remembering through music, the remembering of slavery, the re-creation of traditions and so on. Could you say something about how that performing of memory features in your work and why you see it as important?

AA: The first thing to say is that the essay that you refer to was a part of a conversation that I now would see as an excessively formalist conversation, not that I think that its main idea is a bad idea, but it was a very formal piece, innocent of much of what we learnt later about memory, about even indeed the invention of traditions. Its main point was to argue with anthropologists of a certain type – a functionalist type who had a certain interpretation of Malinowski – who argued that somehow myth and thus anything else of that type was just a thing people functionally produced in relation to contemporary interests. It was an argument good in its politics but bad because it suggested that this just happened somehow and that anything was possible. I argued that anything was not possible. I would write that argument very differently now, and at the time there was much less for me to work with on memory or even on temporality – no LeFevbre, for example – so it was a confined literature. Nevertheless, I think your intuition that it does have to do with later concerns of mine, ones that are connected to the politics of pastness, broadly, is correct. I think it allows me now, in my current work, to think more about the political economy of the relationship between nationalism, remembering and forgetting. Forgetting is a much more recent problem in cultural studies – the issues of erasure and removal – but in India for example, Veena Das's work has shown how much had to be forgotten for Sikhs to be seen as enemies of Hinduism and as instruments tied up with Islam. They were in fact historically the friends of Hinduism and directed against Islam, but on all sides that story has changed, and extremely fast, so the economy of forgetting is even more striking here than the economy of remembering. One interesting question that I think many people will have to engage with is how to connect the idea that under different cultural or ideological regimes the past has different shapes which ordinary people produce, as historians, etc., with both the notion of different temporalities and the questions of memory and forgetting. If those things can be co-configured somehow I think we would come up with better understandings of the ways in which history is mobilized, whether in everyday life or elsewhere. So let me leave it at that. I have not yet taken that up myself and I'm interested in it, and I'm interested to hear what Paul is going to say about it.

PG: The political economy of remembering and forgetting and the place of nationalist thinking in its circuits is something that was raised very very sharply and early here. This was done not only by a kind of black movement but also by a number of white critics of the morbidity of English nationalism. I'm thinking particularly here of my friend Patrick Wright who had taken on rather more than he bargained for when he published his influential and important book *On Living in an Old Country*. The conversations that I had with him around that time were very important in focusing my attention on the mutability of history, memory, heritage and place. So the political currency of the assault on memory – on *official* memory – and official patterns of commemoration around national heritage which have flourished all around us in the period since, is something that had an immediate significance. I would also want to say that my own thinking, and this is something that I have been much more comfortable with in writing the book that I'm writing at the moment, was very much shaped by reading those closing pages of Fanon's *Black Skin, White Masks* when I was an undergraduate, those pages where Fanon is turning his eye simultaneously both against white supremacy and its black nationalist shadows on the other, and he's saying, we are not bound to the past. He is giving his version of revolutionary palingenesis, a sort of Sorelian aspiration toward the production of a new man, a new humanity, and that stages a very interesting political conflict that I've been trying to see through. I want to endorse his argument, to the extent that it says 'the authoritarian nationalist voices in my own political community have to forget certain things in order to instantiate a particular pattern of official memory from which I disengage'. He is saying that we must find opportunities to be more creative, to be more future-oriented than their love affair with the past allows us to be. Embracing that orientation towards the future and looking at the syncopated temporalities of the dissonant modernity he's conjuring up through his critique of Western philosophical traditions or his uncomfortably ambivalent relationship to the anti-fascist struggle in Europe (Fanon had returned from fighting the Germans when he's thinking about this) means we have to be more creative, because to be bound to the past is to become hostage to patterns of political work in our communities which are strongly authoritarian in character. I've become very interested in how a future-oriented political language can or cannot break with those patterns of authoritarian irrationalism. That has become a central issue for me. Black Protestantism has elements of looking forward, but it's always been limited by its eschatology, it always says 'well, you know those utopian questions are for another, better world'. When the authoritarian nationalism of the early 20th century comes along and makes that utopian aspiration into a worldly thing – you have a very strange result – with people like Garvey turning around and saying 'we were the first fascists, I was the one that Hitler and Mussolini stole their act from.' He goes to Germany in 1928 and looks at Hitler and says 'I did this before.'

AA: Just a small comment. I've been hinting, in some small way here and there, especially in the recent book *Modernity at Large*, at something that partly comes to me out of Stuart Hall. That is, the idea that identity, especially that form of identity that we still for lack of a better word, rightly I think, call ethnic, has somehow, not only analytically but historically, become in the etymological sense, a *project*. That is to say, one can see ethnic identity as projected, so that it has a future, without entirely giving up the idea that it is produced by histories that are marked, and that identities are particular, and cannot therefore be completely expansive. Moreover, if one looks at identity movements, and sees them as *projects* that have futures, then one has a completely different sense, first, of the question of the past in relation to those projects and second, to put it simply, of who can join. This allows a kind of openness to inclusion in the project, although not necessarily to inclusion in the history. One does not have to say that the history is open and unmarked and anything might have happened, but at the same time, while resisting that, one can open the project up, so that the project can tie up with other projects, and so on. That becomes politically really interesting.

PG: Well, I was thinking about that essay that you wrote about your father's Indian nationalism and struggle to make the history of the nationalist movement in India complex enough to accommodate his formation. That was one thing that came to mind. There are other questions of memory that we haven't addressed, like what happens when commemoration becomes work, and the very formal ways that the diaspora intercultural has for staging those trials of identity, often ritualized in quite extended ways.

VB: Could I ask, Arjun, whether you could take up that lead in relation to the ideas of movement and authenticity as they figure in your work? There's a real relationship between what Paul has just been saying about ideas of diaspora, but also earlier about ideas of mimicry and borrowing, that cluster around the notion of looking for authenticity and creating authenticity, and what you have written yourself in relation to active consumption as involving the question of authenticity and the creation of 'taste'. I would like to bring together what you say about objects in some parts of your work, and what Paul is saying in his about the creation of subjectivities, and, if you like, to take away the distance between them.

AA: To open this, I would just say that in *The Social Life of Things* I tried in my own essay and in a sense in the whole collection, to milk very hard the conceit that we need to forget people for a moment and think of things themselves, as in some kind of way having a *life*. And then we read out from that to the human contexts, agencies, forms, socialities. It has its merits, but clearly it's a weak way of capturing the other moment, which is the consumption moment or the subject moment, to which it gives one only the most indirect clues. In the work I did a little bit later, on duration and consumption, I tried to think more of what the work of imagination *is*, and to see consumption as a privileged site for looking at the imagination, not as a romantic heroic individual practice but as a social practice which is often quite tedious and difficult in all the ways that capitalist labour is, and not metaphorically, but actually. But still, I know that what I don't have, and would like to think about more, is a more complex idea of subject, which brings us back to the disciplinary question. I, and others, sometimes prefer the default idea – something like 'person' – which is anthropologically important, as it is a constant reminder that there are other constitutions of agency, in say, the Pacific. So that word is important for that reason, but when used it may appear to be markedly in preference to (which it is not), say, 'subject' in the sense that comes out of Hegel. So right now, in my current work, one of my struggles, is to determine whether there is a way to keep that slightly dated sense of self or person, as a culturally constituted thing, which is not natural, which is not everywhere the same, etc. but still bring it into some configuration with the Hegelian idea of subjectivity. I'd love to hear what Paul has to say on this.

PG: I think you're being unduly modest about some of the formulations that came out of that work – *The Social Life of Things* – because what that work set in train for me was a set of questions about the critical role of particular objects, and particular technologies, in mediating precisely that relationship between subjectivities and political life. Not wanting to give any hostages to the notion of a phenomenology of bodily experience, I suppose I've got very much drawn into thinking about the technological processes, objects and systems that mediate our relationship to the constitution of racialized bodies. I've been trying to sketch that unfolding through a number of particular phases: the birth of political anatomy, the advent of microscopy, different notions of the miniature, assumptions about the body and its visual cultures as they move into the phase that we're in now. Here we encounter a number of technologies that operate on scales beneath the microscopic – nanotechnologies – and see the end of those to do with the impact of the play of light on the body. This change offers us an opportunity to reflect upon ourselves, our humanity and our species life in a very different way. Yesterday as I was going out to the library, I was looking at the Stroke Association billboards. The first one showed one of those brain scans done by PET. It superimposes a beautifully coloured image in the way that only computer images do, of a person's brain who has had a stroke, over a sheet of cracked glass, and it says 'every twenty seconds a stroke shatters somebody's brain'. Now the new one has a black doctor sitting at a computer screen looking at the rainbow PET image of the brain, and it says something else about strokes as a species hazard. My particular fantasy about what was going on in the minds of the people who made that particular campaign was confirmed by the fact that that they troubled to put a black doctor – albeit a male, but never mind – sitting at that screen. It confirms my own sense of the value of the technological intermediation of our corporeality and the possibility of turning some of that in a more political way to our understanding of embodied difference. That's a very minimal example of a much longer argument which involves thinking a lot about the history of optics and visuality, about the visualization and observation of racial difference over a long period of time. That's something that seems to me very important and that's only one way of trying to reconcile the problems that you offered, and it is something that I've drawn very directly from.

AA: Yes, that is interesting because this mediation question certainly is a key one. In some of the work that I'm trying to do now, I have an idea that in thinking about things like mass mediation you can deploy some idea about subjectivity and some idea about embodied experience while keeping on board this anthropological idea that persons are constituted fundamentally differently, which is a good heuristic position even if in the end it turns out not quite right. It's a good thing to imagine that in the first instance somebody you meet when doing field work in New Guinea doesn't come out of the same regime of things as oneself.

I'm working now on violence, and I won't say more about it except that for the first time ever, I have to think very hard about embodiment and this business of technologies allowing you to 'see in' and so on. I'm keenly interested in enriching my hold on the 'body question' which has a classical status in anthropology. The talk I'm about to give at the LSE is called 'Purity and Certainty: Towards an Anthropology of Ethnic Cleansing', and it is centrally about the body question which I have written about before but have never had to think so hard about.

PG: Bringing this back into the context of the argument about memory, it is also important to remember that we have a strong suit, where we can show how unreliable, how intermittent, how partial, how selective incorporated memory is, how incorporated memory lacks the kind of authority that we want to invest in it. There are counter-histories of modernity that we may want to summon up, whether it's a carefully reconfigured reading of the material that the slaves themselves produced, or a look at situations of extremity where there is the failure of embodied memory, a renunciation of memory's authority, something that comes out very strongly in Primo Levi's work about his own memory and the tricks it has played upon him for example.

VB: There are two questions which follow on really nicely from that, and I'll mention them both so you can see my points of connection, Paul. First, that idea of the failure of embodied memory makes me want to leap to ask about the relationship that both of your work might have to ideas of performativity, as they figure in Judith Butler's work, and those moments of disjuncture. Let me save that line of questioning, and take you into it again later. Instead, let me pose the second question which concerns the issue of globalization, and maybe what you have both been saying about technology would be one way to lead into that. I know that you've thought about technology in terms of the Internet and diaspora, in relation to the production of locality, Arjun, and issues of reterritorialization. But I feel that you are both quite critical of the sociology of globalization in some versions, and so I wondered if you would take me through why there is that implicit critique, and what you do with the term?

PG: I read the collection *The Social Life of Things* around the time that I discovered John Ellis's (1976) extraordinary little book on the history of the machine gun as a piece of technology. That might be a way to think about why I felt an unease about the way in which formulations of globalization were offered, as if to resolve prematurely a number of important things that anthropologists were prepared to delve into. So I'm uncomfortable with the periodization of those notions, and I'm uncomfortable because the history of the diaspora that interests me is never acknowledged in the narratives that culminate in the theory of globalization. Here we are in London. The work of Peter Linebaugh, a social historian, always reminds me that London was around prior to the instantiation of either the nation or the state, you know, and its important to reflect upon the legacies of those kinds of histories. Of course, sociologists have a good alibi for setting those problems aside, and obviously if one wants to be a sociologist in that sense one has to respect it, but I suppose that's another way of conjuring up my own ambivalence about what one loses when one isn't prepared to take a longer look. When I was a school boy doing my A-level history, we were doing the expansion of Europe, and I remember thinking at that time (I suppose I was 16 or 17) about what it meant for these Spanish and Portuguese navigators to stand in the prow of their boats bellowing the papal requirement into the darkness 3 miles off the shore. I've never seen any of this even hinted at in the constitution of globalization, and it's not because the historical materials aren't freely available. They have been for a long time, and so to be absolutely basically crude I think this is often a truncated and trivialized way of showing that the same cosy assumptions and developmental stories that sociologists tell themselves about the identification of modernity with the formation of European nation states can just persist happily and undisturbed. There are a number of very heavily routinized ways of answering that critique, but I don't think any of them work. That's been a big disappointment to me.

AA: It's interesting what Paul says. It's a reminder of two things. One, the work of one person, among many others, which relates to and forms part of the context of my own reacting to reading *The Black Atlantic*, is the work of my friend and colleague Rolph Trouillot who is constantly asking what if one wrote the whole history of not just a triangle but quadrangle of the two Americas, Europe and Africa, perceived from for example, Haiti. It's not just the trick of saying let's look from the margins. He has an idea specifically of what it means to put oneself where one is hearing that bellow. From there, Spain looks very different. I think that one of the very important things about *The Black Atlantic* was to shape that new look at space and, as it were, to reconfigure the geographies with which we teach. For example, in Area Studies in the US a lot of the understanding of the world is organized area by area. Thus my own training was in South Asian Studies, whereas the whole world could be seen as a series of oceanic formations, quite equal to those of land. The Indian Ocean is important to see in this way, and God knows, the Atlantic, and then the Pacific Rim and its peculiar histories and so on. Some people are beginning to think like this. They just drop the land markers, not that there is anything wrong with them, but there is so much created around them. If you just start with water, then the whole picture changes. Then there is the big question, which has been a troubling and challenging one for me in recent years, which is how to write the positive statements about globalization, knowing full well the difficulties with these things, without appearing to fetishize the present – in other words, one must attend to the global that existed before. The question is: how do you both recognize that continuity, in different parts of the world, *and* speak for breaks, for changes? That's a deep and difficult question, but the first step is of course not to act as if the history of globalization begins in 1970, any more than the history of capital.

There's something that I'd want to throw in about my own project. The way I find comfort and illumination, wherever I find the formulaic dead end that Paul was talking about, is twofold. One is that I see this recent book of mine as an effort to bring back to what in the US one would call the social sciences, ideas from cultural studies. These ideas open up old and classic questions – of identity and of nationalism – that have been around forever. But these can be asked and answered I think, richly and differently, informed by 15 years of work in feminism, and media, and race, and so on. So that's in one way where I see my project, and where I find things that are helpful. And this enables me to address social scientists, even if I think their social science is faulty, and I think that's important. The other thing I wanted to say which is not so clear in my work, but is very much on my mind in respect to globalization, even more than the important and positive debate about its present or its past, or its occluded geographies, and this ties up with some institutional work that I'm involved with, at the University of Chicago, is to see whether and how one can draw in scholars or intellectuals, anybody who is thinking critically about these matters, from other places and to ask them: what really matters to you? Is the 'g' word good? So for example, in Africa scholars I know will often say it is not a good word, they don't like its sound, the way it's tied up with structural adjustment. They have other ideas about it too, but basically they see it as something worrisome both as a process and as an academic term which is floating around. So I'm interested not just out of the broad liberal impulse to say 'What do other people think?', but actually I think that this process peculiarly demands that we should first ask that question. I think I have done very little of that so far, but it informs my sense of what is wrong with this or that theory in a way that I can't yet articulate, because I know there are people in Japan, in Kuwait, in every place I know, who have a picture of this large 'thing' and its forms.

PG: I agree with that absolutely. There's something else that I wanted to say which I think that draws out, which is a question about imperialism, and the abuse of notions of postcoloniality which assume that we now inhabit a safe space beyond the grasp of all of those dynamics. I think you talk for many of us in the way that you mention questions of debt, and the relationship between the overdeveloped countries and the underdeveloped countries. I think that's right, but I'd also want to link it specifically to the argument about American imperialism, I mean, now I've been very critical and I would want to be very critical of the anti-American elements in English social science and social history. But we are left with the political dynamics and periodization of American imperialism. This is something that I've begun to think about in approaching the Cold War, the constitution of black intellectuals and their critical reflections on geo-politics during the Cold War period. I think that we're in a position now to see the constitutive force of the Cold War period in a much more sustained and thoughtful way, and I'm sure that when we begin to do that it will transform all sorts of things about the way that we understand the idea of globalization.

AA: Again the time and space issues come together. There's a question of the locations of these theories – disciplinary locations, national locations and so on – which are always important, but with globalization, possibly especially important. The optics and ontology are really very intimately linked. In my own work I've wanted to put some distance between my style of expression, which can be loosely seen as postmodernist and so on, and my actual account. I would like to see people engage with the account. Everything is not flowing and fluxing; that position seems, to me, thoughtless. So I have taken pains to make positive statements. I think it is important to say what I think, *definitely*, from the belly of the beast, from anthropology, or from American social science, which are not other people's locations. This century is about to end and is now becoming, if you like, historical, and the second half, which is substantially the story of the Cold War, is a large historical story which we may be for the first time in a position to prevent being arbitrarily divided among the fields, or periods, so that some specialists monopolize some decades. Very few historians write about it, and of course they should. I think the idea is worthy of some collaborative work. I think that it is important to reflect collectively both on the Cold War, and on the position of the US, which is still a looming force, not least in defining the terms on which topics get engaged in other places. A note on that is never enough – to say 'note that the US academy has put x on the agenda' – because that power is not unrelated to other things about the US and its force.

VB: Could I press you Arjun to say something about the issue of reterritorialization in relation to ideas of movement around the globe. There's a little phrase in your work on the production of locality where you talked about the implosion of forces within cities, and you do a list – Belfast, LA, Sarajevo, Mogadisho – it was one of those moments when you're reading and you think that 'yeah'. Globalization tends to be seen as a kind of movement 'out', the connection of London with Tokyo, with New York, and it seemed that your use of the idea of reterritorialization was partly because you were turning attention to the way in which these processes have created cities where identities and affiliation were actually implosive.

AA: Absolutely. In some of my early work, drawing partly unconsciously on Deleuze, I used the 'd' word – deterritorialization – like other people did, and was of course instantly reminded that there's not only de- but reterritorialization, and I thought, yes, that's quite right. Indian, or South Asian, populations in the US reterritorialize, but they are also involved in the politics of India, so they are reterritorializing in more than one place. It's really very important – refugees move, but then they can be in camps for 20 years – that's reterritorialization! Not the best kind but ... Then on a different register there's the other question which you put nicely that globalization can seem expansive – but as somebody said, there are flows, but there are also bumps. There's on the one hand that sense of reaching out, connecting, and linking which I think is very important, even for poorer people – you can go and be a fitter in Dubai from being a sweeper in Bombay – that's not a minor matter. But on the other hand, something I'm struggling with especially in relation to the work I'm doing on violence – and I can only draw on geological ideas here – is the way that smaller spaces are being deformed by the pressure of the others. That pressure makes certain kinds of cities not just violent but violent in certain ways. What I want to talk about is the folding in of national violence, partition and so on, into cities in very concrete ways, so that that in Bombay, for example, one street 'is' Pakistan, to put it crudely. You have to see that both spaces and subjectivities have been deformed in the technical sense, because things are folded in, so the implosion idea is trying to catch that phenomenon without falling into the use of metaphors that are too biological or too organic ... language is limited.

PG: I would want to support that very strongly as part of the critique of the sociological parties constituted around globalization. I don't like to use that word. There is a good sociological heritage of a different, a counter-tradition, not that I would call it that, but you could make it into one, if you were to look at people who have addressed these questions. I think for example of Ernst Bloch, and his argument about non-synchronicity in accounting for the particular quality of conflict and violence in which the fascist movement grew in Germany. And I've always been influenced by André Gorz and his notions of what he calls South Africanization: service sector employment, the return of domestic servants, the development of gated communities, the systematic privatization of important civic functions. I do prefer to name those processes South Africanization, although it's harder to call them that now. That's what I've always called them, and they rely on the spatialization of identities, the relationship between the territorialization of identity, the territorialization of power, particular kinds of configurations and sanctions on movement, and yet a premium placed on movement because of the expansion of certain kinds of work, and so on. I always thought that South Africanization was a very useful heuristic way of pursuing these questions. Again one goes back to Fanon and the paradigmatic way that the configuration of space and power and identity in South Africa supplies him with an interpretive key to a whole range of different colonial, decolonizing and postcolonial instances. So I want to find another vocabulary for talking about these things even when I share a concern with the sociological agenda that is beginning to emerge under the sign of globalization.

VB: There are two remaining clusters of things that I would want to ask you both. The first cluster is about politics, because I wanted to come back, Paul, to the point earlier where I was wondering about the phrase you used – the 'failure of embodiment'. I want to link that, if it's not too big a leap, to the things that Judith Butler has been saying about performativity, the performance of gendered subjectivity and the trope of interiority. It feels like there is in your works the same kind of political impulse to find those moments of disjunction.

PG: I would very much like to make that connection, and I think Judith Butler has been very acute in drawing all our attention to the kind of moments of anxiety and instability in what we, often against our better judgement, and she sometimes against her own better judgement, sees as closed systems for the production of both meaning and subjectivity. So yes, I would want to make a similar kind of critique and identify the radical forms of anxiety that flow from uncertainty about racialized identities. I would want to link them to the remarks Arjun made earlier on about the authenticity question which you raised, citing Arjun at himself. For me, authenticity is something which very often circulates as an antidote to those anxieties. This raises a number of critical political problems in wanting to make an analogue of that 'Butlerian' critique. I'll put this in its crudest and simplest form. The political configuration of race in America right now means that to take a deconstructive approach that is both radical and principled to the forms of certainty that people feel about the racialization of their lives and their victimage, is something that for some good historical reasons is very much associated with positions on the Right rather than the Left in America. It's hard to recover the liberatory moment in the process of freeing ourselves from the bonds of raciology and compulsory raciality. That goal has raised all sorts of difficulties for me. She doesn't have to negotiate these problems in quite the same way though I know that as part of the wider attack on 'cultural studies' and its betrayals she's recently been accused of not really being political at all! That seems a quite extraordinary measure of how feminism has been forced into defensive positions. There are tactical limits to how much I'm prepared to be 'out' about my own radically deconstructive aspirations, with regard to race and its observance, but at the same time, I draw great inspiration from the rigour with which she has made that argument about gender, bodies and discourse in ways that always open it to the question of race.

AA: I have a less clear sense of how my own work might link up with Judith Butler's work, which has pressed us hard on the question of performance, on the breadth of the resources upon which such a performance may draw, and how to think about that without evacuating politics. So she's stretched us all to the maximum, and therefore put a challenge to all of us, around gender particularly, but I think generally on other identity projects, in which she may be less engaged, i.e. racial or national or ethno-racial, and in my case on the whole question 'Hindu'. Having been brought up under that sign, which is now a deadly sign, I ask myself again 'Where did I enter into that sign, and its now completely deadly contemporary history?' So I guess I think two things: one is how to relate that kind of general ideal of performance to the work of imagination, trying in other words to draw in ideas about fantasy in relation to the global. Not the imagination in the older sense, but as a kind of modern work. This must be done, it's non-optional as it were. But second, how does that work then relate to the emancipatory implications of the idea of performance? So for example, when you see that great early film called *India Cabaret* by Mira Nair, which I refer to occasionally, there are these extraordinary recorded statements by cabaret dancers who are in fact prostitutes, sex-workers, in Bombay. Clearly what they are doing is very complicatedly placed in that space of performance, both in terms of femininity and in other ways. It's clearly not emancipatory in any obvious way. Where do we place these women in light of these questions about work, sexuality, representation and fantasy?

There is an interesting slightly more technical question, and perhaps I don't have the resources yet to deal with it, and which is something Judy Butler and others may have taken up and I just don't know about yet, and that is how performance as a question in terms of language, in pragmatics, discourse study and in Austinian terms, is related to the other sense of performance which comes out of the study of cinema, theatre and other bodily practices. These are not clearly connected although Bourdieu tried in his early work to bring together these two senses. I'm not clear about that ground – it's a genuine and broad ground – because if I could identify that then I would know how much weight the idea of identity as something you *perform* can carry. What I do like about it is that it goes back to the idea of the projected, that is, to say these things are not only ideologies, not only histories that people automatically propel and enact, but are things that are more visions, utopian and otherwise. In political movements, and we're talking here about politics of many kinds, but especially those relating to identity – not party politics, although perhaps that too – there is in this idea of performance a new angle on bodily actions as invitations or exhortations to others, as possibilities or instruments for mobilizing. That is what I would like to find out more about. Is that built in? Is it only sometimes that these performances have that exhortatory or invitational quality that says 'join me in my product'?

PG: In a kind of homage to Judy Butler, I'd like to call that 'interpellative' process soliciting! I think that is right. The question is how one holds to that openness, keeps the invitation open. I think that this is something which she has really tried to do. [The question is] how one holds to that possibility without being overcome by voluntarism? I think as her work has developed, she has moved this way and that to try and duck that sort of voluntarist appropriation of it, whilst at the same time holding on to the possibility of historical and structural features. I think that has been very difficult. I share her discomfort with voluntarism, although I don't always share the ways that she has tried to describe the closures of that more systematic aspect. For me it's very hard to do both simultaneously at a very high level of abstraction. We all struggle to do it in different ways.

AA: I think it does make a difference which location one comes from, so if one comes from say the cluster composed of gender studies, studies of sexuality, and feminist theory, as opposed to that of sociology, 'race' or anthropology, it sets the terms of the way in which one catches the issue, and the way in which one experiences the anxiety about it. If you come from South Asia Studies, all of these questions have to run through the sieve of some form of the Saidian critique, some form of the subaltern critique. If they don't make it at all out of that [sieve] then you know something is wrong, or something more has to be engaged. Probably for some one like Judy, I imagine, there are other kinds of discussions in the US that have to do with gender and other philosophical problems which, if you don't come to the other side of, the thing doesn't work.

PG: I think what I would like to see is a way of complementing her enquiries into the histories of subjectivity with a kind of enquiry into the history of solidarity, and intersubjectivity. I think that's more difficult really, and again raises the tension that you cited earlier between notions of personhood and histories of subjectivity. A lot of the time we use the word 'identity' to blur all of these. In a way what we need to do is to unpack that in a much more rigorous manner so that those different problems, some of which are more readily seen as questions of politics than others, come more clearly into view.

VB: Do you mean moments of solidarity both in the positive and the negative sense? Is that what you feel you are writing about now where you're thinking about the Cold War and the responses to fascism and other forms of extreme politics?

PG: Yes, and thinking not just about the Cold War, but about 'hot' wars too, war in general actually, and principles of fraternity and solidarity which are explicitly contradicting other noble modern aspirations towards brotherhood, equality and liberation. I think one of the reasons I was drawn to the idea of fraternity as a problematic value was precisely prompted by Judy's work. I think the emphasis on fraternity as a particular value is something that in a very useful way troubles our understanding of authoritarian irrationalism cross-culturally. It takes us away from notions of patriarchy, forms of male domination according to the dynamics of power that derive from men's hold over women as husbands and fathers, into a rather different domain of a kind of collected masculine power, the value of brotherhood assumes a different shape and the psychodynamics of power are altered remarkably. There's a whole literature there that's useful and valuable – some of it by sociologists even! – some of it by sociologists in the 19th century even! – but it isn't always put together in that way. I'm thinking for example of Simmel's work on secrecy, fraternity and fraternal organizations or Weber's essay on ethics and fraternity, things of that kind.

AA: I am struck and very delighted at the interesting convergence between some of what I gather, Paul, you are up to now with this interest and a cluster of things of things that I am working on which centre on the question of ethnic violence. This is of course a very overcrowded field so I take it on with trepidation, but I'm now compelled to do it. With the enquiry into ethnic violence – with particular reference to Hindu–Muslim violence in India, but of course also trying to think about Eastern Europe, Rwanda and so on – I find myself asking questions which people have been asking for 15 years or so now, not least Ben Anderson but also others, concerning the issue of *affect* that surrounds nation. I have returned to the question of love of the nation, the question of how such a plainly abstract, contingent, artificial and violent form actually persuades people to live for it, to die for it. It's a classic question, of course, but I think we are now in a position to ask it again, and to ask about the role of violence, both in the macro sense – warfare, mobilization, conscription – which has been pointed out by others, and less discussed, in the everyday practices of violence. One of the things that I will be talking about this week, at SOAS, is arson, or burning, which is very frequent in public acts of violence. What is it doing? It's very much part of everyday life, it's not a macro-historical statement ... it's one example of a problem that I hear underneath or between the things you're saying, Paul, I hope rightly: what is the economy of sentiment surrounding the nation form?

In turn this question opens up the propaganda question, which is always brought in as if once said, we know – 'that's because of propaganda' – but what do we know about propaganda? We know nothing ... when it works we don't know why it works. So what are the practices which produce affect for the nation?

Today I was reading Gordon Craig's review of a book on Hitler. Hitler said very early, in 1923 or so, that the important thing was that you have to have certain things in place and then teach people to hate, hate and hate again. We also know that there is some complex kind of love involved. But we know little about either of these things. To me, they surround the question of ethno-national violence. In my current work, therefore, one question is: what are the practices through which this set of feelings about this entirely abstract form are produced, and more importantly, reproduced?

These questions tie up of course to classic concerns such as crowd behaviour, the work of Le Bon and others, people who had good ideas, but whose questions we may be in a better position to ask now. Questions about the micro-physics of crowds, for example, or about what parades do, or other institutional forms through which the movements of positive affect for the nation can be rehearsed. In some situations, we also have to attend to the way people, in Hirschmann's terms, 'exit', and say, 'Hang on, I don't care for this bloody thing, I'm gone from here.'

PG: I agree, absolutely. I'm much more inclined to think about the sort of iteration of hate as a much more substantial component of what an irrational authoritarian movement does, how it works with its members, how it manages its own institutional life. That is, to see those forms in their positivity – it's difficult for me. What's most powerfully connected with what I'm doing at the moment from how you've described your project is this question of love, and how bad I think we've been as social scientists in thinking about love, and thinking about the forms of love. I had all sorts of trouble when I tried to name it homophilia or whatever, because people immediately accuse me of betraying a project in queer theory, I suppose, which suggests that what counts most about this is the specifically erotic dynamic involved in love between men, the forms of love that men practice when they have banished women, got women out of the way so they can get on with the very intense business of loving each other. I still think that what's most important there is the idea that that form of love might be extremely compromised and destroyed by the erotic dynamic, and a great deal of work, a great deal of technology, is invested in managing and containing that problem. That interests me a great deal.

AA: It connects with issues of remembering and forgetting, that can play into this question of the economy of love for these abstract, large projects or institutions. There is the issue of what it takes to accomplish or to sustain that love, and which everyday forms of it are models of the larger forms. I think, coming back to the comment right at the beginning, that at least in anthropology of a type, but also in sociology, there has been the banishing of psychology, either classic Freudian psychology or American-style clinical psychology.

I'm now finding – as a personal note here – reading Žižek very useful, not because I either understand nor endorse the whole project, but because I think his alertness to how a kind of Hegelian retake of Lacan can directly illuminate the peculiar ironies of certain charged ideological situations, or those wonderful examples of communist trials where people have to confess that they are communists but confess that they are not communist because they recognize the importance of such confessions.

PG: We learnt this from Kafka a long while back! I think there are elements of that which have been alive in the experience of the literary culture of Eastern Europe. People were under the pressure that you describe, an almost geo-physical kind of pressure.

AA: I think you're right. I'm speaking more of these disciplinary habits about where one can move. For me I have read little and understood less of the whole Lacanian thing, and I feel tempted to say well if that's the place that illuminates a kind of split subject – and it may not! – then I have to go for it. We have a disciplinary habituation to bracketing the question – either the psychological question, or the affect question, which is broader – which is to say 'well that's somebody else's job' so we'll take that theory and plug it in. I think that's a mistake.

Interview conducted on 12 November 1997, London.

References

Appadurai, A. (1981) 'The Past as a Scarce Resource', *Man* 16.

Appadurai, A. (ed.) (1986) *The Social Life of Things: Commodities in Cultural Perspective*. Cambridge: Cambridge University Press.

Appadurai, A. (1996) *Modernity at Large*. Minneapolis: University of Minnesota Press.

Ellis, J. (1976) *The Social History of the Machine Gun*. London: Random House.

Fanon, F. (1986) *Black Skin, White Masks*. London: Pluto Press.

Gilroy, P. (1993) *The Black Atlantic: Modernity and Double Consciousness*. London: Verso.

Wright, P. (1986) *On Living in an Old Country*. London: Verso.

Vikki Bell is a lecturer in the Department of Sociology at Goldsmiths College, University of London. She is the author of *Interrogating Incest: Feminism, Foucault and the Law* (Routledge, 1993) and of *'We Feminists': Genealogies in Feminist Theory* (Sage, forthcoming 1999), as well as several articles on the thought of Michel Foucault, feminism and theories of difference.

Paul Gilroy is a Professor in the Department of Sociology at Goldsmiths College, University of London. He is the atuhor of *Ain't No Black in the Union Jack* (Routledge, 1987), *The Black Atlantic: Modernity and Double Consciousness* (Verso, 1993), *Small Acts* (Serpent's Tail, 1993) and of *Between Camps: 'Race' and Culture at the End of the Colour Line* (Penguin, forthcoming 1999), as well as several articles on the politics, history and philosophy of 'race' and cultural processes.

Arjun Appadurai is a Professor in the Department of Anthropology, University of Chicago. He is well known for his work on the sociology of objects, South East Asia studies and anthropological theory. His most recent publications include *Modernity at Large* (University of Minnesota Press, 1996).

Re-Membering Places and the Performance of Belonging(s)

Anne-Marie Fortier

If Veni Vidi, Can Vici Be Far Behind?

(Bill Nichols, 1994: 67)

IN THE WORLD of contemporary theory, identity is widely understood as lived and imagined in ways that break down its contiguousness with a geographically bounded locality. Much has been written about the transnational public sphere as a new space for cultural, economic, technological and political exchange, the paradigmatic figures of which are refugees, exiles and migrants, whose 'ethnoscapes' (Appadurai, 1990) are increasingly documented. Within these theoretical circles, fixity and rootedness are positioned as experiences from which we withdraw from the world and take a look at it, whereas movement and travel are much more viewed as the 'reality' of the experience of daily life in the contemporary world. However, although some theorists suggest that we are in a transnational era which undermines any concern with roots, immigrant populations often project themselves in relation to specific origins that do not necessarily undermine multi-locality or transnational connections (Calhoun, 1994: 19). As Caren Kaplan points out, 'even theories of nomadic rhizomes include "nodes"' (1996: 143).

In this paper, I discuss the formation of an Italian émigré culture[1] within different forms of representation of the Italian presence in Britain. I shall explore how efforts of settlement and rootings manifest themselves in locally specific ways, and how they articulate with multi-local terrains of belonging. One theme I address in my analysis is the relationship between the construction of the identity of places and the construction of terrains of

■ *Theory, Culture & Society* 1999 (SAGE, London, Thousand Oaks and New Delhi), Vol. 16(2): 41–64
[0263-2764(199904)16:2;41–64;008254]

belonging. Against the assumed isomorphism of space, place and culture, on the one hand, and the reification of uprootedness as the paradigmatic figure of the postmodern experience of identity, on the other, I raise here the ways in which cultural identity, in migration, is at once deterritorialized and reterritorialized. Questions of what it means to speak of 'home', 'origins', 'continuity' and 'tradition' are paramount in this project. Imagining a community is both that which is created as a common history, experience or culture of a group – a group's belongings (Probyn, 1996) – and about how the imagined community is attached to places (Gupta and Ferguson, 1992: 10) – the location of culture.

The line I follow here moves through 'the imaginary possessions that are created in the name of an identity project, the belongings that . . . a group, a people cobble together from the past and the present' (Probyn, 1996: 68). Belongings refers to both 'possessions' and *appartenance*. That is, practices of group identity are about manufacturing cultural and historical belongings which mark out terrains of commonality that delineate the politics and social dynamics of 'fitting in'. As will become clear in the following pages, some of these belongings may be physical places: St Peter's Italian church and its surroundings, in central London. In short, they constitute Italian *(terrains of) belonging(s)*: they are at once appropriated as Italian historical and cultural possessions, and used as privileged sites for the iterated performance of a collective 'body', the formation of which also implies the construction of differentiated subjects.

The second theme that ties into my analysis, then, concerns the ways in which the formation of group identity is woven through the formation of particular subjects. As I unpack various forms of cultural practices that mark out spatial and cultural boundaries for the Italian immigrant population, I will follow male and female bodies (especially the latter) as they circulate, and embody, thresholds of belonging. I shall pay close attention to the ways in which ethnicity and gender circulate, articulate, are embedded and simultaneously produced in representations of collective identity. Feminist accounts of ethnicity and 'race' have alerted us to the ways in which ethnicity is essentialized or rendered absolute through its intersection with gender systems of differentiation (Anthias and Yuval-Davis, 1992; Brah, 1992; Juteau, 1996; Yuval-Davis and Anthias, 1989). Others, however, question the fruitfulness of conceiving identity as the result of the intersection of distinct systems of differentiation (Anzaldúa, 1987; Butler, 1993; Di Leonardo, 1994; Gunew and Yeatman, 1993; Probyn, 1996; Trinh, 1989). Moving beyond add-on models of identity formation, these writers explore the embeddedness of social categories and the extent to which they rely on each other for their construction. In the pages that follow, I draw from Judith Butler's work of performativity (namely in *Gender Troubles* and *Bodies that Matter*) to unpack the mutual construction of social categories through performative acts of gender and ethnicity.[2] I ask how gender regulations and ethnic conventions relate to each other in their simultaneous performance.

For Butler, performativity is not merely about routine or the reiteration of practices within one individual's life. Nor is reiteration 'simply replicas of the same' (Butler, 1993: 226). Rather, she argues that performativity is primarily about citationality, that is that it is 'through the invocation of convention' (1993: 225) that 'acts' derive their binding power. Performativity is about the 'reiteration of norms which precede, constrain, and exceed the performer' (1993: 234). Performative acts include 'legal sentences, baptisms, inaugurations' and other forms of 'statements which not only perform an action, but confer a binding power on the action performed' (1993: 234). Viewing identity as performative, then, means that identities are constructed by the 'very "expressions" that are said to be [their] results' (Butler, 1990: 45).

Butler's main object is to explore the materiality of sex; she de-naturalizes it and locates it as a product and enforcement of regulatory discourses. Likewise, I want to de-naturalize ethnicity, for within British new racism, the naturalization of culture diffuses 'race' and racism in ethnic-related discourses of differentiation. This is what Paul Gilroy calls 'ethnic absolutism' (1987: 59). Consequently, some cultural practices are reified and naturalized as 'typical expressions' of an ethnic identity; they are seen as resulting from that identity, rather than performing that identity. This is how Paul Gilroy approaches musical performances within the 'Black Atlantic' and their impact in the construction of a 'racial' identity. Gilroy's reading of music illuminates how signifying practices are mediated through the body and 'produce the imaginary effect of an internal racial core or essence ... through the specific mechanisms of identification and recognition that are produced in the intimate interaction of performer and crowd' (1993: 102).

In short, it is as performative acts that I approach institutional discourses and practices through which an Italian émigré culture is produced. In what follows, I present four episodes drawn from the daily life of St Peter's Italian church: written renditions of former Little Italy, where the church stands,[3] a weekly Mass; the annual procession; a first communion. Each episode constitutes a different kind of statement of the Italian presence in London; they come out of the mandate that the leaders of St Peter's have set for themselves, that is to 'preserve' the community and its traditions, and as such, they enunciate that enduring presence. As performative acts, these episodes are part of regulatory practices that produce social categories and the norms of membership within them. They are sites where hegemonic definitions of the collective body relate to multiple injunctions of individual bodies; in the words of Minoo Moallem (1998), they are 'sites of repetition'. What interests me here is not so much bodily enactments in and of themselves, but rather the ways in which different statements (textual or performed in rituals or commemorations) constitute signifying practices that are mediated through the interpellation of individual bodies. How different displays of presence operate through the repetition of regulatory norms that produce an effect of materialization and naturalization of cultural belonging through the ethnicizing and gendering of individual bodies.

The four episodes are to be read as a collage rather than an organized sequence that composes a plot. They capture a number of layers embedded within the process of identity formation, and which tie in with broader theoretical questions about the reterritorialization of identity, the invention of tradition and the embodiment of culture. I begin with written renditions of life in former Little Italy. These stories construct an Italian historical environment (physical and temporal) that serves to legitimate the actions undertaken in the name of an identity project. As such, they partake in the formation of a broader context of conventions (and traditions) within which the performance of collective belonging(s) take place.

First Episode: 'The Hill' as a Second Place of Origin

As one of two religious-cum-social clubs of Italian London,[4] St Peter's is a main focal point of the population's associative life. Founded in 1863, it stands in the centre of what used to be 'Little Italy', in Clerkenwell, central London. Its initial name was to be St Peter's Roman Catholic Church of all Nations, but when it opened in 1863 it was simply called St Peter's Church. At that time, it ministered to the religious needs of the large number of Catholics residing in, or constantly hurrying through, London: Irish, Poles, French, Germans and of course Italians. Gradually, as this multicultural presence moved on, or established their own separate churches[5] St Peter's catered predominantly to Italians and acquired the status of being the Italian Church. Today, St Peter's occupies a mixed position within the local Catholic hierarchy. On the one hand, it has a national parish status, which means that its membership is based on ethnicity instead of place of residence. On the other, it answers to the diocese of Westminster. In the Mass celebrating the 130th anniversary of St Peter's (9 May 1993), Padre Carmelo, the parish priest, publicly assured Cardinal Basil Hume, the archbishop of Westminster who was invited for the occasion, that St Peter's considers itself part of the British Roman Catholic Church, dismissing its national parish status as 'not important'. By stressing that it is part of the 'British Catholic family', Padre Carmelo at once deterritorialized and reterritorialized St Peter's, by way of its de-ethnicization and re-ethnicization. Yet as I will show, St Peter's plays a significant role in the formation of a specifically Italian presence in London.

St Peter's acquires a special significance within London Italian historicity as a result of its association with its immediate surroundings. Known as 'The Hill', this section of former 'Little Italy' is repeatedly retraced, its history retold and its confines redefined through written recollections published in St Peter's monthly magazine, *Backhill*.

Started in November 1992, 'The Hill', as the column's title goes, is written by a British-Italian woman, Olive Besagni. Its typical pieces are about families or are portraits of individuals, all of which emerge from stories told to Besagni by former residents of *Il quartiere italiano*, or their descendants. These short biographies are set against the backdrop of the everyday life of Little Italy in the late 19th or early 20th centuries. A striking aspect of Besagni's column is the way in which genealogy and geography are worked into the creation of new grounds of belonging.

In Besagni's accounts, readers are introduced to the characters of each story through their links – kinship, professional or other – with other former residents, some of whose stories could have been told in previous issues. In other cases, the genealogy is more conventional and retraces the family tree of the characters. Such genealogical tracings usually provide a transgenerational backdrop to the main story, linking past to present, linking memories to 'real' people, linking former Little Italy residents to the present-day, geographically dispersed, Italian population.

> The Nastri sons . . . all married to English girls, all had good marriages and as you can imagine there are plenty of young Nastri's growing up in England today. All as a result of that journey made by Trofimena and Alfonso way back in the year 1908.[6]

Olive Besagni resorts to genealogy as a metaphor for continuity. It may be argued that languages of descent trace blood-lines between generations, thus concealing racist notions of culture and belonging as genetically endowed (Michaels, 1992). Without denying that family-trees emphasize a kind of continuity that follows blood-lines, I want to suggest that Besagni does not imply that the culture of the present-day 'community' is *biologically* determined by its lineage. To paraphrase Daniel Boyarin and Jonathan Boyarin (1993), there is a difference between saying that I am Italian because I have Italian ancestors, and saying that I *behave* like an Italian because I have Italian ancestors. In short, my point is that as Besagni's chronicles extend into one another through the generational trope, ideas of duration[7] surface and support the creation of an Italian terrain of belonging predicated on remembrances of beginnings. Generations are called upon as images of duration and continuity, the origins of which are located in The Hill.

To be sure, The Hill is remembered in a variety of ways: as a rough, poor area where outsiders were less than welcome, or, in contrast, as a place of close-knit community life of solidarity and mutual support – which some remember as equally enclosed upon itself. For some, Little Italy is not worth remembering and Besagni's nostalgia is condemned as a useless wish to retrieve an imaginary and romanticized past which, they argue, 'actually never existed'. She is berated for what is perceived as a naive longing for things to be as they once were. Others, however, bask in the memories of past times which 'bring Little Italy to life again', and warmly recall the daily life on The Hill. Others, still, simply appreciate Besagni's series as a source of historical knowledge: 'it tells us about the history of the place, the history of the community', thus providing added texture to their immediate experiences of the place and of the 'community', and allowing them to claim the Italianness of St Peter's and The Hill. Finally, The Hill may also appear as an Italian enclave where the 'community' is tightly woven through stifling 'traditional' family values and injunctions about womanhood (Ferrari, 1993).

These contested meanings and histories are constitutive of the creation of Little Italy as an ancestral space for Italians of England or Britain. Indeed, Besagni's column identifies sites and places people can return to and re-member, that is, they cobble together elements of a(n imagined) past, projected on to the area. One reader wrote to her, telling of his journey to St Peter's: 'I really felt that I [was] re-tracing the surroundings and traditions that would have been familiar to my ancestors.'[8] Besagni's stories constitute a form of 'memory work' (Gillis, 1994: 3) that is rich with images of duration. There is more to this series than simply juxtaposing images from the past on to the present. It is part of a creative process that constructs and locates an historical environment, adding substance to the immediate, lived experience of the present. Besagni's series conjures up lives of the past to create a habitable space for her contemporaries (De Certeau, 1990: 162).

The 'Italian Quarter' (as she also refers to it) emerges from Besagni's narrative as a space distant from the rest of the world. Yet a constitutive feature of this space is migration. While *e*migration from Italy is construed as the inaugural moment of the formation of Little Italy, migration appears as an inherent component of the lives of its residents. Flows of migration act upon the delineation of *Il quartiere italiano* as an enclosed space, surrounded by an imagined boundary. We rarely go beyond its limits, in Besagni's stories, and when we do, it seems like a temporary migration. Even the daily journeys of workers to the West End (or other parts of London) convey this sense of moving between two separate worlds.

In one article, Besagni cites Victor: 'Whenever we represented the school in competitive athletics or football, we always felt that we were competing for Italy, rather than the school.'[9] This suggests that in the minds of some of the residents, Little Italy *was* Italy. However, overlaying the boundary between Little Italy and Elsewhere is another boundary that separates this Italian quarter from another 'Little Italy' in nearby Soho. Histories of the area (Colpi, 1991a; Sponza, 1988) provide accounts of the well-known rivalry between the two areas. For former residents of The Hill, the 'West End Italians', as the Soho Italians were known, were the 'posh lot', as opposed to their own poorer, working-class community. Interestingly, in her column Besagni retraces a boundary line between these two areas by obliterating the presence of the 'others', rather than by emphasising their differences and rivalries. It is as if Italians from each sector had no contact; as if there had never been any cycling trips joining 'The Hill Italians' and 'West End Italians', like those Olive and her husband Bruno recall in the conversations I had with them. Memory and forgetting work together in the struggle over differing histories and geographies that construct the identity of a place.

In British Italian historicity, 'The Hill' is construed as the original settlement, the second place of origin for Italian immigrants. 'The history of Italian immigration to Britain', writes Lucio Sponza, 'is to a great extent the history of the Italians in [Holborn]' (1988: 19). The Hill is both an end point and a starting point; a point of arrival and a point of departure. It is an interval; a spatial and temporal 'moment' that marks off the passage from migrancy to settlement. A passage that is also highly gendered: settlement is grounded on a distinction between sojourners and settlers configured around masculinized definitions of mobility and movement – migrant workers – and feminized representations of stability, sedentariness and continuity – settler wives and mothers. In sum, the 'foundations' of the Italian presence in Britain are associated with the arrival of women-wives-mothers (see Colpi, 1991a; Marin, 1975; Sponza, 1988).

The Hill emerges as an 'envelope of space-time' (Massey, 1995: 188) constituted out of particular claims about the history and geography of the original settlement. It is part of the communal project of recovery; of the 'rediscovery' of a past, of a place, a *grounding* which, as Stuart Hall points out, is grasped through reconstruction (1991: 36). It is remembered in a way that draws essentialist and exclusionist borders – indeed it obliterates the presence of Irish and other residents in this area at the time, while it traces generational blood-lines of belonging and continuity. Yet although it is place-*based*, this history is not univocally place-*bound*. The Hill is arguably elevated as the emblem of Italian settlement in Britain, but it inserts itself within a network of many similar 'Little Italies' scattered in Britain (and elsewhere). 'Origins', here, are multiple. The image of the rhizome comes to mind: diaspora as a rhizomatic network of nodes that foreground the possibility of new beginnings (Glissant, 1981: 196–7). Little Italy, here, is a space of belonging that proceeds from remembrances of beginnings (Probyn, 1996: 113) and that roots them, as it were, within English territory.

Second Episode: Untitled

When I first entered St Peter's Italian church, I was overwhelmed by the sense of *déjà vu* conveyed by the surroundings: the aromas, the light, the statues and icons, the holy water, the pews, the priests' robes. . . . I easily performed the proper bodily movements, drilled by the cues of rising, sitting, kneeling, crossing, heart-pounding with a closed fist while whispering *mea culpa*. . . . Despite the fact that I had renounced Catholicism years before, the familiarity of these weekly Masses alleviated the sense of estrangement one might feel when engaging in a new research world. This place constituted a strange terrain of familiarity and comfort in a country where I had recently arrived from Montreal. Even though the ceremonies were not performed in the French vernacular I was brought up with, my first visit to St Peter's struck me because it was a 'habitual space'.[10] A space where I need not try to make sense of what was going on: all was familiar, intelligible, even if unpleasant and troubling.

My engagement with Judith Butler was crucial in these initial stages of my study. Her insistence on repetition helped me come to terms with understanding 'ethnicity' as more than a mere social construct. As I sat there in the pews, it seemed as if I was watching a re-run of part of my identity *in the making*: the 'stylised repetition of acts' (Butler, 1990: 140) reached into some deep-seated sense of selfhood that had sedimented into my body. The rituals, in turn, cultivated a sense of belonging. This short episode made me realize the extent to which cultural identity is embodied, and memories are incorporated (Connerton, 1992), both as a result of iterated actions. And how these, in turn, are *lived* as *expressions* of a deeply felt sense of identity and belonging. This small experience gave me some insight into what it may mean, for some Italians, to return to St Peter's. Going to the Italian church momentarily solves the ontological problem about belonging to the Italian Catholic culture in a non-Italian, non-Catholic world.

With Butler, I began articulating what Angela K. Martin (1997) refers to as a corporeal approach to group identity. More broadly, I am informed by recent developments in feminist theory that explore how bodies constitute the raw material through which place is both experienced and inscribed, and how bodies, in turn, are inscribed by and become the signifiers of particular notions of place (Grosz, 1994; Martin, 1997; Valentine, 1993). Identity, here, 'is formed and continually reinforced via individual practice within culturally defined spaces, which are themselves in turn continually constituted out of these same practices' (Martin, 1997: 92). But it seems to me that the focus on the sexing of bodies neglects the processes through which bodies (and spaces) are also ethnicized. In other words, embodiment is reduced to sexualization and thus becomes the matter and symbol through which identities and spaces are sexualized within already culturally defined spaces. As my above noted experience hopefully makes clear, I believe that ethnic identity can also be performative.

My version of a corporeal approach to group identity takes account of the simultaneous genderization and ethnicization of both bodies and space. In the next two episodes, I examine commemorations and rituals insofar as they constitute performative sites of communal and individual subjects at once. That is to say that the shared performance of patterns of behaviour not only produces a communal appreciation of belonging, but it simultaneously produces particular kinds of subjects which cannot be dissociated from the collective project. In a manner akin to Angela McRobbie's appraisal of Catholic Glasgow (1995), I investigate how bodies and space produce each other in both ethnically and gender-specific ways.

Third Episode: The Annual Procession as a 'Display of Presence'

The most important affair of St Peter's is its annual procession in honour of Our Lady of Mount Carmel. It occurs on 16 July or the first Sunday thereafter, and attracts diverse segments of the Italian population. This is not unique to the procession: a yearly pilgrimage to a monastery in

Aylesford (Kent) and an annual picnic at the Villa Scalabrini (a home for Italian retirees), also draw people of different generations, classes and Italian regional origins. What distinguishes the procession from other Italian gatherings is its association with a multiculturalist discourse. The procession is a 'public' event, held in selected streets of Clerkenwell, open to a public of spectators who are not overwhelmingly, though perhaps predominantly, Italian. It symbolizes the multicultural fabric of London by publicly displaying the presence of an enduring Italian culture. It is not as well known as the Notting Hill Carnival, but it has been listed as an 'Ethnic London' event in the *Time Out London Guide* and attracts many tourists and non-Italian Londoners. The procession, then, is marked out as an 'Italian event'.

It is easy to label such manifestations as 'ethnic' and to encase them as traditions that testify to the continuity of some authentic, original culture. Yet the devotion to Mary is not specifically Italian, nor is the feast in honour of Our Lady of Mount Carmel. Moreover, the event is not only held in London. On the contrary, this is what I call a diasporic moment: that Sunday, each in their own way, Italians of London, Toronto, Montreal, New York, as well as in some parts of Italy, hold a procession in honour of Our Lady of Mount Carmel, and in some cases re-map, through walking the route, areas known as Little Italies. As Olive Besagni puts it, on that day 'the streets of "Il Quartiere Italiano" come to life once more, just as they did in the old days "Down The Hill"'.[11] For these occasions, Italians from different parts of the world join families and friends, like Besagni's relatives from the US who 'strive to get [to London] for that day'.[12]

The first London procession did not result from the spontaneous re-enactment of some ancient devotional practices. Rather, it appeared in the context of Catholic emancipation among Irish residents of Holborn and Islington and was instigated by an Irish priest (Sponza, 1988: 315 n78). Today, as one of the organizers explained to me, the procession is the re-enactment of village feasts which are dedicated to patron saints: 'Since we cannot have feasts for each village of origin of London Italians, we hold this big event for all of them and we chose to honour Our Lady.' In short, the procession is a form of a cultural reprocessing that may be viewed as a response to the dispersal, fragmentation and transformation of Italian émigré cultural life. This is what Paul Gilroy calls the 'changing same' (1993: 101): tradition as cultural reprocessing, as a response to the inherent transience of modern life. The changing same raises the question of the relationship between sameness and differentiation by propelling those who agree that 'we are more or less what we used to be' in a conflict about whether it is the more or the less that should be privileged in the project of identity (Gilroy, 1995: 26). The disputed meanings of The Hill are a good example of such conflicts. The changing same seizes the ways in which the tension between having been, being, and becoming is continually negotiated, conjugated and resolved.

At one level, the invention of tradition is tightly bound to the (re)creation of ethnicity that surfaces from reprocessing history and memory (Hobsbawm and Ranger, 1983). Ritualization and formalization lie at the basis of the invention of tradition, thus exalting into timelessness a culture that is said to be *re*presented by the different forms of remembering. Yet beyond the processes through which a tradition is invented, I want to emphasize how it becomes, when performed, a ground of remembrances and how, as such, it becomes an open site for multiple memories.

The annual feast features several kinds of events at once: it is an ethnic festival in a plural society, a village feast, a demonstration of enduring Roman Catholic devotion, an occasion for 'family unification', a 'community' gathering and a reprocessing of popular religious practices – Italian and Irish – within a new environment. The procession itself is a trail of different temporalities, histories, boundaries and 'communities'. Italians from Birmingham and Gloucester 'return' to London, signalling their presence with a banner, thus projecting the 'community' beyond London. Elderly women pray in earnest, while young British-born teenagers and children pose as angels, or proudly represent St Peter's Youth Club, and young girls parade in 'traditional' regional dress. A band of Irish pipers also participates each year in the procession, recalling the Irish presence in the neighbourhood.

Whether it is a display of faith, culture, enduring presence, pluralism, or all of these at once, the procession nonetheless states the unquestionable presence of Italian Catholicism in London. The very performance of the ceremony defines this 'truth'. In this respect, the procession consists of what Barbara Myerhoff has called 'definitional ceremonies': 'performances of identity which state the unquestionability of truths, made unquestionable by their performance' (1979: 32). As it unfolds the procession simultaneously traces the confines of a territory and reiterates the identity of The Hill as an Italian place.

For many participants or bystanders, the procession is a moment of nostalgia; a return to the neighbourhood they grew up in: 'I lived just around the corner, here. I come here for nostalgia.' 'I lived down the road, down there. . . . Ooooh, we was a tough lot!' 'When I was kid, the *festa* went on for four days!' Memories flow into the air, weaving a net of nostalgic remembrances which wrap the procession and tie it down as a moment of attachment. This is what the procession means to Francesco Giacon, editor of St Peter's *Backhill*. For him, it constitutes:

> . . . a base, a closeness, a point of reference, *a point of refuge*; without them, you are a drifter. It's to preserve a particular way of life, a particular community. It's about bridging the gap between generations. You do what your forebears did. I do it out of some sense of duty; to keep the traditions up. (Giacon's emphasis)

However invented, the procession is lived by many as an ossified tradition, that which constitutes, as Giacon says, the 'kind of ground work on which we base our lives'. It is a display of presence, where Italians – and increasingly non-Italians – are called upon to bear witness to the Italian past and present/ce.

As Doreen Massey writes: 'The invention of tradition is . . . about the invention of the coherence of a place, about defining and naming it as a "place" at all' (1995: 188). Commemorations such as the procession allow for memories to be not only lived and reprocessed in a ritualized pattern of continuity. They are also located within a specific territory in a collective claim of belonging. Streets are blocked, taken over for a day when 'we show our faith to the world', in the words of Padre Carmelo. The procession, in short, is a version of the living memory of Italian presence in London. The living memory of the church and The Hill as a place of belonging for all Italians, past and present, living in London and elsewhere.

But there is more to the procession than tracing London Italian culture on to a map. This is where most accounts of processions in other Italian diasporic communities come to a halt (Migliore, 1988; Primeggia and Varacalli, 1996; Swiderski, 1986; Trebay, 1990). In contrast, I want to suggest that the procession of the Madonna is not exclusively about cultural (re)production or territorial claims. It also concerns the construction of an ideal of femininity that relates back to the creation of local particularity – and, in this respect, I also move beyond the general argument that confines the Marian devotion in her relationship to family and family roles (Carroll, 1992; Orsi, 1985). Rather, I propose to examine how this devotion takes on a particular significance as a threshold figure of collective belonging.

In the booklet for the 1993 procession in honour of the Madonna, we find the following text:

> Today we honour a woman who, in human terms, should hang her head in shame. She gave birth to a child, not fathered by her husband. Her son had the audacity to claim to forgive sins. Her son was condemned to death as a blasphemer who dared declare to be the Son of God. But throughout her life she never questioned the motives of the Lord, never doubted His actions, never criticized His ways. Her Faith, her trust in the Lord, never faltered or wavered, however little she understood. Rather than condemning God she praised him. 'My soul proclaims the greatness of the Lord' (Luke 1: 46). When we look at Our Lady's life, not through a rose-coloured filter, but in the harsh reality of how it must have been, one can understand why she is revered above all other human souls.

As this text illustrates, the location of 'woman' is not a thing of her own. It is contingent on that of a father, a husband, a son. This is what leads Amy-Jill Levine to remark that 'woman is, in effect, in perpetual diaspora' (1992: 110). In turn, it may be argued that the Italian diaspora is figured as 'woman'. 'First-generation Italian women of the southern Italian communities', writes Terri Colpi, 'are the living embodiment of the difficulty and sadness of emigration' (1991a: 218). The isolation of these women, confined in the home, not speaking English, becomes the epitome of the sacrificial émigré condition of existence.

For Levine, the exaggeration of women's captivity and passivity asserts the freedom of male migrants and exiles, and simultaneously stabilizes the world of the exile (1992: 117). Yet when contemplating the feminization of the Italian diaspora through the body of the Madonna in the light of Catholic popular religious practice, the figure acquires both utopic and dystopic aspects. This ties in with the historical paradox that has invested definitions of 'woman' in Western thought. A number of feminists have pointed out the mixture of attraction and repulsion (Julia Kristeva), or recognition and wonder (Luce Irigaray), that makes ' "woman" . . . the eternal pole of opposition' (Braidotti, 1994: 83). Mary, as 'woman', is indeed a paradoxical figure, one who is both loved and feared; giving and narcissistic – 'Italian Catholics . . . see Mary as a goddess who craves veneration' (Carroll, 1992: 54) – unitary and splintered – in contrast to Protestants, Catholics have tended to splinter the image of Mary into a range of personalities, including Our Lady of Mount Carmel, each of which has become the object of an extensive cult (1992: 2). The 'unnatural' birth of God suggests that Mary was, in some ways, not quite human, not quite flesh, indeed not quite 'mother' given the present-day obsession with 'natural parents', as it manifests itself in discussions over adoption. To paraphrase Rosi Braidotti, the birth of Jesus through divine intervention 'inscribes an antimaternal dimension at the very heart of the matter' (1994: 84).

But within contemporary Catholic discourse, voiced by the London Italian clergy, Mary's ambiguity is levelled through the sanctification of motherhood. Likewise, the multiple bodies are unified within the single body of femininity as motherhood. Mary's is a vulnerable body, a body that has been invaded, hurt and its desires utterly suppressed – the virgin. But it is also a fecund body – the mother – and celebrated as such. To be sure, this constitutes one version of Italian *mammismo*, that is the veneration of the mother figure as 'the symbol of what is most sacred within a family' (Bottignolo, 1985: 59; Colpi, 1991a: 216).[13] Historically, in Italy, the singling out of women as a group and their location within the family has been variously systematized through the concerted efforts of Catholic teaching and Fascist policies (Caldwell, 1986; De Grazia, 1992; Passerini, 1996; Pratt, 1996).[14] It is difficult, in this regard, to speak of Italian *mammismo* outside of the Catholic discourse of motherhood deployed in the cult of the Virgin Mary, or of the nationalist discourse of women as reproducers of the nation.

It bears repetition that St Peter's is a national parish and serves as the repository of British-Italian history. For instance, up the stairway, in the portico, are two war monuments. One is dedicated to the memory of London-Italians who died in the war of 1914–18. The second honours the 446 Italians who lost their lives in the sinking of the *Arandora Star*, a ship headed to Canada and Australia, transporting Italians who had been interned as 'enemy aliens' by the British authorities during the Second

World War. It was torpedoed on 2 July 1940 and sunk: a total of 700 men died.[15]

The location of these national memorials on the church's premises brings together nation and religion and testifies to the national status of St Peter's. Moreover, they mimic widespread practices of nation that honour the soldier-citizen as an exemplar of national allegiance. Indeed, the nationalist discourse distinguishes between masculinized representations of national allegiance, and feminized representations of the nation itself (Mosse, 1985; Parker et al., 1992), where women are interpellated as mothers of the nation, bearers of national culture and in charge of its reproduction. Consider, in this respect, how the narratives on the foundations of the community mimic nationalist discourses, by associating them with the arrival of wives-mothers, founders of the family and, by extension, of the 'community'.

As for the religious discourse, the Catholic Church has displayed an obsessive interest in the mysteries, duties and obligations of motherhood. This became particularly explicit in recent discourses which appeal to women as descendants of Mary, as it were, and where ideals of love and devotion are woven through the conflation of femininity and motherhood and the sublimation of female sexuality (Kristeva, 1983; Warner, 1990). The Pope's letter to women published in 1995 goes one step further: womanhood, in his discourse, *is* the essence of a divine and pure humanity by virtue of the effects of the 'love work' of motherhood. It is through the care of their mothers that men learn about 'loving thy neighbour'. Mary, then, is no longer 'alone of all her sex' (Warner, 1990), for she joins all women in the accomplishment of her 'natural' gift of motherhood. Women's bodies, their wombs, become the sites of authentic human experience that clear the path to redemption and divinity (Pope John Paul II, 1995). In this respect, the integrity of humanity is interchangeable with womanhood/motherhood. Yet the affirmation of the primacy of womanhood, of the maternal function, is defined within a gender position. In Catholicism, languages of authority are written on male bodies, while languages of purity are inscribed on female bodies, and they are arranged in a hierarchy.

The procession at St Peter's works within universalist discourses that essentialize and celebrate motherhood as the supreme experience of human life. Leaders of the Church view its role as one of displaying the presence of a 'community'. Rather than seeking transcendence from the 'drama of emigration' – as is the case at the Centro Scalabrini – St Peter's re-members a place of origins, a place of nostalgia, a place of being and of 'living-in-the-present, of simple reproduction, which has been termed immanence' (Massey, 1996: 113). And immanence, in Western philosophical thought, is female (Lloyd, 1984; Massey, 1996). Woven through Mary's body, the procession becomes a narrative of presence-as-immanence. That which is contained in the very nature of being.

The signs of Italian Catholic presence, then, are not just engraved on the church's stones, its adjacent deli, or in the re-tracings of boundaries on

Figure 1 The Madonna is carried out of the church

to a map. They are also displayed on women's bodies that emphasize the primacy of womanhood: as the Madonna is carried out of the church gates (Figure 1), leads the motley file and travels through the winding streets of former Little Italy, she marks out the boundary of an Italian Catholic presence. The female body is a symbolic threshold in the process of inventing traditions and naming places. Here, the living memory of The Hill as (former) Little Italy is given substance through the circulation of female bodies that are interpellated through gender. The following episode further explores this process.

Fourth Episode: The Sacraments of Ethnicity

> She's standing in front of the church, in her white dress, with her white gloves and her hair adorned with white flowers. She smiles shyly as her mother takes some photographs before the ceremony begins.
>
> The interior of the church is decorated as for festive days. Flowers hang on the pews of the central aisle, flowers at the altar, all lights brightly shining. This is a big day.
>
> After the photograph, she must get ready to enter the church. 'We don't want to keep the assembly waiting, do we?' She kisses her mother on the cheek and, nervously, lets go of her hand. The mother enters the church and finds her seat.
>
> The church is packed. Families meet, laugh, hug, wave to each other or call out to those who still haven't found their seat. Men in dark suits, women in colourful dresses move around, wafts of perfume and after-shave trailing

behind them. Children run around while teenagers look on indifferently, sticking together near the entrance, at a safe distance from their parents.

The ceremony finally begins and all fall silent. They enter the church, in a double file. Girls in white dress, boys in suit and tie. There are thirty-six who are receiving the first communion.

The first communion is part of what an Italian priest of London has called 'familistic religion' (Parolin, 1979), that is a religious practice which is mediated through the family frame of reference.[16] Familistic religion includes the rites of passage that punctuate individual lives: christening, first communion, confirmation, wedding and funeral. The celebration of these life-cycle events are viewed by some as expressive of an Italian specificity: 'steeped in ritual and tradition ... it is mainly in this area that differences between British and Italian Catholicism are highly visible' (Colpi, 1991a: 235). That is to say that the particular manner in which rites of *passage* are celebrated is where Italian Catholic specificity is located. The ritualized *passings*, or ritualized *becomings* are displayed as emblems of ethnic difference. In other words, performances of generational *differences* are reified as emblems of Italian émigré *identity* and *continuity*.

Within the array of practices that comprise familistic religion, the first communion is invested with a special significance for it is viewed as an event that brings young Italian children in touch with Italian culture and institutions (Colpi, 1991b: 126). St Peter's church, *the* Italian church, is, for many London Italians, the preferred location for the celebration of the rites of passage. It is the space where transgenerational discontinuity is challenged head on. 'My father took me here for my First Communion, and I want my children to have their First Communion here.' The church, here, provides a stage for the performance of continuity. It offers a 'refuge', in Francesco Giacon's words, against the threat of discontinuity.

As I argue elsewhere (Fortier, forthcoming), generations, in immigration discourses, are the living embodiment of continuity and change, mediating memories of the past with present living conditions, bringing the past into the present and charged with the responsibility of keeping some form of ethnic identity alive in the future. Called upon as bearers of an 'original' identity and culture, and an 'adopted' one, they embody both continuity and change, 'identity-as-conjuncture' and 'identity-as-essence' (Lavie and Swedenburg, 1996: 13) that decant into each other and combine in the formation of a distinct émigré identity. Here, however, their very presence seems to be a defiance to discontinuity and they are regularly wheeled out as a public testimony to the enduring life of Italian émigré culture: girls in regional apparel and first communicants in their elaborate dress, parade, each year, in the procession (Figure 2).

Images of generations work differently on male and female bodies. Boys wear dark suits and ties, dressed up like little men. But when seen standing next to the girls, the 'little men' become grooms. A woman volunteer working at the preparations for the ceremony agreed: 'Parents

Figure 2 First communicants in procession

tell their daughters that they are the brides of this big event. But they tell their sons that they are little men. I've never heard boys referred to as grooms.'[17] Boys will be men. Girls will be brides. The first communion is a wedding rehearsal.

Within Italian émigré culture, the wedding acquires a special significance as a result of its association with sacrifice. Sacrifice stands as an outstanding symbol of the Italian émigré condition of existence (Cavallaro, 1981; Colpi, 1991a).[18] The world of the Italian émigré is a world normalized by a system where sacrifice guarantees redemption, embodied in the future generations. The wedding serves as the ultimate reminder of the drama of emigration where sacrifice becomes the binding element of a system of intergenerational responsibility (Cavallaro, 1981: 84). In a wedding reception, a guest expressed his congratulations and best wishes to the newlyweds, as well as to all 'young persons' present:

> . . . so that they appreciate and follow the example and the sacrifices of their parents, who do all that is in their power to support their children throughout their lives and to accompany them to the altar on their wedding day.[19]

Sacrifice becomes the key principle of a teleology which charges parents with the responsibility of transmitting to their offspring this founding value. A teleology that assigns the children, in turn, with a responsibility towards their parents, more specifically toward the father. As Renato Cavallaro writes, 'the family develops a *centripetal* reciprocity that stems from the family head and that results from the daily imperatives founded upon "sacrifices"' (1981: 112 my emphasis). The 'author' of sacrifice, he adds, is the father. In short, the relocation of sacrifice within the family setting emphasizes kinship ties, reinstates patriarchal authority, and invests them with a special significance in the context of migration.

Both the first communion and the wedding, then, are stages for the enactment of intergenerational responsibility and, as such, are elevated as emblems of collective continuity within the project of identity formation. In other words, these 'definitional ceremonies' are institutional sites of repetition steeped in ritualized patterns of behaviour that repeatedly perform gender differences. It is by *passing* as/in particular *kinds* of boy/manhood, girl/womanhood, that generations enter the communal fold.[20] As young girls and brides mirror each other, and boys mirror men (grooms), gender and generation blur into the display of an enduring Italian culture in London.

On Gendered Ethnicities

Informed by the work of Mary Douglas (1981), Aiwha Ong and Michael Peletz suggest that 'discursive constructions of bodies are frequently plotted against divisions that maintain social order, and that women's bodies in particular are commonly used to symbolize and threaten transgressions of social boundaries' (1995: 6; see also Levine, 1992; McClintock, 1995). More broadly, this concerns the extent to which the performativity of gender is not only most intensive (Ong and Peletz, 1995: 3), but perhaps most imperative at the borders of communities, classes, nationalities and cultures. For Italian intellectuals in London, the issue is precisely to 'create a community', as one leader told me, or to create 'a new identity,'[21] at a time when the population is fragmented, dispersed, and when migration from Italy has radically changed; at a time when the 'community' is perceived as being at the threshold of indeterminacy, assimilation and invisibility.

One notable aspect of the émigré culture of St Peter's is that women embody the threshold of identity/difference as they are both moving and fixed figures of identity and change. Grand narratives about the supremacy of 'virgin-motherhood' as the essence of womanhood are inscribed on female bodies as they mark out and enact the thresholds of identity and difference, while they display the certainty of presence. The female body – the multiplicity of female *bodies* is repudiated in the notion of the Italian 'woman' (*la donna italiana*) – becomes the 'flesh' (Grosz, 1994) through which local particularity and collective identity are inscribed. It is offered as a guarantor of individual and collective selfhood and continuity. To be sure, '[g]ender is a project which has cultural survival as its end' (Butler, 1990: 139). Gender is the key stabilizing principle of Italian émigré culture. The Italian project of identity is moulded out of deeply held ideas about gender differences and generational responsibility, which are products of a patriarchal regime of knowledge that reasserts the universality of male authority and that naturalizes the different positions of men and women.

One conclusion that may be drawn from my findings is that gender, in

Italian émigré culture, is the ultimate trope of difference, insofar as cultural specificity is viewed as best expressed in practices that emphasize gender differences. This, however, seems problematic to me, namely because I am fully aware of the conditions of continuing racism in which the Italian project of collective identity has developed. This project was instigated in the aftermath of Britain's integration in the European Union, which cleared a space for Italian immigrants to claim some form of equal status in relation to Britons on the grounds of their shared European heritage. In this context, Italians projected themselves as 'invisible immigrants'[22] which in Britain, is best understood as the product of the racialization of immigration, where 'immigrant' means black. 'Invisibility' is a notion caught up with 'race' struggles that makes its appropriation by Italians both an instantiation and a challenge of white hegemony. First, its meaning emerges from the very racialization of immigration and 'multicultural' politics, and its adoption by Italians may be read as a gratuitous claim for equality by a population whose invisibility is the product of its integration and acceptance within British society, rather than from conditions of marginalization and imposed silence which configure the 'invisibility' of blacks in Britain. Second, the project of 'visibility' is couched in a politics of difference that both mimics and calls into question the 'invisibility' of whiteness (Dyer, 1997). Indeed, this self-labelling brings to the fore the very assumption that white immigrants have no 'ethnicity', not only as racialized whites, but as culturally diverse people with a variety of backgrounds. In addition, their project evolved in the context of new racism, where culture and difference, rather than skin colour and hierarchy, are the founding principles of differentiation. Hence the project of 'visibility' challenges totalizing conceptions of whiteness on the grounds of claims about cultural difference, but it operates through the privileges of whiteness.

Ethnicity is undeniably worked into British Italian belongingness. That is to say that the quest for, and location of, cultural particularity is deeply intertwined with the construction of ethnic boundaries that hem in differences and enclose them into the fold of a hegemonic 'Italianness'. But the point is that the very simultaneity of ethnic and gender formation in institutional practices of identity signals that clear distinctions between such categories are not so easy to maintain. They are deeply embedded in one another, and their entwinement is to be understood as the outcome of their construction along similar bodily lines. This is particularly the case in the sacraments examined above, where both ethnic and gender differences are inscribed on bodies. Though the body may not figure as the bearer of immutable cultural or biological difference in the formation of cultural ethnicity, it is conscripted to render 'visible' what is not. Moreover, it is called upon as a *gendered* body. Imperatives of gender and ethnicity are dependent on each other for their mutual construction. Gender regulations operate through the regulation of ethnic boundaries, while ethnic regulations serve to protect against 'certain socially endangering sexual transgressions' (Butler, 1993: 20). It is in the name of ethnic tradition that younger generations are brought into the communal fold as (little) men and (future) brides. At the same time, injunctions of womanhood operate as guarantors of cultural continuity.

St Peter's is a place of re-membering. It is a place of collective memory, in which elements of the past are cobbled together to mould a communal body of belonging. It is a place where individual lives, present and past, are called upon to inhabit the present space, to 'member' it. Finally, it is a site where individual bodies circulate, come and go; where bodies are signifying actors in claims for, and practices of, the identity of St Peter's and former Little Italy. These bodies, in turn, are projected into a structure of meaning that precedes them and re-members them into gendered definitions of identity and becoming. Re-membering 'The Hill' works through bodies that are ethnicized and gendered at once, while the circulation of these bodies ethnicizes and genders a space in the process of claiming it as an Italian (terrain of) belonging(s).

Notes

I wish to express my deepest gratitude to those who have generously commented on different versions of this essay, especially David Leahy who read numerous drafts with sustained thoroughness and interest, and Kate Nash whose notes have been most useful in refining my argument. I also thank Vikki Bell, Diane Lamoureux, Minoo Moallem, Anick Druelle, Colette St-Hilaire and two anonymous referees. An earlier version of this article was presented at the international conference 'Transformations: Thinking Through Feminism', at Lancaster University, 17–19 July 1997. I thank those present for their supportive comments and useful questions.

1. Following Kerby Miller's (1985) model of the 'culture of exile', and Matthew Frye Jacobson's 'migrant culture', I use émigré culture to speak of a culture 'for which the experience of geographical movement and resettlement [is] formative' (Jacobson, 1995: xi). Though not all London Italian immigrants regard themselves as émigrés, the trope pervades different forms of representations of the Italian presence in Britain (see Fortier, 1996a).

2. Sneja Gunew (1996) also uses Butler in her exploration of performative acts of cultural ethnicity. Though she does not address questions of embeddedness (with gender or 'race' for instance), her article is an original contribution to conceptions of the performativity of cultural ethnicity.

3. In contrast to Butler's emphasis on embodied acts or speech acts, I expand my field of enquiry to include other forms of representation such as written remembrances, which I view as equally performative by virtue of the fact that they produce the 'History' they claim to be retrieving and re-presenting (De Certeau, 1983).

4. The second is the Centro Scalabrini in Brixton (south London). Its church is called Chiesa del Redentore.

5. Such as the Irish church, St Etheldreda's Catholic Chapel, that was also established in Clerkenwell, in Ely Place, in 1879.

6. *Backhill* (March 1993: 30).

7. I am using here the notion of duration that the French philosopher Henri Bergson has developed. For Bergson, memory is an act of duration where different states and

moments have no beginning nor ending, but rather extend into one another (1993: 31). As Butler rightly points out (1993: 244–5 n8), this implies a notion of temporality that is not to be construed as a succession of distinct and equivalent units of time called 'moments'. For Bergson, memory consists of accumulating 'moments' from the 'past' and congealing them to the point of their indistinguishability. Yet in contrast to Bergson, I do not completely refute the possibility of spatial mappings of temporality. Further on in this article, I explain how The Hill operates as a spatio-temporal interval within Italian émigré historicity.

8. *Backhill* (June 1993:10).

9. *Backhill* (March 1993: 30).

10. I borrow this phrase from Padre Gaetano Parolin who used it in reference to the other London Italian religious social club, the Centro Scalabrini (*La Voce degli Italiani*, no. 967, February 1997: 5).

11. *Backhill* (September 1996: 9).

12. *Backhill* (September 1996: 9).

13. Some define *mammismo* as Italian men's excessive attachment to their mother (Gundle, 1996: 317). But I prefer to expand the definition of *mammismo* to a collective fascination for motherhood, especially for mothers' devotion, suffering and sacrifice for other human beings, namely their sons and husbands.

14. Though in the years following Mussolini, the project of an Italian liberal democratic state has also attended to women. As Leslie Caldwell (1989) demonstrates, progressive politics of post-war Italy substantially reproduced those of the fascist era when it came to the regulation of women-as-mothers.

15. Aside from Italians, the ship also included German prisoners of war and Jewish refugees. For a more detailed analysis of the tragedy of the *Arandora Star* and its significance within British-Italian historicity, see Fortier (1996a, chapter 2).

16. And what Bruno Orsi has labelled the 'domus centered' Italian-American popular region (Orsi, 1985).

17. It is worth noting that she added that these parents were, in her view, subverting the 'true' meaning of the white dress, which is 'purity and joy'. To be sure, the bridal gown projects girls' bodies into a metaphysical realm, where their sexuality is sublimated into the more venerable virginity. This denial of female bodies is deeply enmeshed with Catholicism's distates for 'things of flesh' that work through a particular connection with injunctions of womanhood.

18. The difference between émigrés and exiles is captured in the trope of sacrifice, which connects with a migrant culture that, according to Italian-Montreal poet Filippo Salvatore, is shaped through the 'spiritual possibility' of return which sustains a sense of continuity with the homeland that displaced people do not share (in Caccia, 1985: 158). To put it simply, sacrifice is configured around notions of continuity, in contrast to suffering, which is founded on notions of discontinuity and rupture.

19. *La Voce degli Italiani* (no. 869, July 1992: 10).

20. For a fuller account of the particular kind of injunctions of womanhood deployed in London Italian social clubs, see Fortier (1996b).

21. *La Voce degli Italiani* (no. 831, October 1990: 15).

22. The phrase was first coined in a statistical survey on Italians, Spanish and Portuguese immigrants in Britain (see MacDonald and MacDonald, 1972). It was

subsequently used by Marin (1975) and by Father Graziano Tassello, a leading advocate of Italian émigré identity, in a speech he gave in 1983 which was reprinted in Britain's leading Italian newspaper (*La Voce degli Italiani* no. 831, October 1990: 15).

References

Anthias, F. and N. Yuval-Davis (1992) *Racialized Boundaries: Race, Nation, Gender, Colour and Class and the Anti-Racist Struggle*. London: Routledge.

Anzaldúa, G. (1987) *Borderlands/La Frontera: The New Mestiza*. San Francisco: Aunt Lute.

Appadurai, A. (1990) 'Disjuncture and Difference in the Global Cultural Economy', pp. 295–310 in M. Featherstone (ed.) *Global Culture: Nationalism, Globalization and Modernity*. London: Sage.

Bergson, H. (1993) *Matière et mémoire*. Paris: Presses Universitaires de France. (Orig. 1939.)

Bottignolo, B. (1985) *Without a Bell Tower: A Study of the Italian Immigrants in South-West England*. Rome: Centro Studi Emigrazione.

Boyarin, D. and J. Boyarin (1993) 'Diaspora: Generation and the Ground of Jewish Identity', *Critical Inquiry* 19(4): 693–725.

Brah, A. (1992) 'Difference, Diversity and Differentiation', pp. 126–45 in J. Donald and A. Rattansi (eds) *'Race', Culture and Difference*. London: Sage.

Braidotti, R. (1994) *Nomadic Subjects: Embodiment and Sexual Difference in Contemporary Feminist Theory*. New York: Columbia University Press.

Butler, J. (1990) *Gender Troubles: Feminism and the Subversion of Identity*. New York and London: Routledge.

Butler, J. (1993) *Bodies that Matter: On the Discursive Limits of 'Sex'*. New York and London: Routledge.

Caccia, F. (1985) 'Filippo Salvatore', pp. 150–65 in *Sous le signe du phénix: entretiens avec 15 créateurs italo-québécois*. Montréal: Guernica.

Caldwell, L. (1986) 'Reproducers of the Nation: Women and the Family in Fascist Policy', pp. 110–41 in D. Forgacs (ed.) *Rethinking Italian Fascism*. London: Lawrence and Wishart.

Caldwell, L. (1989) 'Women as the Family: The Foundation of a New Italy?', pp. 168–83 in N. Yuval-Davis and F. Anthias (eds) *Woman-Nation-State*. London: Macmillan.

Calhoun, C. (1994) 'Social Theory and the Politics of Identity', pp. 9–36 in C. Calhoun (ed.) *Social Theory and the Politics of Identity*. Oxford: Blackwell.

Carroll, M.P. (1992) *Madonnas that Maim: Popular Catholicism in Italy since the Fifteenth Century*. Baltimore, MD and London: Johns Hopkins University Press.

Cavallaro, R. (1981) *Storie senza storia: indagine sull'emigrazione calabrese in Gran Bretagna*. Rome: Centro Studi Emigrazione.

Colpi, T. (1991a) *The Italian Factor: The Italian Community in Great Britain*. London: Mainstream.

Colpi, T. (1991b) *Italians Forward: A Visual History of the Italian Community in Great Britain*. London: Mainstream.

Connerton, P. (1992) *How Societies Remember.* Cambridge: Cambridge University Press.

De Certeau, M. (1990) *L'Invention du quotidien, 1: arts de faire.* Paris: Gallimard. (Orig. 1980.)

De Certeau, M. (1983) 'History: Ethics, Science, and Fiction', pp. 125–52 in N. Haan, R. Bellah, P. Rabinow and W.M. Sullivan (eds) *Social Science as Moral Inquiry*. New York: Columbia University Press.

De Grazia, V. (1992) *How Fascism Ruled Women.* Berkeley: University of California Press.

Di Leonardo, M. (1994) 'White Ethnicities, Identity Politics and Baby Bears' Chair', *Social Text* 41: 165–91.

Douglas, M. (1984) *Purity and Danger. An Analysis of the Concepts of Pollution and Taboo*. London: Ark Paperbacks. (Orig. 1966.)

Dyer, R. (1997) *White*. London and New York: Routledge.

Ferrari, L. (1993) *Fortunata*. London: Michael Joseph.

Fortier, A.-M. (1996a) 'Gender, Ethnicity and Power: Identity Formation in Two Italian Organisations of London', PhD dissertation in Sociology, Goldsmiths College, University of London.

Fortier, A.-M. (1996b) 'Troubles in the Field: The Use of Personal Experiences as Sources of Knowledge', *Critique of Anthropology* 16(3): 303–23.

Fortier, A.-M. (forthcoming) 'The Politics of "Italians Abroad": Nation, Diaspora and New Geographies of Identity', *Diaspora: A Journal of Transnational Studies.*

Gillis, J.R. (1994) 'Memory and Identity: The History of a Relationship', pp. 3–23 in J.R. Gillis (ed.) *Commemorations: The Politics of National Identity.* Princeton, NJ: Princeton University Press.

Gilroy, P. (1987) *There Ain't no Black in the Union Jack*. London: Unwin Hyman.

Gilroy, P. (1993) *The Black Atlantic: Modernity and Double Consciousness.* London: Verso.

Gilroy, P. (1995) 'Roots and Routes: Black Identity as an Outernational Project', pp. 15–30 in H.W. Harris, H.C. Blue and E.E.H. Griffith (eds), *Racial and Ethnic Identity: Psychological Development and Creative Expression.* London and New York: Routledge.

Glissant, E. (1981) *Discours Antillais.* Paris: Seuil.

Grosz, E. (1994) *Volatile Bodies: Toward a Corporeal Feminism.* Bloomington and Indianapolis: Indiana University Press.

Gundle, S. (1996) 'Fame, Fashion and Style: The Italian Star System', pp. 309–26 in D. Forgacs and R. Lumley (eds) *Italian Cultural Studies: An Introduction.* Oxford: Oxford University Press.

Gunew, S. (1996) 'Performing Australian Ethnicity: "Helen Demidenko"', pp. 159–71 in W. Ommundsen and H. Rowley (eds) *From a Distance: Australian Writers and Cultural Displacement.* Geelong (Aus.): Deakin University Press.

Gunew, S. and A. Yeatman (eds) (1993) *Feminism and the Politics of Difference.* St Leonards (Aus.): Allen and Unwin.

Gupta, A. and J. Ferguson (1992) 'Beyond "Culture": Space, Identity and the Politics of Difference', *Cultural Anthropology* 7(1): 6–23.

Hall, S. (1991) 'The Local and the Global: Globalization and Ethnicity', pp. 19–39 in A.D. King (ed.) *Culture, Globalization and the World-System.* London: Macmillan.

Hobsbawm, E. and T. Ranger (eds) (1983) *The Invention of Tradition*. Cambridge: Cambridge University Press.

Jacobson, M.F. (1995) *Special Sorrows: The Diasporic Imagination of Irish, Polish, and Jewish Immigrants in the United States*. Cambridge, MA and London: Harvard University Press.

Juteau, D. (1996) 'Toward a Pluralist Citizenship: Accounting for Ethnicity', paper presented at the conference États, nations, multi-ethnicité et citoyenneté, Montréal, 30 May–2 June.

Kaplan, Caren (1996) *Questions of Travel: Postmodern Discourses of Displacements.* Durham, NC and London: Duke University Press.

Kristeva, J. (1983) 'Stabat Mater', pp. 225–47 in J. Kristeva, *Histoires d'amour.* Paris: Denoël.

Lavie, S. and T. Swedenburg (1996) 'Introduction', pp. 1–25 in S. Lavie and T. Swedenburg (eds) *Displacement, Diaspora, and Geographies of Identity*. Durham, NC and London: Duke University Press.

Levine, A.-J. (1992) 'Diaspora as Metaphor: Bodies and Boundaries in the Book of Tobit', pp. 105–18 in J.A. Overman and R.S. MacLennan (eds) *Diaspora Jews and Judaism: Essays in Honour of, and in Dialogue with, A. Thomas Kraabel.* Atlanta, CA: Scholar Press.

Lloyd, G. (1984) *The Man of Reason: 'Male' and 'Female' in Western Philosophy*. London: Methuen.

McClintock, A. (1995) *Imperial Leather: Race, Gender and Sexuality in the Colonial Context*. London and New York: Routledge.

MacDonald, J.S. and L.D. MacDonald (1972) *The Invisible Immigrants*. London: The Runnymede Industrial Unit.

McRobbie, A. (1995) 'Catholic Glasgow: A Map of the City', *History Workshop Journal* 40: 172–80.

Marin, U. (1975) *Italiani in Gran Bretagna*. Rome: Centro di Studi Emigrazione.

Martin, A.K. (1997) 'The Practice of Identity and an Irish Sense of Place', *Gender, Place and Culture* 4(1): 89–119.

Massey, D. (1995) 'Places and their Pasts', *History Workshop Journal* 39: 182–92.

Massey, D. (1996) 'Masculinity, Dualisms and High Technology', pp. 109–26 in N. Duncan (ed.) *BodySpace: Destabilizing Geographies of Gender and Sexuality*. London and New York: Routledge.

Michaels, W.B. (1992) 'Race into Culture: A Critical Genealogy of Cultural Identity', *Critical Inquiry* 18(4): 655–85.

Migliore, S. (1988) 'Religious Symbols and Cultural Identity: A Sicilian-Canadian Example', *Canadian Ethnic Studies/ Etudes éthniques canadiennes* 20: 78–94.

Miller, K. (1985) *Emigrants and Exiles: Ireland and the Irish Exodus*. New York and Oxford: Oxford University Press.

Moallem, M. (1998) 'National Belonging and Sexed Corporeality', paper given at the 14th World Congress of Sociology. Montréal: 26 July–1 August.

Mosse, G. L. (1985) *Nationalism and Sexuality: Middle-Class Morality and Sexual Norms in Modern Europe.* Madison: Wisconsin University Press.

Myerhoff, B. (1979) *Number Our Days*. New York: E.P. Dutton

Nichols, B. (1994) *Blurred Boundaries: Questions of Meaning in Contemporary Culture*. Indianapolis: Indiana University Press.

Ong, A. and M. Peletz (1995) 'Introduction', pp. 1–18 in A. Ong and M. Peletz (eds) *Bewitching Women, Pious Men: Gender and Body Politics in Southeast Asia*. Berkeley: University of California Press.

Orsi, R.A. (1985) *The Madonna of 115th Street.* New Haven, CT and London: Yale University Press.

Parker, A., M. Russo, D. Sommer and P. Yaeger (1992) 'Introduction', pp. 1–18 in A. Parker et al. (eds) *Nationalisms and Sexualities.* New York and London: Routledge.

Parolin, G. (1979) 'Foreign Catholics: The Religious Practice of the Emilian Community in London', unpublished MA dissertation, Kent University in Canterbury.

Passerini, L. (1996) 'Gender Relations', pp. 144-59 in D. Forgacs and R. Lumley (eds) *Italian Cultural Studies: An Introduction*. Oxford: Oxford University Press.

Pope John Paul II (1995) *Letter of Pope John Paul II to Women.* London: Catholic Truth Society.

Pratt, J. (1996) 'Catholic Culture', pp. 129-44 in D. Forgacs and R. Lumley (eds) *Italian Cultural Studies: An Introduction*. Oxford: Oxford University Press.

Primeggia, S. and J.A. Varacalli (1996) 'The Sacred and Profane among Italian American Catholics: The Giglio Feast', *International Journal of Politics, Culture and Society* 9(3): 423–49.

Probyn, E. (1996) *Outside Belongings*. New York and London: Routledge.

Sponza, L. (1988) *Italian Immigrants in Nineteenth-Century Britain: Realities and Images.* Leicester: Leicester University Press.

Swiderski, R.M. (1986) *Voices: An Anthropologist's Dialogue with an Italian-American Festival*. Bowling Green, OH: Bowling Green Popular Press.

Trebay, G. (1990) 'Our Local Correspondents: The Giglio', *New Yorker* 4 June: 78–89.

Trinh, T.M.-H. (1989) *Woman, Native, Other*. Bloomington and Indianapolis: Indiana University Press.

Valentine, G. (1993) '(Hetero)sexing Space: Lesbian Perceptions and Experiences of Everyday Spaces', *Society and Space* 11: 395–413.

Warner, M. (1990) *Alone of All Her Sex: The Myth and the Cult of the Virgin Mary.* London: Picador. (Orig. 1979.)

Yuval-Davis, N. and F. Anthias (eds) (1989) *Woman-Nation-State*. London: Macmillan.

Anne-Marie Fortier teaches Sociology at Lancaster University. Her forthcoming book *'Italians Never Die, They Just Pasta Away': Indeterminacy, Continuity and the Location of Culture* is on the formation of an Italian émigré culture in London. Her current research interests are on diasporic identity formations and the articulations of 'race', ethnicity, sexuality and gender.

Ethnic Absolutism and the Authoritarian Spirit

Chetan Bhatt

Introduction

WITHIN BOTH 'racial politics' and the broadly conceived discipline of race relations sociology, it has become difficult to describe some of the new black political and cultural formations that reside inside or nearby fairly authoritarian discourses of race, nationalism, religion and ethnicity. Those seemingly autocratic, seemingly 'radical' formations and movements have gathered together new languages and practices around race, ethnicity and nationalism that appear to defy comprehensive description or explanation from within both older Marxist and liberal theoretical paradigms or the newer ones that name themselves postmodern or postcolonial. Importantly enough, those formations and movements pose formidable and often stark political challenges to black or white sensibilities that may be called democratic, anti-authoritarian or egalitarian, even if we agree that the meanings of the latter terms, and the political structures they announce, have changed.

With some important exceptions (Gilroy, 1993, 1996; Sahgal and Yuval-Davis, 1992; Solomos and Back, 1996), relatively few writers in the UK have discussed directly the philosophical and political challenges posed by black authoritarian ethnic and cultural movements. While there certainly has been considerable intellectual debate on issues of multiculturalism and anti-racism in the UK and US, it can still seem that this is framed by questions of identity and 'difference'. Many theoretical discussions of identity are bounded by an overarching, always innocent question of metaphysical identity. Much contemporary theory tends to assume that the question of identity is an ontologically innocent one, that identity is a virtue as well as a natural necessity. Its ontological status must necessarily

▪ *Theory, Culture & Society* 1999 (SAGE, London, Thousand Oaks and New Delhi), Vol. 16(2): 65–85
[0263-2764(199904)16:2;65–85;008255]

be of greater analytic importance than its actual content, the latter always defined as emergent only subsequently.

Consequently, theories of identity can formulate the question of identity as one that is also epistemologically innocent. Postmodern or cultural studies work abounds with discussions of identity but it is rare to find a discussion that has moved into the messy business of the evaluation of the democratic or authoritarian, egalitarian or totalitarian content of identities. In many current discussions, typically framed by aphorisms such as 'the problem of modern society is the problem of difference', neither the question of identity itself nor its content are made amenable to ethical judgement.

Both these 'naturalized' conceptions of identity are the preconditions for an 'innocence of subjectivity' that can impel the subject towards an enunciation of the most authoritarian sensibilities. The historically wounded subject of innocence can fill its subjectivity with the most abhorrent rational and affective – and metaphysical – material, and it can be very difficult to criticize or oppose it (Gilroy, 1996; Levinas, 1990). Perhaps this kind of innocence is best described as a claim to moral authority that actively disavows a capability in and responsibility towards engaging the moral complexities of the lifeworld that confront it. More generally, we can speak of an active complicity in reconstructing or reducing moral or ethical questions into ones that are concerned only with upholding the simple unity of one's ownmost being ('I think black, therefore I am'). If, at this stage, absolutism emerges, it can be of a distinctly metaphysical kind that need not rely on varieties of nature or culture to legitimize it. Finally, questions of identity are often framed at the level of epistemic generalities, whereas the actual material of identity arises through historical and social processes, institutions, networks, associations. Metaphysical identity does not simply arise metaphysically but requires comprehensive practical labour for its realization.

Similarly, while there has been a significant move away from the dogmatism that dominated some aspects of UK anti-racist practice in the early 1980s, many current theoretical, political and policy-oriented tendencies around race and ethnicity continue to be based around the following broad axioms: an acknowledgement of multiculturalism that is invested in a celebration of cultural, ethnic, national and religious *incommensurability* regardless of the ethical consequences which may follow; an acknowledgement of difference that hinges on its reification but is epistemologically, and in practice, unable to evaluate the political tendencies and material that constitute the basis of a claimed difference; an explicit, perhaps even socialist or social democratic anti-racism that seems unconcerned with its practical affiliation with varieties of corporatist or cultural black nationalism whose ethics may not travel as far as any kind of universal democratic anti-racism; the resurgence of theoretical epistemologies of liberation and emancipation that seem fixated on contriving various racial and ethnic affiliations based on a philosophical anthropology of ancient riverine civilizations and varieties of mysticism and personal growth (the latter expected to substitute for a considered analytics of the socioeconomic and cultural conditions of the Western black underclasses or of the 'Third World'.) Each of these tendencies has the possible consequence that affiliates to an identity have no common obligations (such as those of solidarity, care or love) to non-affiliates, except perhaps those that comprise pure transaction in economic and cultural products and are enacted selectively by the pure. However, the internal 'we' of identities typically assumes obligations that are not about equality, a 'universal franchise' or democratic ideals but about strategies for internal stratification and discipline, fairly typically gender-based and reliant on systems of patronage. It is perhaps these kinds of structures that have elicited the description of late modern identity formations as 'neo-tribal': primordial proto-humanist obligations that cease completely and finally for those outside the group boundary; an internal discipline based on forms of masculine authority and the family trope; authority based on normative patronage and deference; and an irreducibly antagonistic conception of group boundary.

Ethnic Absolutism and the Description of Fascism

There are immense political and irreducibly philosophical difficulties that new ethnic and religious authoritarian movements expose for a politics of anti-racism that now necessarily has to deal with the 'absolutisms of the powerless'. In this political exchange, what is anti-racist and what is apparently 'racist' has become, in several instances, indistinguishable. A consequently easy generalization that *some* have found relatively easy to make again is that projects of anti-racism necessarily lead to varieties of absolutism or nationalism (Kristeva, 1993; Žižek, 1997). A much older problem of reductionism is the possibility (if any) of an anti-racism that cannot reify 'race' or 'racial' categories.

It is from within this complicated environment that the stimulating critiques by Paul Gilroy of black nationalism, ethnic absolutism, 'unanimism' and even varieties of minority 'fascism' (Gilroy, 1987, 1993, 1996) become valuable, especially because Gilroy's project taken as a whole tends to avoid these kinds of reduction by considering in some detail other black movements that refuse the valorization of essential categories. The movement in his work from a critique of racially exclusive Englishness and British nationalism, to a consideration of the various ideologies produced by some of its racial victims has illustrated a range of general problems that can extend far beyond a demonstration of the congruencies between right-wing English nationalism and the types of black nationalism that would claim to confront it.

Gilroy's critiques of both racism and black nationalism fundamentally question the claims of high modernity. They expose how languages of liberty, solidarity, revolution or care can become transformed into particularist idioms that innocently celebrate ideas of racially or ethnically exclusive solidarity, authoritarian revolution and a liberation based on masculinist regimes and gendered stratification. In such a scheme, 'care' can only be self-directed and primordial, and effective only as a form of 'nihilism'. More specifically, in his critique of black radical conservatism, Gilroy asks how universalist emancipatory ideas allow their appropriation by tendencies which seem to be proximate to 'fascism'. In a period that is troubling for foundational or universal ideas, or even comparative political generalizations, what then is the critical ground for one's own description of particular ideas as 'authoritarian' or 'fascist', or of one's opposition to such ideas? What exactly is it about 'our' sensibilities that makes ideas from National Socialism or fascism feel as if they have some semblance to some ideas present in deconstructionist theory, Nietzschean philosophy or Heideggerianism? Conversely, how can progressive sensibilities disavow the possibility of their appropriation by authoritarianism (Gilroy, 1996)?

Some of these questions inhabited an older space of radical dissent in Europe in the 1930s and 1940s. Its key thesis was put forward in Emmanuel Levinas' critique of the Heideggerian subject (Levinas, 1990). For Levinas, the possibility always exists that the foundations of Western philosophy have made it insufficiently inured to its own embedded potentiality for 'elemental Evil', for absolutism, terror and erasure.[1] Is the Heideggerian a priori for the 'subject', or the 'pre-ontic-ontological Dasein', universal to Western philosophy and the necessary precondition for Western modernity (Heidegger, 1962)? Is Dasein simply a discovery by Heidegger of the previously unacknowledged presuppositions that allow the subject(s) and ontology of Western philosophy to exist or is it his absolutist prescription for Western philosophy? What is it about the metaphysics of the subject that allows its easy philosophical identification with a metaphysics of Volk? Conversely, what are the possible ethical contents for the place of identity, communion, solidarity and care that the racially oppressed and exploited themselves create and which is 'inside', 'outside', 'adjacent to' or in some other way fundamentally, though not uncritically, influenced by the modernist 'subject of humanism'?

It is from within this broad context that Gilroy's work bears extension and elaboration to a different area that has preoccupied South Asian writers (Basu et al., 1993; Das, 1992; Gopal, 1990; Jaffrelot, 1996; Ludden, 1996; Nandy et al., 1995; Sarkar and Butalia, 1995; Vaniak, 1997). Paradoxically, a critical engagement with some of the themes derived from Gilroy's varied assessments of primarily African-Caribbean and black American nationalisms serves, reflexively, to highlight important themes in the development of specifically South Asian varieties of nationalist, 'racial' and religious identification. This is not to imply that the historical and political contexts or ideological issues are the same, or even remotely similar. However, some of the themes that emerge in Gilroy's earlier critiques of ethnic absolutism, and their development in his subsequent work towards what appears to be a critique of some specifically metaphysical formations, bear extension to other ideological phenomena that are primarily about religion.

This is explored below through an engagement with some of these themes for assessing the kinds of political ideologies that have come to animate contemporary Hindu authoritarian religious movements. The latter are particularly interesting since they are firmly preoccupied with the metaphysics of a distinctive South Asian concept of 'race' that is manifestly embedded in spiritual discourse (Bhatt, 1997; Jaffrelot, 1996). This opens up the possibility of ideas of 'race' in Hindu nationalism that are not simple inversions of English or colonial racism (though that exists), but of other 'racisms' that can accommodate lineage, typology, classification and hierarchy (Banton, 1987). These ideas also carry a troubling but characteristic spiritual orientation towards a variety of Aryanism.

This movement from hereditarian and cultural racisms to a privileged and expressly 'metaphysical xenology' provides an additional, potent ingredient that requires analysis in its own right, and which can assist in extending discussions about the characterization of contemporary proto-fascisms. This tentative and temporary phrase aims to describe the core sense of being that is at the basis of some of these movements. It describes the cultivation of self and Being that is based on an archaic hereditarian ethnology that slides between culture and nature, history and the present, without ever having any epistemic responsibility around the use of these ideas. It does not need to specify the actual mechanics of heredity or biology that are related to its key trope of 'blood' from which the ethnology of self, as well as a totalizing xenology, are derived.

The Civilizational Shift and the Aryan Memory

A distinctive characteristic of the authoritarian religious movements that claim hegemony over the political representation and cultural, community and familial activities of South Asian communities in the UK is their reliance on a complex discourse of renewal that embodies not simply 'ethnic tradition' or 'authenticity' but also key ideas about novelty and innovation. Paradigmatically, traditions that have never existed (such as the idea of an Islamic government) and ethnicities that have never been (such as a recent and dogmatic idea of *hindutva* – the 'transcendental essence' of Hinduness) can be claimed as primordial but also in need of rejuvenation. What is deemed to be 'the authentic' can also be 'the novel'. Actual ethnic traditions can be compared with the measuring instrument of authenticity and then discarded.

A key strategy in much South Asian ethnic or religious revival – and in other cultural-political formations arising in Caribbean and African-American groups – is related to posing a question of originary civilization (Jain, 1994). This civilization methodology is a perpetually shape-shifting, mesmerizing technique that superficially seems concerned to aggrandize those contemporary groups that wish to claim their descent from one of the despotic ancient riverine civilizations that existed along that resonant line that stretched from the Nile Valley to the Indus Valley.

Paul Gilroy's discussions about Afrocentricity (Gilroy, 1993) bear on these areas, because there are striking similarities and correspondences, often mirror-images of each other, between varieties of Afrocentricity and the burgeoning literature arising from India and Pakistan on the 'Indus-Saraswati' civilizations (Gupta, 1996) and on the Vedic Aryans. Both are mirrored in each other spatially, since each can claim its own narrative of civilization as primordial and the cause of the other. If the Buddha is claimed for Africa, ancient Egypt can also be claimed for India (Rajaram and Frawley, 1997). The ethnic and mythical narratives of both, their 'epistemologies of time and space', create an epic story of a primordial, spiritual and sublime civilization that fell to degradation and struggle (typically with external, colonial invasions, or because of deviations and corruptions of the original wisdom). The (perpetually) present moment is one of renewal and return, manifested as a declaration of becoming, a shedding of internal metaphysical impurity, an exhibitionism of the body. Futurity is enclosed in a coming to collective civilizational being, typically the return of an archaic hierarchy and despotism that is imagined as an authentic liberation, a natural order and a state of peace. Similarly, both Afrocentric and Indocentric tendencies are preoccupied with ideas of 'race', 'race inferiority', chromatic divisions or gradations, physiognomy and craniometry, archaeology and anthropology.

It seems impossible for any contemporary project to discuss ancient civilizations without confronting at some point Europe's own originary civilization myths based on some key ideas of Aryanism. Both Afrocentricity and Hindu nationalism embody a substantial anti-racist critique that engages very directly with specifically 18th- and especially 19th-century 'race thinking', particularly German, French and British Egyptology and Indology. Both are concerned with a critique of variants of Aryanism and both reject ideas of *external* Aryan influence upon their pristine indigenous civilizations, especially where these relate in both cases to a familiar thesis: the southward migrations of nomadic pastoralist 'Indo-Aryans' or to nomadic pastoralist 'Hamitic', 'Nilo-Hamitic' or 'Nilotic' Aryans. Both, finally, believe their favoured civilization was the cradle of all world civilization.

To be sure, the current impact of 19th-century Aryanist thinking needs to be actively and consistently opposed. However, the contemporary and horrifying resonance of 19th-century 'Aryan hypotheses' not only controverts the belief that these ideas are now marginal or inconsequential, but also demonstrates how their effects are unpredictable. The systematic genocide of Tutsis in Rwanda during 1994 was informed by a Hutu supremacist view that the Tutsis were 'originally' descendants of invading or usurping Aryans ('Hamites') from the north, a view whose origins can be traced to the travel writings and 'anthropological' observations of Western explorers in eastern and central Africa towards the middle of the last century (Speke, 1864). A central component of Hutu supremacist ideological mobilization was the rhetoric that Tutsi 'Aryans' would implement a strategy of genocide against the Hutus that would be similar to that undertaken by the other 'Aryans', German National Socialists (African Rights, 1995: 39–42.) The 'Hamitic hypothesis' and its variants are still central to discussions about the nature of political antagonism and tribal conflict in Africa (African Rights, 1995; Seligman, 1957: chapter 7). The recent civil war in Uganda was itself inflected with a view of nomadic pastoralist Nilotic or Nilo-Hamite 'Aryans' (identified with the northern Acholi) that had usurped Bantu lands.

If the perceived descendants of 'Aryans' are the target of official genocide, as in Rwanda during the 1990s, this makes the progressive nature of counter-Aryanist ideology problematic in a number of ways. Clearly, it is the reification within a paradigm of Aryanist 'race thinking' of particular groups, ethnicities and nationalities that is the fundamental problem. But the Rwandan genocide, and as we shall see, Hindu nationalism also signal the possibility that those national and ethnic absolutists who oppose Western 'racial Aryanist' ideas can still create their own totalitarianisms based on their civilizational methodologies.

The Possibilities of Volkish Anti-Racism

The importance of 'indigenous civilization' for many new contemporary ethnic formations is accompanied by exhaustive definitions of exclusionary identity and it is worth briefly examining these in the paradigmatic case of Hindu nationalist ideas about civilization. For the founders of contemporary Hindu nationalism, Aryanism presented an epistemic problem: the evidences of English and German linguistics and Indology suggested Aryans entered from outside physical India, and hence the idea of an immemorial cultural hearth in which the physical land, culture and people intermingled to give rise to Hindu civilization is already disturbed at its origin by a founding presence which is alien to the land. Vinayak Damodar Savarkar, the founder of modern Hindu nationalism during the period of the 1920s, indeed initially argued for a hybrid origin for Vedic civilization: it was the commingling of the blood of the incoming Aryans and the people they encountered that gave rise to Hindu civilization. That civilization was formed through a Lamarckian conception whereby the physical land and environment impresses upon, and is conversely affected by the people so as to instil a peculiar *hereditary* quality to land, culture and people. The essence of that culture was hindutva, the 'beingness' of a Hindu that defines a common nation (*rashtra*), 'race' (*jati*) and civilization (*sankskriti* culture). Hindutva is transmitted by blood and apprehended by a feeling, a structure of emotion that makes a Hindu realize his or her true connection with the sublime civilization of the Vedic Aryans (Savarkar, 1989). There is a powerful 'race concept' here that was created by an Indian nationalist hero who was actively fighting British colonialism and its conceptions of 'race' and racial supremacy. This leads to a further examination of some of the historical basis of these ideas, within which a kind of chauvinistic ethnic particularism rests easily with an 'anti-racism'.

Savarkar's 'race concept' combines land, blood and heredity, affect and emotion, superlative originators (Aryans), an ancestral blood community and a particular Vedic view of religion. Many of its elements are proximate to German Romanticism and some of the ideas that informed German Idealism. However, all these elements can also relatively easily be derived, from a particular gaze, from existing Hindu-Vedic traditions, especially the Rig-Veda and Manusmriti. There is little doubt that European Aryanist race thinking owed much to an already pre-existing white supremacist racial paradigm in which the discovery of Vedic Sanskrit had to be both explained and made use of. That short history of 'the discovery of Aryan' is replete with numerous conjectures and nuances that have become strangely animated today in a complex series of Hinducentric arguments. Perhaps ten years ago, they would have been seen simply as anti-racist arguments. Today their proponents hold up a powerful banner of anti-colonialism and anti-racism in order to create a project that seems barely removed from the fascism they claim to distance themselves from.

The Hinducentric project closely follows the intellectual trajectory of early Indology, expressed through that German love affair with India during the late 18th century, in the period during and after the French Revolution. Charles Wilkins's translation of Sanskrit, and Sir William Jones's discovery in the 1780s of the philological similarities between Greek, Latin and archaic Sanskrit, and his laudatory discussions of the antiquity and perfection of the Sanskrit language and its grammar provided rich material for those who sought a new, non-biblical, and importantly a non-Semitic, non-Hebraic origin for 'the obscurer portions' of European, especially German history and civilization (Mosse, 1966; Poliakov, 1974). In both France and Germany from the mid-19th century onwards, this later became a major justification for the fascination with India. Frederick Schlegel's *On the Language and Wisdom of the Indians* (Schlegel, 1849), published in 1808 contained several key points that were to become so effective later: India received the primordial revelation (though Indians were also the first to commit the primordial error, the fall from grace); all world civilization came either from Indian migration out of India or from Indian influence; Greek, Latin, Hebraic[2] and Arabic language and mythology are already both superseded and captured in Sanskrit and in the Vedic religion; Indian spiritual and mystical reverence for a 'northern place' was the basis for Indian outward migration, which led ultimately to the formation of the Teutonic races in northern Europe.[3]

Herder similarly wrote of India as the absolute cradle of world civilization and culture and opposed the Hebraic or Old Testament chronology. (The latter became an important strand in the opposition by many Enlightenment writers to biblical authority – indeed any alternative chronologies that threatened the Noachian or Mosaic 'history of humankind' were mobilized against clerical dogmatism.)

> We Germans would, like the Indians of North America, still be living contentedly in our forests, waging cruel wars as heroes, if the chain of

> foreign cultures had not pressed in upon us, and with the impact of centuries, had not forced us to join in. Roman civilization hailed from Greece; Greece owed its culture to Asia and Egypt; Egypt to Asia, China perhaps to Egypt, and so on; thus the chain extends from its first link to the last and will one day encircle perhaps the whole world. (Herder, 1969: 174)

While ancient Chinese civilizations (and their apparently more austere, refined and rational characteristics) were the archetypal inspiration for Enlightenment thinkers, a distinctive Indomania[4] became very important, not just for the more romantically inclined philosophers, but also as rationalist ammunition against clerical authority for writers such as Voltaire. India's superiority in philosophy and metaphysical speculation, taste, the arts, 'cultivation', nobility was compared with the inferiority of culture and proto-nationalism in Europe, especially as it related to that fierce differentiation between the French and the Germans. Herder was to distinguish this later as the inferiority of French 'nationalism' in comparison with his idea of the Germanic *Volk*. Herder's 'anti-racism' was fairly definitive: against Kant and other writers who were occupied with the question of 'race', Herder unequivocally argued that there was no such thing, there was only one and the same human essence (*Humanität*), and there is only 'nation' or Volk. Similarly, his attacks on black slavery and European slavers were important for his justification of his idea of Volk and ultimately a volkish nationalism:

> No words can express the sorrow and despair of a bought or stolen Negro slave when he leaves his native shore, never to see it again in his life.... What gives you the right, you despicable slave-drivers, you inhuman brutes, even to approach the land of these unfortunates, let alone tear them away from it by cunning, fraud and cruelty? For ages these regions were theirs by heritage; it belonged to them just as they belonged to it ... (Herder, 1969: 286)

This early combination of anti-racism and volkism, combined with an ancestral Indian civilization recurs in strikingly similar forms in modern Hinducentrism. However, most contemporary Hindu nationalists oppose the turn that followed, from the mid-19th century onwards, regarding the origins of the Europeans and the Indians. That shift was not simply reducible to the complete inversion of Frederick Schlegel's thesis (after which the Teutons became the ancestral community and the Vedic *Arya* their racially degenerate descendants). It was instead a complex and changing series of inventions, fabrications and refabulations that, in the very specific case of Indian scriptural influences, require much further and careful research. The anti-Semitic project to invent a German ancestry that was untouched by Jewish or Judaeo-Christian influences was dominant, as were Social Darwinist and evolutionary ideas. But this is not entirely the specific point being made here.

There is some kind of complex attachment between the formation of nationalisms in 18th- and 19th-century Germany and the substantive inspiration that proponents of these ideas derived from their reading and understanding of the Vedic and other scriptures. This philosophically important link can be dismissed by invoking the later horrific appropriation of Aryanism in National Socialism, and the latter's corruption and distortion of Vedism. However, it should not work against the interests of progressive Hindu and Indian sensibilities to acknowledge the enduring efficacy of Vedic and vedantic (post-Vedic) philosophy on the founders and the later practitioners of European Romanticism, nationalism and idealism. Despite the evident, though uneven, distaste for aspects of Hinduism, certain aspects of archaic Vedic literature (and the Zend Avesta) had great metaphoric, philosophical and spiritual appeal, at some time or another, for Herder, the Schlegel brothers, Kant, Hegel, Goethe and Max Muller. Vedism also variously appealed to Schopenhauer, Fichte, Nietzsche, Wagner and the Bayreuth Circle, Paul Lagarde, Edouard Drumont, Arthur de Gobineau, Houston Stewart Chamberlain, various pre-Nazi volkish associations, Alfred Rosenberg,[5] Dietrich Eckhart,[6] Walther Darré and Carl Jung.

The complex impact, transvaluation and distortion of Vedism and Hinduism can perhaps be seen to result in three tendencies: one concerned with the philosophical and metaphysical contents of the texts, one with a speculative anthropology of the myths, and the last with philology and mythology. One can read Vedic and Upanishadic metaphysical discourses about the nature of a priori, the conditions that allow ontology 'to be', extra-causal non-spatial non-temporal 'emergence', and so forth in various contributions of 19th-century (and later) German Idealism.[7] Several verses in the Rig-Veda and several of the Upanishads were preoccupied with abstract ideas of ultimate reality and subjectivity, the relation between subject and object, how to explain emergence that is necessarily non-causal (how to explain the emergence of time and space), and questions such as 'What ultimately is the thing-in-itself?' At the same time, Vedic and post-Vedic ideas of caste superiority, superhumanity and lesser humanities, a noble caste, noble and ignoble qualities, foreigners-others, colour and physiognomy, war, caste and caste-mixing, primordial blood communities, purity, mystical origin and belonging, and an obsession with description, classification and hierarchy, however much later transfigured, distorted or manufactured, were also important, and from a Western gaze, could relatively easily be read into various Vedic and post-Vedic texts. It is difficult to deny the complex impact that some ideas in Vedic Hinduism did have in the reformation of some versions of German and French nationalism. If the lavish praise for Vedism by the Schlegel brothers and Herder, from which they drew their own histories of humankind, constituted one ideological pole, consider, for example, Schopenhauer's 'pessimistic' philosophy, and the endless cycle of birth, death and rebirth, which was fairly comprehensively indebted to Hindu and Buddhist metaphysics, the latter superior to the 'Jewish metaphysics' that he hated. Similarly, if Gobineau simply inverted the civilizational myth of earlier German romanticism, the influences upon him were not restricted to his use of the word 'Aryan'.

There is considerable debate about whether or not the Vedas and subsequent literature contained concepts that led directly to ideas of phenotypical 'race'. Are the extremely few often metaphoric, or allegorical references to colour, phenotype and physiognomy in the Rig-Veda important in the contemporary period *only* because of their 19th-century distortion in German racial anthropologies? Can we ignore the admittedly numerous and fundamental references to caste, nobility, purity and natural hierarchy throughout Hindu literature, and their continuing impact, as if these become innocent concepts at the moment that the idea of 'race' or 'colour' is shown to be a Western or German invention? One can accept that the word *arya*[8] in the Rig-Veda (*airya* in the Avestan literature), referred to a quality that is usually translated as 'noble', rather than an ethnology, and certainly not an 'Aryan race'. But accepting this can defer consideration of (Western or non-Western) ideas about 'nobility' and 'aristocracy' themselves, as if these again become innocent once it is shown that *arya* is not a racial term.

Much historical work needs to be done on explaining these associations of ideas,[9] especially as they related to the maintaining of aristocracy and nobility in western Europe. The centrality of the blood trope also needs to be noted. 'Blood', like 'civilization', compresses together a large and wide-ranging bundle of philosophical ideas that deserve much further elaboration especially since many of these ideas have become animated in more recent racial politics. 'Blood' invokes immediately the sexual metaphor and the heterosexual act itself. These sexual metaphors are allied closely to the patronymic of the ancient fathers (not the actual father, who is typically made to disappear) and the genealogical quest that shows one's descent from and identity with them. In this project, time is both collapsed and is seen to be congruent with the travel of the patronymic, or with that quality which is transmitted patrilinearly. The mother, the 'empty vessel' (Theweleit, 1987) is also created as disappearance in this mythical genealogy, but frequently reappears in various ancient geographical or spatial tropes. This 'genealogy' is a pure form, an immediate purity of the male self, or the purity of the substance that is transmitted unchanged, that provides a powerful mythical idea for one's ownmost and purest history.

From the Arya to the New Age

Even though most contemporary Hindu nationalists would consider any links at all between National Socialism and their versions of Hinduism disagreeable,[10] the resonance of Aryanism in their movements is powerful, though fundamentally different in content to the versions of Aryanism that provided the materials for Nazism. These areas can supplement discussions about the nature of fascism after its classical period, because they can provide a distinct xenology and ethnology in which a purely metaphysical and spiritual chauvinism is dominant, but is in negotiation, as it were, with a different metaphysics that is reliant on the blood trope.

The new Hinducentrism demands comprehensive evaluations and judgements about the fruits of traditional, disciplinary scholarship, especially those related to archaeology, anthropology, history and linguistics, and particularly where the latter have been judged to be soiled by foreign influences such as Western imperialism, progressive secularism, socialism and Marxism. These epistemological efforts, also manifestly apparent in Afrocentric and Islamist ventures, have provided the contents, and even the metaphoric shape of some of the new ethnicities that are recovered under Hinducentrism. They raise fundamental and difficult questions about epistemology, discipline, canon and ultimately the nature of the whole intellectual process itself. The methodological importance of epistemic relativism for these projects, including explicit, if rather careless, use of anti-foundationalist, postmodern and deconstructionist ideas is significant, and will continue to aggravate those intellectual tendencies that view both foundationalism and anti-foundationalism as problematic.

Western critics of teleological reason or foundationalism, such as Kuhn and Feyerabend, are mobilized in support of a project that seeks to create the human civilizational record anew in fundamentally particularist directions. If this illustrates the ease with which anti-foundationalist ideas can allow themselves to be used for chauvinistic enterprises, it perhaps also raises a more elemental question about the nature of the philosophical debate about foundation. For within these projects, the methodological content is a melange of naive empiricism, positivism and realism, a Cartesian rationalism, varieties of syllogistic reasoning that sit happily alongside a fundamental critique of inductive reason, and a strident, sceptical anti-foundationalism. The positivist and mechanistic-rational content, particularly horrifying in its orientation towards human cultural societies, may well be the result of the disciplines of the intellectual founders of Hindu nationalism (engineering, as well as chemistry, physics, medicine and classical economics). However, it is mobilized in a non-antagonistic alliance with varieties of anti-positivist mysticism.

One manifest consequence of these Hinducentric methods is their all-embracing claims about the contemporary human and natural sciences. These are part of a broad civilizational claim which occurs in similar forms in varieties of Afrocentrism. These projects seem concerned both to condemn Western scientific materialism and its technological products and to demonstrate how its discoveries were already present in ancient texts, glyphs or cuneiform. However, natural science is also seen as materialistic, mechanistic, determinist and particularist and in some consequent way evil, and this is compared with a totalizing, holistic, 'infinite' and completed religious discourse. This critique of materialism elides the rather materialist obsessions of religious fundamentalist discourse – those of land, nature, state, political power, technology, economy and so forth.

Interestingly, 'materialism' is seen as evil and particularist, whereas 'nature' is universally constructed as benevolent, amiable and infinite.

To be sure, much of this is the result of the necessary need to 'cultivate civilization' against the erasures and distortions of Western colonialism, imperialism and racism, to demonstrate the rich classical and mediaeval traditions of learning in the natural and human sciences that existed in Indian traditions, particularly in philosophy, astronomy, arithmetic, literature, the arts, mathematics, optics, cosmology, historiography and natural history. However, the insertion of non-Western traditions into the process of world history that imperialism has erased is not necessarily what is being undertaken by these movements. Of particular importance in recent years has been the labour devoted to illustrating the congruence between modern physics and the philosophical speculations about ontology that result from mystical apprehension, as elaborated in the Vedas and Upanishads. This semiological approach to the text allows readings of the Vedas to discover helicopters, submarines, atomic theories, Dalton's chemistry, time dilation, the theory of gravitation, electricity, interplanetary travel, civil engineering, organ transplants and so on.[11] Though many of these projects are inconsequential, one should not underestimate the impact such ideas have in forming quite tenacious common senses in their subject communities. Similarly, that nothing like actual quantum physics or relativity or electromagnetism or Newtonian mechanics or gravitation has existed in any ancient texts seems irrelevant to the civilizational reconstruction being undertaken. These projects are also not simply about the single-minded dedication to demonstrate that every other ancient civilization (Egyptian, Sumerian, Mesopotamian, Babylonian, Greek, Mayan, Persian, Chinese) came from or was a direct product of Vedism, or that it was fundamentally arya-Vedic, or even part of aryavarta (the 'best land' of the Aryans). They are however, important for the hegemonic history of the present that they seek to create that in and of itself provides the disciplinary cultural tools with which a unified, ultimately chauvinistic and repressive neo-Vedic Hinduism can exist in the late modern world.

That much of this has also emerged in right-wing New Age contributions should not be surprising. This is best illustrated in the works of writers such as the American David Frawley and the Belgian Koenraad Elst, two Westerners who decry the historic distortions of Hinduism that Westerners have created, and who are without hesitation, the key ideological supporters of far right-wing Hindu nationalism in India, and key Western apologists for the kinds of militant and chauvinistic Hinduism that the Rashtriya Swayamsevak Sangh (National Volunteer Servers Corps – RSS), the Bharatiya Janata Party (BJP) and the Vishwa Hindu Parishad (World Hindu Council – VHP) seek to create. Both Frawley and Elst discovered Hinduism through their New Age activities. Frawley is a Vedic astrologer who is especially important in the Western context for his numerous New Age books and publications on astrology, *ayurveda* and spirituality. There is little that distinguishes his work from the glut of New Age aphoristic manuals available. In India, his chauvinistic Hindu nationalist work is published by the far right-wing Voice of India press (Frawley, 1994), a key publishing house for RSS, BJP and Hindu nationalist writers, that also publishes much of Elst's vituperative work.

A key recent New Age publication, virtually a trademark of the civilizational method of much Hindu nationalism, is *In Search of the Cradle of Civilization* (1995) which Frawley co-authored with George Feuerstein, founder of various Hindu-influenced New Age, yoga and tantric-sexuality projects in the USA, and Subhash Kak, a US computer scientist and Kashmiri poet. Kak has a substantial and long-standing publications record on Indo-Aryans in the journal *Mankind Quarterly* (see Kak, 1989, 1992, 1993), the latter perhaps the most influential academic far-right racist and eugenicist journal in the world. At this stage it is worth stepping back from a certain, perhaps necessary tendency in anti-fascism that seeks to demonstrate the fascist content or leaning of a work by noting the company that its author keeps. This is not to dismiss the importance of investigating those connections, which always involve extensive work to bring them about, but brings to the fore a different strategy that allows for the possibility that the character and nature of what is named 'fascism' has itself become transformed precisely because of the history of National Socialism and the Italian and Spanish fascist regimes (Gilroy, 1996). Consequently, the appearance of Kak's work in a journal whose founders or current editors were anti-Semites, racists, eugenicists and neo-Nazis (and actual Nazi race scientists) should not draw attention away from projects and agendas in right-wing 'New Age' Hinducentricty that are not describable in the languages of Nazism or Western white supremacist racism. A similar claim needs to be made about the New Age movements themselves. It is not implied here that there is an immediate congruence between contemporary New Age mysticism and Nazism or fascism, and the variety of political strands in New Age thinking is acknowledged. However, there is an established and documented history of connections and overlaps between varieties of syncretic, Eastern- influenced Western mysticism and actual Nazism or fascism. How, for example, has it come to be that Julius Evola's Hindu and Buddhist writings[12] are published by both neo-Nazi publishers and under New Age imprints, that these books by perhaps the foremost *racial* ideologue within Italian Fascism can be found nestling among books on feng shui, lesbian and gay spirituality and Lakota drum medicine.

The project appropriated by Frawley, Kak and Feuerstein is dependent on a recent intellectual reassessment of India's and Pakistan's antiquity in which more recent archaeological and geographical discoveries might suggest that the pre-Aryan Indus Valley civilizations were both more extensive and older than may have been assumed. However, the pace of actual archaeological scholarship, the possibilities of rethinking Indian antiquity against Western colonial distortions, and the speculations and fancies of Hindu nationalism have become mixed up in these recent interventions. Hindu nationalism has instead largely succeeded in setting the agendas for debate and creating 'commonsense' world-views about India's and Pakistan's antiquity that bypass the methods of traditional scholarship, and would have relied, in different circumstances, on a necessary mobilization of the whole critical intellectual process itself.

There has been considerable debate about the Indus Valley civilization since the urban ruins of Harappa and Mohenjo-Daro were discovered in the 1920s, followed by subsequent discoveries of numerous ancient towns in northern India and then Pakistan. These new discoveries demonstrated a considerably advanced *pre-Aryan* urban civilization, contemporaneous with the earliest civilizations in ancient Egypt and the Near and Middle East. The abandonment of these vast urban centres was explained in colonial knowledge as resulting from a subsequent barbaric and destructive Aryan invasion from what is now Iran. It has since been accepted that no such destructive invasion occurred. The Indus Valley civilization declined well before Aryan-speaking tribes migrated over an extremely long period into India and gave rise, through complex and syncretic processes, to what later became Vedic culture. The idea of a conquering Aryan invasion that destroyed Mohenjo-Daro and Harappa was little more than the result of Western Aryanist thinking in the first decades of this century. Its original archaeological thesis was put forward by Sir John Mortimer Wheeler, the British archaeologist who implicitly equated the arya language with an Aryan race. The discovery of the Indus Valley civilization however, threw up numerous conundrums, of which perhaps the most pertinent is its script, which is still undeciphered and may well remain so in the absence of further archaeological discoveries that contain larger continuous examples of the script. Seals bearing motifs and writing from the ancient Indus Valley have also been discovered in other parts of the ancient world (this is partly responsible for the claim that ancient Middle Eastern and Egyptian civilizations are in essence arya or Indian).

It is in the interests of Hinducentric projects to claim, despite the impressive evidence to the contrary, that the Indus Valley civilization was Indo-Aryan or Indo-European in language, fundamentally arya in culture and ethnicity (even if the latter is viewed as syncretic and distanced from any ideas of 'race'), Vedic in religion, and Sanskritic or proto-Sanskritic in civilization. Several other consequences immediately follow, for such claims imply that Aryans were autochthonous and not usurpers, that a fundamentally Aryan civilization was the first world civilization, that all other civilizations were its direct or indirect products, that the differentiations between Indo-Aryan and Dravidian languages are racist, colonial creations, and that, instead, all Indian languages and cultural products are essentially derived from one ethnic, indigenous, non-invasive arya culture and civilization. This, of course, also provides a far greater lineage for Hinduism, and confirms not only its primordial antiquity, but its superlative and original genesis in that first civilizational hearth, 'the first and best land of the Aryans'. The congruence of this arya 'prehistory' with that of early

German orientalism, and its exact mirroring in the Western racial Aryanism that animated the pre-Nazi and Nazi periods, is less important than the general epistemic space that all these tendencies share, which is dominated by a primordial Aryanism.

It is methodologically necessary that Frawley, Feuerstein, Kak and their ilk ignore or gloss over all the evidence to the contrary, primarily linguistic, archaeological and archaeo-anthropological. Their particularist move, though, does result in the perhaps incongruous phenomenon of left-wing secular Indian scholarship defending an external and invasive Aryan influence against right-wing white Americans who accuse the latter of racism and the propagation of colonial and imperialist ideas. As interesting is a methodological manoeuvre that has also preoccupied critics and defenders of Afrocentricity and of Islamism. This is best summarized as a negligent, semiotic disciplinary eclecticism in which text, monument and sign become history and culture. 'Text' itself is removed from its historical development and presented as always completed and hermetic. One selects some agreeable hymns of the Vedas as pure reflective history (the land of the Aryans as equivalent to the physical geography of India), others, less agreeable, as simple whimsy and harmless metaphor (the wars by the Aryan-speaking tribes against the dark-skinned *dasyus*). In this register, what the Rig-Veda says is both absolutely true and completely open to reinterpretation from the vantage point of the late modern period.

A much more problematic consequence is the advancement in these activities of a primal and innocent subjectivity that is universal, transcendental, exemplary in its virtuousness and kindness, and possessed of a superlative wisdom and insight that has never been matched. The 'ancient Vedic seers', or *rishis*, living in a kingdom of peace, plenty and harmony, apprehended fundamental primordial truths and wisdoms about the universe. It is our human failure not to see this. It would be easy to dismiss the tropes of ancient 'wisdom', 'secrets', 'knowledge', 'truth', 'light', 'seer' and so forth that animate both new cultish Hinduisms and Western New Age movements. These various projects seek to discursively restrain Third World cultures in a natural state of blissful, innocent, primitivism. There is a long Western tradition, both Romantic and scientific that has sought to do just this. However, the idea that ancient 'wisdom' and 'light', the (perpetually deferred) 'secrets' of nature and the universe were apprehended by superhuman 'seers' function exhaustively in modern projects as dogmatic but barren signifiers. These projects are not about the enormously complicated social and cultural histories of Hinduism that are shielded from their followers, but are concerned instead to create subjects anew, subjects whose 'ownmost being' is automatically equated with the qualities of purity, righteousness, truth, innocence and bliss. This subjectivity that arbitrarily demands acknowledgement of its superlative, transcendental, primal wisdom is a subjectivity that is constituted by a fundamental arrogance that its claims of rectitude, bliss and purity can barely mask.

Conclusion

The example of right-wing Hindu nationalism, and its New Age apologists in the West, lends itself to a different or supplementary critique of ethnic absolutism or 'generic fascism'. Many of the substantive themes that emerge in varieties of cultural 'unanimism' are ones of land, blood or *ethnos*/'race', or hermetic views of culture or ethnicity, and a unique gendered personality or affective dimension. However, in this metaphysical chauvinism, there is no need to rely on the resources of scientific or cultural racism. One can invoke an atemporal association with an ancestral blood community – a philosophy of hereditarianism – without ever having to specify the actual mechanics of scientific racism, of heredity, lineage or typology, without even having to rely on a mutilation of Darwin or Mendel. One can invoke an animism that tidies up the relation with nature without ever having to grasp what nature is. Culture becomes symbolic, 'occultish' material. These ideas seem resistant in the face of reason to reason itself – or conversely they can demonstrate 'a rational application of irrationality' (Gilroy, 1996: 84).

Gilroy asks 'what is at stake in the desire to find an entirely pure mode of particularised being' (1996: 79)? The 'particularised' and the 'being' condense a fundamental metaphysical idea that is manifest in many of the political formations described above. In the main, what we see as 'particularism' is rarely manifest as a particularist claim, but invariably a universal one – it is not in the nature of absolutisms to develop limited epistemologies. Perhaps the importance of metaphysics is best illustrated by considering the identity they assume between that tenacious idea of the ancestral blood community and the idea of existent, or more accurately that relation between Volk and Dasein. This relation allows a consideration of 'generic fascism' of the powerful or the powerless outside of the boundaries of nature and culture within which some or much of their substantial content may lie. It is instead a purely speculative, metaphysical relation and its foundational claims harbour two difficult questions: whether the relation is a necessary one; and what is its fidelity to '*humanität*'.

From inside this association between Volk and Dasein a universal idea emerges that, as in Heidegger's own dismissal of the forms of rationality and reason that existed prior to his own pre-philosophy, need not have any completed allegiance to any forms of modern rationality, nor any reason to engage them. This does not imply that these ideologies cannot be transplanted into the machinery of modern rationality. However, this metaphysics shields itself from reason or rational critique because of its claim to exist prior to the emergence of reason. This is a striking attribute of many of the writings emerging from ethnic-religious movements that seek to create their own exceptional 'ontologies' or privileged 'angles of vision' that are freed from the burden of difficult epistemic, moral and ethical questions. In its specifically racist form, this metaphysics of being need not explicitly rely on its difference from an other, or even concern with the other, because that is irrelevant to it, or has already been subsumed into it. If it is now conventional to stress an ontology of unity only through its endogenous relation to difference and otherness, this can elide the more difficult task of describing the normative making up of the wholesome subject. Perhaps despite Levinas, one can actively choose to ignore the face of the other, and celebrate only the poetics of the self. In modernity, one need not be a member of an already described chosen people; one can choose oneself, and can manufacture mythical narratives, folk genealogies, political symbols and histories; a cultivation and nurturing of a metaphysical self that identifies both the archaic and the futuristic with itself.

Notes

I would like to thank Stephen Cross and John Solomos for comments on an earlier draft. I also want to acknowledge the support of the ESRC in relation to some of the material used in this article.

1. Compare Kant (1960: 32): 'Now if a propensity to [the inversion of the ethical order] does lie in human nature, there is in man a natural propensity to evil; and since this very propensity must in the end be sought in *a will which is free* . . . it is *morally* evil. This evil is *radical*, because it corrupts the ground of all maxims; it is, moreover, as a natural propensity, *inextirpable*, by human powers, since extirpation could occur only through good maxims, and cannot take place when the ultimate subjective ground of all maxims is postulated as corrupt . . .' (first two emphases added).
2. Schlegel did not wish to 'exalt one chief branch of the language exclusively, or to the disparagement of the other. . . . Who can deny the lofty power and energy of the Arabic and Hebraic languages?', but considered that 'languages in which the grammar is one of inflexion are usually preferable' (1849: 451).
3. This critical idea of the mountainous cold north derived from an interpretation of the Rig-Veda and the reverence with which the arya held for mountains, possibly the Himalayas, has influenced numerous writers, up to the present period. Kant held this cradle to be Tibet, and later writers assumed the Caucasus. A North Pole origin for the Aryans gained currency from various interpretations of the Rig-Vida and was pronounced again this century by Tilak, a founder and leader of the Indian National Congress.
4. The characteristics of English and Scottish Enlightenment 'Indomania' were uneven, and in many respects very different from later French and German obsessions with India. However, certain formative links were evident – for example, Schlegel was a student of Sanskrit under Alexander Hamilton, and indeed had been inspired by the earlier works of Charles Wilkins and William Jones, among other British orientalists. It needs noting that the fascination with Indian literature and philosophy was frequently accompanied by an extremely strong distaste for what were perceived as the vulgarities and monstrosities of Hinduism in 18th- and 19th-century India: both these orientations not only coexisted, often in the same individual, but in many respects provided the inspiration for the theory of temporal degradation of Hinduism which eventually, and in a complex way, lead to ideas about primordial Aryanism.

5. The younger Rosenberg was a student of Indian religion and metaphysics. He read the Vedas and other Indian religious writings, admired the caste system and viewed India's 'degeneration' as resulting from the adulteration of its original Aryan blood. In his *Myth of the Twentieth Century*, he makes stark equations between the Indians, Greeks and Romans and his Aryan Germans (Cecil, 1972). It has also been suggested that Rosenberg supplied Hitler with much of the material for his Aryanist thinking (Lane and Rupp, 1978).

6. It seems difficult to read Eckhart's 'Jewishness In and Around Us' (1919) without some appreciation of at least some of these influences. 'Jewishness' in this piece, represented a *quality* (rather than a race) primarily manifested as materialism, 'this-worldliness', anti-spiritualism and the denial of life after death. This was contrasted to the supreme turn towards spirituality, to 'other worldliness', to the fundamental idea of a soul that transcends death that was needed in cultivating Aryanism. See 'Jewishness In and Around Us: Fundamental Reflections' in Lane and Rupp (1978: 18–26).

7. These affinities are well known and there is a significant body of literature in this area. The work of, for example, Wilhelm Halbfass and Indian philosophers such as Sarvepalli Radhakrishnan has been influential in highlighting the often striking similarities between Vedic or classical Indian thought and Western philosophical ideas (especially idealism).

8. It is a supreme and tragic irony that Max Muller's use of the term 'Aryan' to describe the Indo-Aryan languages (and in his earlier discussions, the 'Aryan people') was intended to provide a neutral, technical, relatively unknown archaic foreign word that implicitly could not be appropriated for the purposes of national or chauvinistic pride in Europe.

9. There is a complex relation between the rise of the New Thought movement, especially Theosophy, in Europe towards the last decades of the last century (a movement so vividly described by William James) and volkish thinking. The New Thought movement depended heavily on varieties of Hinduism and Buddhism for its content, and its eclectic, aphoristic methods bear very strong comparison with current New Ageism. Goodrick-Clarke (1985) presents a brilliant discussion of the complex ways in which Theosophy became transmuted into a specifically Germanic 'Ariosophy' in the works of Liebenfels and the (pre-)Nazi occult movements and supplied much of the mythological and symbolic material for Nazism. Along the way, Goodrick-Clarke demonstrates the fundamentally novel, hybrid and syncretic origins of Nazism. See also James's (1985) description of the New Thought movement.

10. Though there are instructive exceptions: Madhav Golwalkar, the second Supreme leader of the Rashtriya Swayamsevak Sangh not only admired Hitlerism but positively based his prescriptions for India on Nazi thinking, at least in the late 1930s. Savarkar himself was attracted to both Italian and German fascism in the mid 1930s. More recently, the current leader of the Shiv Sena, Bal Thackeray, openly praises Hitler's actions, the latter his obvious source of emulation. These fascist tendencies were (and are) outside the mainstream of Hinduism which was comprehensively and unequivocally anti-fascist and anti-Nazi (Bhatt, 1997; Jaffrelot, 1996).

11. Most of the series of *Exploratory Papers* (1995) published by the Dharam Hinduja International Centre of Indic Research (Delhi, Columbia and Cambridge)

and dedicated to the scientific study of the Vedas are more recent, if notably extreme, examples of this phenomenon.

12. Evola's recent re-publications give an idea of his racial and Hindu interests: *Revolt Against the Modern World: Politics, Religion and Social Order in the Kali Yuga*; *The Yoga of Power: Tantra, Shakti and the Secret Way*; *Race as Revolutionary Doctrine*; *The Doctrine of Awakening: The Attainment of Self-Mastery According to Early Buddhist Texts*.

References

African Rights (1995) *Rwanda: Death, Despair and Defiance*, revised edn. London: African Rights.

Banton, M. (1987) *Racial Theories*. Cambridge: Cambridge University Press.

Basu, T., P. Datta, S. Sarkar, T. Sarkar and S. Sen (1993) *Khaki Shorts and Saffron Flags*. New Delhi: Orient Longman.

Bhatt, C. (1997) *Liberation and Purity*. London: UCL Press.

Cecil, R. (1972) *The Myth of the Master Race: Alfred Rosenberg and Nazi Ideology*. London: Batsford.

Das, V. (ed.) (1992) *Mirrors of Violence: Communities, Riots and Survivors in South Asia*. Delhi: Oxford University Press.

Feuerstein, G., S. Kak and D. Frawley (1995) *In Search of the Cradle of Civilization*. Wheaton, IL: Quest.

Frawley, D. (Vamadeva Shastri) (1994) *Arise Arjuna: Hinduism and the Modern World*. New Delhi: Voice of India.

Gilroy, P. (1987) *There Ain't No Black in the Union Jack*. London: Hutchinson.

Gilroy, P. (1993) *The Black Atlantic: Modernity and Double Consciousness*. London: Verso.

Gilroy, P. (1996) 'Revolutionary Conservatism and the Tyrannies of Unanimism', *New Formations* 28: 65–84.

Goodrick-Clarke, N. (1985) *The Occult Roots of Nazism*. New York: New York University Press.

Gopal, S. (ed.) (1990) *Anatomy of a Confrontation*. Delhi: Penguin.

Gupta, S.P. (1996) *The Indus-Saraswati Civilization*. Delhi: Pratibha Prakashan.

Heidegger, M. (1962) *Being and Time*. Oxford: Blackwell.

Herder, J.G. (1969) *J.G. Herder on Social and Political Culture*, trans. F.M. Barnard. Cambridge: Cambridge University Press.

Jaffrelot, C. (1996) *The Hindu Nationalist Movement and Indian Politics*. London: Hurst.

Jain, J.K. (1994) *The Hindu Phenomenon*. New Delhi: UBS Publishers.

James, W. (1985) *The Varieties of Religious Experience*. Harmondsworth: Penguin. (Orig. 1902.)

Kak, S. (1989) 'Indus Writing', *Mankind Quarterly* 30: 113–18.

Kak, S. (1992) 'The Indus Tradition and the Indo-Aryans', *Mankind Quarterly* 32: 195–213.

Kak, S. (1993) 'Understanding the Caste System', *Mankind Quarterly* 34.

Kant, I. (1960) *Religion Within the Limits of Reason Alone*. New York: Harper. (Orig. 1791.)

Kristeva, J. (1993) *Nations without Nationalism*. New York: Columbia University Press.

Lane, B.M. and L.J. Rupp (1978) *Nazi Ideology before 1933: A Documentation*. Manchester: Manchester University Press.

Levinas, E. (1990) 'Reflections on the Philosophy of Hitlerism', *Critical Inquiry* 17. (Orig. 1934.)

Ludden, D. (ed.) (1996) *Contesting the Nation*. Philadelphia: University of Pennsylvania Press.

Mosse, G.L. (1966) *The Crisis of German Ideology*. London: Weidenfeld and Nicolson.

Nandy, A. et al. (1995) *Creating a Nationality*. Delhi: Oxford University Press.

Poliakov, L. (1974) *The Aryan Myth*. London: Heinemann.

Rajaram, N.S. and D. Frawley (1997) *Vedic Aryans and the Origin of Civilization*. New Delhi: Voice of India.

Sahgal, G. and N. Yuval-Davis (1992) *Refusing Holy Orders*. London: Virago.

Sarkar, T. and U. Butalia (eds) (1995) *Women and Right-Wing Movements: Indian Experiences*. London: Zed.

Savarkar, V.D. (1989) *Hindutva – or Who is a Hindu?* Bombay: Veer Savarkar Prakashan. (Orig. 1923.)

Schlegel, F. (1849) *Aesthetic and Miscellaneous Works*, trans. E.J. Millington. London: Henry G. Bohm.

Seligman, C.G. (1957) *The Races of Africa*, 3rd edn. Oxford: Oxford University Press. (Orig. 1930.)

Solomos, J. and L. Back (1996) *Racism and Society*. Basingstoke: Macmillan.

Speke, J.H. (1864) *What Led to the Discovery of the Source of the Nile*. Edinburgh: W. Blackwood.

Theweleit, K. (1987) *Male Fantasies*, vol. I. Cambridge: Polity.

Vaniak, A. (1997) *The Furies of Indian Communalism*. London: Verso.

Žižek, S. (1997) 'Multiculturalism, or, the Cultural Logic of Multinational Capitalism', *New Left Review* 225: 28–51.

Chetan Bhatt is Lecturer in Sociology at the University of Essex.

'She'll Wake Up One of These Days and Find She's Turned into a Nigger'

Passing through Hybridity

Sara Ahmed

THE TITLE of this article announces the threat of becoming black as a joke: 'She'll wake up one of these days and find she's turned into a Nigger!' (Larsen, 1994: 171). This joke, in its contractual declaration not only of a shared desire to stay white, but also of an assumption that a white subject cannot possibly become black (its humour residing in the impossibility of its status as event), leads to an outbreak of laughter. That laughter is so excessive, so brutal, that it threatens to destabilize the conceptual order of racism through which the joke becomes tellable. The audience have to stop themselves laughing; they have to be careful not to let slip the humour that lies beyond the form of the joke and doubles its movement back at the expense of the teller. For the joke is an exchange between a white man and three black women in Nella Larsen's *Passing*, a short novel first published by one of the few women writers of the Harlem renaissance in 1929. The irony in which the reader shares as a knowing witness is precisely that the woman who is its object (the wife of the teller) is 'a Nigger'. That is, the woman, Clare, is a black woman who is passing as white, partly through assuming the role of wife to a white man. The logic of the joke is then: the black woman who is (mis)read as white (becomes white) may (or may not) become black.

Here, the identity of the other as white or black becomes destabilized by the very relation of looking which assumes, in the first place, the visibility of blackness in the joke's humorous untruth. The deferment and

■ *Theory, Culture & Society* 1999 (SAGE, London, Thousand Oaks and New Delhi),
Vol. 16(2): 87–106
[0263-2764(199904)16:2;87–106;008257]

slippage between identifications that are not simply visible on the surface of the subject's body – black to white to black – can be traced only if we give up the conviction that we can tell or see the difference. That conviction (we all know she is white and can't turn into a nigger) is the organizing principle for a system of racial classification which assumes that racial identity marks the subject in the form of the absence or presence of colour. This joke about the joke opens out the possibility of hybridization: hybridization, not as the struggle between two racial identities (the tragic mulatto who is half-white and half-black), but as the very traversing of the notion of the two that can be distinguishable in space and time: hybridization as the very temporality of passing through and between identity itself without origin or arrival.

Indeed, in an earlier encounter in the novel, Irene, who could pass for white but generally chooses not to, finds herself passing on a particular occasion. She is stared at by a woman opposite in a cafe. Her immediate response is fear. Has she been detected?:

> Did that woman, could that woman, somehow know that here before her very eyes on the roof of the Drayton sat a Negro.
>
> Absurd! Impossible! White people were so stupid about such things for all that they usually asserted they were able to tell; and by the most ridiculous means, finger-nails, palms of hands, shapes of ears, teeth and other equally silly rot. (Larsen, 1994: 150)

The immediate fear of being caught out is dealt with effectively. The idea that 'they were able to tell' is mocked as a sign of cultural arrogance implicated in whiteness. This passage reminds me of Marjorie Garber's consideration of the desire to 'tell the difference' as a way of guarding against a, 'difference that might otherwise put the identity of one's own position in question' (1992: 130). In *Passing* the impossibility of telling, or the impossibility that her difference could be seen under a regime of detection, enables her survival. But there exists yet another irony. Irene assumes the other woman is white. This assumption constitutes a misrecognition. The woman is also a black woman passing as white; indeed, it is Irene's old friend Clare, whom she fails to see or recognize given her own assumption of whiteness. The impossibility of telling returns to the teller to undercut her positioning of the dupe as always the other. Indeed, the exchange dramatizes that passing dislocates the relation between self and other through the movement of desires which are crucially instituted by differences that both command and resist the scopic regime.

Passing and Transgression

One could argue that it is narratives like these which invite a political discourse around passing. This discourse tends to position 'passing' as a radical and transgressive practice that serves to destabilize and traverse the system of knowledge and vision upon which subjectivity and identity precariously rests. The subject who passes, or the passing of subjects through each other, has increasingly become a point of entry for an approach to identification which emphasizes the phantasies, ruptures and breakages which prevent identity from being assured as the ontological given of the subject. For example, in Lola Young's *Fear of the Dark: Race, Gender and Sexuality in the Cinema*, passing is read 'as a sign of racial duplicity which threatens to undermine the stability of racial categorisation' (1996: 85), and as 'transgressing racial boundaries' (1996: 91).

I want to emphasize from the outset that I don't want simply to repeat the terms of this discourse around passing as transgression. This is not to say such work is inherently problematic. However, I do think there is a failure to theorize, not the potential for any system to become destabilized, but the means by which relations of power are secured, paradoxically, *through this very process of destabilization* (we all know, I think, how the language of crisis is managed by a conservative politics). How are differences that threaten the system recuperated? How do ambiguous bodies get read in a way which further supports the enunciative power of those who are telling the difference? In what ways is 'passing' implicated in the very discourse around tellable differences? How are social identities fixed and secured? To simply focus on strategies or tactics of destabilization, transgression, mimicry, rupture, hybridity, breakage, travesty, masquerade, iterability, performativity, citationality, camouflage (one must note the proliferation of such terms which celebrate and affirm the structural possibility of a displacement from social norms), is to forgo an analysis of the complex social and psychic mechanisms for dealing with such tactics (such as designating them as undesirable outcomes of the loss of social and familial security). Unless we begin to ask questions about how differences and ambiguities get re-incorporated, then I think the feminist consideration of (the impossibility of) identity will remain inadequate to the task: that is, it will not be able to engender a transformative politics.

In calling for such an analysis of the way in which instability and crisis can enable the stabilization of relations of power, I am inviting you to rethink the shift in Judith Butler's work from *Gender Trouble* (1990) to *Bodies that Matter* (1993). In the first instance, Butler provides a model of gender performativity which suggests a voluntaristic capacity to transgress (or make trouble). Throughout this text, words such as 'rupture', 'breakage', 'destabilization', 'transgression' are repeated. They come to stand for a politics which makes trouble (or which is troubling) insofar as it refuses to assume the subject or sex as an ontological given. Hence she takes the position that the categories 'female' and 'woman', are not only unstable and troubled, but also 'unfixed' (1990: ix). The following sentence suggests how the model of unfixity and disruption implies a certain voluntarism: 'I describe and propose a set of parodic practices based on a performative theory of gender acts that disrupt the categories of the body, sex, gender and sexuality and occasion their subversive resignification and proliferation beyond the binary frame' (1990: x). This sentence suggests that the acting out or performing of gender itself can *occasion* its own disruption or subversion:

that is, that such a performance is, in itself, an occasion which moves 'beyond' the (binary) frame of signification and containment. I would argue that such a sentence implies a certain voluntarism, *not* a voluntarism which assumes the subject as agent, but a voluntarism which is displaced on to the subject's acts, such that *they* become (subjectified as) agents. This voluntarism of acts is tied to a theory of transgression: the acts, as agents, can in themselves occasion a movement beyond *the law* (of signification).

In contrast, in *Bodies that Matter*, the emphasis is much more on the regulatory and normative mechanisms through which subjects are identified and which de-limit the potential for transgression through the re-incorporation of differences. There is hence an account of both systematicity and fixation. The change in emphasis is clear in the following sentence where Butler calls for an analysis of performativity, 'not as the act by which a subject brings into being what she/he names, but, rather, as that reiterative power of discourse to produce the phenomena that it regulates and constrains' (1993: 2). There is more emphasis on how bodies materialize as *intelligible*, and how that materialization both *constraints* and *delimits* embodiment, even as it produces, 'a domain of unthinkable, abject, unliveable bodies' (1993: xi).

But then again, to describe this shift *as* a shift in Judith Butler's work may be unjust. By taking two sentences out of their contexts, I have quite literally sentenced *Gender Trouble* to an unwarranted death. To avoid such a premature sentencing, I think we could understand *Bodies that Matter* as an attempt to explain why *Gender Trouble* does not, in the first instance, support a voluntaristic model of social change (= transgression). However, the reading of *Gender Trouble* as supporting voluntarism through the model of transgression is not, properly speaking, either inside or outside the text, but may constitute its limits. This can be understood in terms of Butler's 'defensiveness' against the potential reading of voluntarism in *Bodies that Matter*:

> Actually, in the recent past, the question was repeatedly formulated to me this way: 'What about the materiality of the body, *Judy*?' I took it that the addition of 'Judy' was an effort to dislodge the more formal 'Judith' and to recall me to a bodily life that could not be theorised away.... Couldn't someone simply take me aside? Matters could not have got much worse, if not more remote, by the questions raised by notion of gender performativity introduced in *Gender Trouble*. For if I were to argue that genders are performative, that could mean that I thought that one woke up in the morning, perused the closet or some more open space for the gender of choice, donned that gender for the day, and restored the garment to its place at night. (1993: x)

Here, the (mis)reading of voluntarism is evoked in the text as a violence against the bodily life of the author, and the refusal of her proper name, 'Judith'. In both instances, she is reduced to, 'an unruly child, one who needed to be brought to task' (1993: ix). But the ironic reading of voluntarism in *Gender Trouble* offered in *Bodies that Matter* is far from a reading: rather, it is a caricature that forecloses the possibilities of reading how voluntarism may operate otherwise in *Gender Trouble* as, indeed, it may foreclose any critical reading of the text at all (could we now dare to bring Judith Butler to task?). Importantly, such defensiveness in the prefacing of *Bodies that Matter* returns us to *Gender Trouble*: it is a defence of a previous text against its (mis)readings. As a result, the mis/naming and mis/reading becomes the condition of possibility for the writing of *Bodies that Matter* (it charges the text into being). Butler names the charge of voluntarism (if I am performed, I can unperform my self) as an inappropriate reading in order then to exclude that reading from the writing of the text. Such a gesture of repeating the name/charge which violated *Gender Trouble* in order to free *Bodies that Matter* from the contamination of the name/charge, renders that name/charge the point of entry for her engagement. So in calling for analysis of how passing works at the level of identification, I am both following Butler's lead *and* not following her lead: I am reading through and against the model of transgression as the condition of possibility for my own analysis.

Acts of 'transgression' implicit in passing do not, then, transcend the systematization of differences into regularities. Indeed, Clare's act of passing in *Passing* leads to her death. Or, as Judith Butler herself puts it: 'the exposure of her colour leads straightaway to her death' as a 'literalization of social death' (1993: 183). Clare is detected as a black woman underneath the assumed white mask and, in terms of the narrative development, this leads to her death. Such a literalized punishment restores the narrative to its rightful order. Her passing, which enables her access to the privilege of assumed whiteness (she is white because she does not look black), is an event which constitutes not simply the impossibility of racial identity being secured through the visual coding of difference (the black woman who is not seeable as black), but also the demand to designate others into categories of identity beyond the visual (for example, categories of blood or genetics). Who counts as white? Who counts as black? Who counts as male? Who counts as female? Who counts as a black woman? Passing may render these questions a matter of social contest: it may in this sense politicize identity; it may demonstrate that there are no absolute criteria for making such decisions about identity, property and belonging. But I would argue that this does not necessarily constitute the basis for theorizing passing as transgression beyond the act or event of passing, when the enunciative power to decide upon criteria for identification remains the very basis of forms of sexism and racism. The dis-organizing of social identities, here, can become a mechanism for the re-organizing of social life through an expansion of the terms of surveillance (how are we to know the other's difference if we cannot see her?). The economy of desire (to tell the difference in Garber's terms) is itself an apparatus of knowledge which already fixes others into a certain place. Such an economy of desire to tell the difference assumes that the difference can be found somewhere on (or in) the bodies of others (on or underneath their skin).[1] Ambiguous bodies that do not fit existing criteria for identification keep in place, or are even the condition of possibility for, the desire to tell bodies apart from each other through the accumulation of knowledge.

Passing and Identification

How else to speak and write of passing? Why use 'passing' itself as a point of entry for a discussion of identification and hybridity? We cannot talk here of a logic of passing. Passing is not identifiable as a discrete practice that has discernible political effects. On the contrary, passing is intelligible only in relation to a complex set of social antagonisms; passing for white as a black subject has a very different relation to power than passing for black as a white subject. Equally, passing may function at the level of the intentional subject (the subject who seeks to pass in order to secure something otherwise unavailable to them), or it may function as a misrecognition on the part of others (one may pass for something other than one's self-identification but not seek to, or know it). Passing may be successful – in which case the difference between the subject and the image assumed becomes unrecognizable – or it may fail – the subject may be detected as 'not being' the identity assumed. Thus, passing may not be a special case that we can speak of as throwing up a crisis of identity in and of itself.

And yet, we must resist the temptation of generalizing passing as simply a condition of identity formation. I hence would want to problematize the shift in Carole Ann Tyler's work from her consideration of passing as 'a politically viable response to oppression', to the argument that, 'all subjects therefore are passing through the signifier which represents them for another' (Tyler, 1994: 212, 220). I would not deny that identity – any identity – involves passing in some form. It involves assuming an image that has no proper 'fit' with the structure of the subject; indeed, it is the act of assuming an image that constitutes the subject (passing demonstrates, in this sense, that the subject is the effect rather than the origin of a phantasy of being). However, the problem that resides with using this model of identification is that we can no longer differentiate between kinds of identifications and particular forms of 'crisis' over identity. Indeed, if we take Lacan's definition of identification – 'the transformation that takes place in the subject when he assumes an image' (1977: 2) – we can consider how the misrecognition which founds or finds the subject involves an economy of difference. Rather than simply understanding identification as something that has already taken place in the formation of subjectivity, we can consider how identifications perpetually fail to grasp 'others' in social encounters. That is, subjects assume images which they cannot be or fully inhabit, but the images they assume are *already differentiated*: subjects and others become differentiated at the very same moment that they are constituted as such.

So while the process of identification involves a form of passing – the transformation that takes place in the assumption of an image – we can still theorize how passing itself involves a form of social differentiation. Not only do we have the difference between images already assumed in social encounters with others (such as 'being assumed' as white or black), but in the temporal lag of passing for an-other, we have the potential of a difference between an image that is already assumed in and by a subject (however much the assumption does not hold or contain the subject), and an image that is *always yet to be assumed*. So, for example, I would argue that we can differentiate between a black subject who passes for white, and a white subject who passes for white. While whiteness is an assumed image which is often invisible, one's relation to whiteness as something which is passed through depends on a prior history of self-identification and identification by others. Would one worry, would one fear being caught out, if one did not *already* perceive oneself to be passing for white? Would there be danger, would there be death? In other words, passing for something that one is not already assumed to be makes a difference to the politics of passing.

The difference between the black subject who passes as white and the white subject who passes as white is not then an *essential* difference which implies that blackness or whiteness simply exist before passing. Rather, it is a *structural* difference that demonstrates that passing involves the re-opening or re-staging of a fractured history of identifications that constitutes the limits to a given subject's mobility. To refuse that difference by arguing that passing constitutes a general logic of assuming an identity (since all identities belong, so to speak, to the Other), is to refuse to recognize the constraints which temporarily fix subjects in relations of social antagonism. The white subject who passes as white (that is, the subject already constituted as white by structures of identification that precede the encounter) has a degree of comfort and security about identity as the crisis of not-being is, so to speak, hidden from memory (it is not representable or livable as such).

Indeed in much black feminist literature, there is a reflection on how passing as white takes place given the invisibility of the mark of whiteness as a mark precisely of its privilege. As Jayne O. Ifekwunigwe argues there is a 'prevailing and inconsistent social and political stance that anyone who does not look white is seen as Black' (1997: 210). We can turn this around and emphasize that one is assumed to be white unless one looks black. Here, 'looking black' becomes a deviation from the normalized state of 'being white'. Passing as white hence guarantees a form of social assimilation in which the gaze of others hesitates only upon those that are already marked as different (such a hesitation on 'exceptional ambiguous bodies' allows the 'community' to imagine itself as unmarked and hence white). In Harryette Mullen's reflection on passing for white, she emphasizes how the individual and familial acts of passing become mechanisms for the re-creation of the nation space (1994: 72). Passing as white supports a national desire to assimilate difference into a generalized white 'face of the nation'.

Here, the spatial configuration of communities of belonging involves the legitimation of passing for white as an individual and national story of progress.

Passing as white allows both the redefinition of (nation) space – the white community assimilates the difference – and a re-narrativization of the history of the nation/subject (a forgetting of the forms of racial antagonism that are concealed by the white nation face). Passing hence becomes narratable as an individual act only through being *joined* to forms of social and national belonging in which being passed as white, by others, allows one to pass into an invisible and privileged community. The difference between the white subject who passes as white and the black subject who passes as white can be understood as determined by a different relation to this imaginary space: the crisis of 'not belonging' for the black subject who passes becomes then a crisis of knowledge, of knowing there is always a danger of *being seen*.

A consideration of passing as constitutive of such contradictory social identifications involves an understanding of the processes whereby subjects come to be seen as 'having' a prior and fixed identity. The erasure of that process from regimes of knowledge involves the erasure of the social conflicts which structure intersubjectivity. If passing can be seen as threatening, it is in the making visible of the fractured history (the time, the labour and the crisis) that is concealed by identity. Through fetishism, identity hides passing, and by hiding passing, identity hides the conflict and antagonism that determines the 'work' needed to be done to reproduce a given sociality.

Passing through Others

Passing then cannot be simply theorized as a logic of the subject (= the transformation that takes place in the subject when she or he assumes an image). Rather, we can consider how passing takes place through encounters with others in which there is a crisis of reading, a crisis that hesitates over the gap between an image that is already assumed and an image that is yet to be assumed. Given this, passing is not best understood as an event that is clearly definable in time and space. Passing, by definition, is a movement through and across. Passing as the literal act of moving through space (in which there is no moment of departure or arrival), can be linked with passing as a set of cultural and embodied practices (passing for the other). In the act of passing through a given place one does not come to a halt and inhabit that place. Likewise, in the act of passing for an-other, or passing through the image of an-other, one does not come to inhabit the image in which 'one' moves (away from oneself).

To this extent, acts of passing cannot be thought of as events: they involve encounters between others whose boundaries are not fixed. Such encounters represent precisely the impossibility of fixing the meaning of passing; it is the undecidable moment that repeats itself as others are addressed, as we address each other. Take the following event.[2] I was stopped by two policemen in a car when walking near my home in Adelaide when I was 14. The first policeman asked, 'Are you Aboriginal?' I replied no, rather indignantly. The second policemen winked and said, 'It's just a sun tan, isn't it?' I smiled and did not reply.

One must note that the first policeman's assumption of his right to stop and interrogate me operated through the politically sanctioned conflation between Aboriginality and criminality. My denial of being Aboriginal and my failure to name or declare my 'race' (which of course was unnoticed or invisible to them) implicated me in their structure of address, by rendering Aboriginality something to be disavowed. The gesture of smiling can here be figured as a collusion, a desire to pass as white, as respectable, as somebody who has a legitimate right to walk in these leafy suburbs. Or it could be read as motivated by fear; fear of being positioned as a suspect who must be excluded. Such a fear may be gendered: the fearful smile may here be readable as a feminine smile.

The exchange of glances and the hailing of the policemen did not simply interpellate me as a subject. It also opened out a space in which the subject becomes 'unfixed' precisely by almost, but not quite, 'fitting' the visual prompt that triggers identity thinking. The difference in passing, as Carole Ann Tyler has suggested, is an uncanny one (1994: 212). Or, to put it differently, it is a disturbance that lacks a sign. I have taken up elsewhere how the reference to sun tanning in this address positions me as a white woman, as a woman whose colour is not natural or real, but is a sign of her proper attention to the cultivation of her body (Ahmed, 1998: 58–60). Tanned colour is understood as an adornment and not a stain, as 'a paying attention to the body'. The colour of my body is read as a detachable signifier, a 'mask' that can be put on and taken off, inessential to the subject, and hence acceptable. By rendering colour a mask rather than essential, the exchange rendered my body something to be valued, adorned, protected. Colour becomes inscribed as a detachable signifier, positioning me as essentially white, as truly and properly white underneath the luxury of a brown veil. Inscribed as a white woman, I became the legitimate object of the policeman's protective gaze.

The reference to sun tanning enabled me then to pass as a white woman. Now, between these two addresses – to the Aboriginal woman and the (sun tanned) white woman – something slipped beyond, something passed through. No, not some-thing. There is no nameable object that was not spoken. The language could not name what was beyond the two identifications: passing here allows a mobility precisely through not being locatable as an object that meets the gaze of the subject; passing here passes through the limits of representation and intentionality. That mobility has its limits precisely in *the re-opening of histories of identification which violate and fix subjects*. The policemen necessarily return to interrogate those they see as not white, or as not quite, not white. So while passing unfixes by the impossibility of naming the difference, it also fixes. In this example, fixation occurs by the policeman resolving the crisis of an uncertain identity by re-reading the ambiguous body according to a pre-existing regime of identity cards: if not Aboriginal, then sun tanned, then white.

Passing here involves both fixation and the impossibility of fixation determined through encounters between others within the context of law. In passing, the act of assuming an-other (imaginary) identity is not just re-forming, it is trans-forming. But passing is not becoming. In assuming the image of an-other one does not become the other. The fit does not constitute a proper identification. It is not a painless merger. Passing, to this extent, makes a difference: the subject does not stay the same through passing. The difference is one that mobilizes both identities: both the identity one 'already has' and the identity one takes on. In moving across identities perceived as inviolably distinct, passing may transform the conditions of their existence.

Passing and Hybridity

So far I have considered how I will not address passing – as either a form of transgression or as a generalized aspect of identity formation – and I have called instead for an account of passing which examines *its implication in social encounters with others, that is, in relationships of social conflict and antagonism*. What I have not discussed is how passing relates to the question of hybridity. Before further analysing particular narratives of passing, I will try and explain why any account of passing as a gendered and racial phenomena must take account of hybridity. Partly, my concern here will be with mixed-race female subjectivity; the reasons for this concern are autobiographical. As somebody from a mixed-race background (my mother is English and my father is Pakistani), I feel that my identification as either white or black involves inauthenticity – I do not feel like a real or proper white or black person. When I was young, passing for white was a matter of need, desire and strategy. Being identified as white was a way of belonging, a way of being included in a consensus. Now, whiteness has not become a matter of the desirable, or of an invisible norm that I repeat through the passage of my desires. Whiteness is something I contest, both politically and personally. I identify myself as a black feminist. Now, but in a different way, I feel as if I am passing. I worry that I will be caught out or detected, that I will be found out to be an inauthentic or improper black feminist. Of course, such a sense of being inadequate to the identity one assumes (either consciously or unconsciously) involves phantasies about who is the real or authentic subject (in my case, who is the 'real' black feminist). Needless to say, the phantasy does not and cannot find a proper object.

However, mixed-raceness cannot be theorized as an already constituted subject position, as a third term which resides simply beyond the binarism black/white. I do not want to introduce hybridity as a way of re-theorizing mixed-raceness as a special case. Rather, mixed-raceness makes uncertain at the level of the subject's self-identification what may appear certain in the formation of racial identity. Mixed-raceness brings to the foreground the crisis of identity which is concealed by the invisibility of the mark of passing. To this extent, being mixed-race is both a particular position which involves a set of dilemmas (for example, the frequency of questions about 'Where do you come from?')[3] and demonstrates the general problems of racialized thinking which assumes that race is secure as an origin. The crisis faced by hybrid subjects who pass is a particular and pressing demand to 'choose' between the 'two identities' that define the limits of racialized thinking: Are you white? Or black? Or just confused?

In Homi Bhabha's account of hybridity as destabilizing, hybridity does not 'belong' to the mixed-race subject. Rather, hybridity is determined by the very structure of the colonial address which demands both the disavowal and affirmation of difference. The colonizing mission is a civilizing one: it assumes that the colonized subject can reflect back the values and practices of the colonizer. And yet that civilizing mission must have its limits if it is to maintain the structure of authority which secures whiteness as the sign or mark of privilege. The colonized subject (who is, of course, always of a certain class) becomes a mimic subject: not quite, not white. But in mimicking the colonizer, the colonized subject opens out a space for resistance. The colonizer can be copied; the epistemic privilege is not founded in nature. As Bhabha argues:

> The display of hybridity – its peculiar 'replication' – terrorized authority with the *ruse* of recognition, its mimicry, its mockery. Such a reading of hybridity of colonial authority profoundly unsettles the demand that figures at the centre of the originary myth of colonial authority. (1994: 115)

In copying and hybridizing the colonizer, the colonized subject demonstrates the inauthenticity of the original as originary; the original itself is a copy which is open to reiteration and hence displacement. Hybridization here traverses absolute distinctions between identities – between the self and other – precisely by affirming a difference that undoes the binarism.

However, I would question any assumption that hybridity constitutes in itself a basis from which to theorize resistance and transformation. The traversing of racial distinctions – manifest most dangerously in the phantasies of interracial sex – can easily be recuperated into the identificatory practices of the master discourse. The danger of the hybrid – of the loss of clearly demarcated identities – may be read, in the term of a master discourse, as constituting the necessity for new forms of policing and surveillance. While hybridity in its travels undermines authorization and property, it nevertheless can become the condition of its possibility. The violence of the 'copy' which undercuts the originality and authority of the original, demonstrating that the identity of the original is already stolen, remains read and seen through the apparatuses of knowledge and vision that inform colonial privilege. Indeed, hybridization, if read as the failure or loss of a proper or authentic identity could then, paradoxically, become a means by which a purified notion of identity is upheld as the origin of truth, value and security (the fate of the hybrid makes clear what 'we' could lose).

Passing and hybridization merge in their use and abuse of mimesis. As Ellen Brinks points out, the passing subject desires to become (like) the other (1995: 4). In this process of miming and approximating the identity of an-other, 'identity' itself becomes decontextualized. In passing for an-other, the subject's movement constitutes the force of hybridization. The traversing of distinct identities materializes itself through *the discontinuities of the subject's biography*. In miming the identity of an-other, identity itself becomes an object of exchange that resists the realms of the proper and property. How to approximate her look? How to look white? Here, in desiring to capture an identity, the subject has to work and labour. It takes time and knowledge to see the difference that one may desire (or need) to become. The labour that is hidden in the assumption of identity as self-presence is re-created on the surface of the subject who passes through hybridity. But passing through such hybridity does not just reveal the labour and antagonism that is concealed by identity. It also reproduces identity as a fetish, by rendering it an object that can be known, seen and approximated. If I desired to pass for a particular other, I can imagine myself saying: 'Look, this is what you are, so I will become you. I will move, talk, eat, smell and be like you. By adopting your dress and manner, I will pass for you.' The subject who seeks to pass may assume the knowability of the place of the other. The contradictions embedded in passing through the hybrid space suggest the impossibility of placing passing on one side or the other of identity politics. While identity may be dislodged through the act of theft, and hence become subject to reiteration, it also determines the economics of passing, that which it takes for granted as the measure of desire.

Passing as a Technique of Knowledge

Passing for black as a white subject can certainly assume a knowable other and can fetishize the other (by approximating its image). Such an assumption of an-other's image in which there is a perpetual re-confirmation of the other's knowability is clearly evident in John Griffin's *Black Like Me*. This text is an autobiographical account of a white man who receives medical help to alter the colour of his skin so that he can 'discover' the truth of being black. It is quite clear that the story about the truth of the Negro involves a fetishizing of skin colour. By altering his skin, the narrator becomes a Negro: 'How else except by becoming a Negro could a white man hope to learn the truth?' (1970: 9). Here, the becoming-black of the skin is reducible to the assumption of a true and proper Negro identity. He asks himself, will they realize I am the same man, 'or will they treat me as some nameless Negro?' The reply is, 'As soon as they see you, you'll be a Negro' (1970: 12). Here, one becomes a Negro in the event of being seen as black, in being found and fixed in the horrified gaze (or 'hate stare') of others. The relation between identity and looking is demonstrated when the narrator catches his image in the mirror:

> In the flood of light against white tile, the face and shoulders of a stranger – a fierce, bald, very dark Negro – glared at me from the glass. He in no way resembled me.
>
> The transformation was total and shocking. I had expected to see myself disguised, but this was something else. I was imprisoned in the flesh of an utter stranger, an unsympathetic one with whom I felt no kinship. All traces of the John Griffin I had been were wiped from existence. Even the senses underwent a change so profound it filled me with distress. I looked into the mirror and saw reflected nothing of the white John Griffin's past. No, the reflections led back to Africa, back to the shanty and the ghetto, back to the fruitless struggles against the mark of blackness. Suddenly, almost with no mental preparation, no advance hint, it became clear and it permeated my whole being. My inclination was to fight against it. I had gone too far. I knew now that there is no such thing as a disguised white man, when the black won't rub off. The Black man is wholly a Negro, regardless of what he once may have been. I was a newly created Negro who must go out that door and live in a world unfamiliar to me. (Griffin, 1970: 19)

Here, the transformation of skin colour from white to black becomes causally linked to a total personal and collective transformation. Skin in this way is seen to hold the 'truth' of the subject's identity (like a 'kernel') as well as functioning as the scene of the subject's memory and history (with a black skin there is no *trace* of his previous identity). The essentializing image of his black skin leading (back) to Africa creates an absolute link between skin colour and racial origin. His transformation into a stranger, where he passes as black in the mirror, produces the naked face of a black man, a face that immediately gets coded as fierce and glaring, as monstrous and bestial. In passing as black in his own mirror image, the vision of the black face is hence overdetermined by the 'knowledges' available of blackness central to the violence of colonialism (it is a 'fierce' face). In other words, what one sees as the other (or in oneself, as one passes for the other) is already structured by the knowledges that keep the other in a certain place. Passing as a phantasy of becoming the other involves an apparatus of knowledge that masters the other by taking its place.

Passing as black as a form of appropriation/knowledge is central to Gail Ching-Liang Low's concerns in *White Skins/Black Masks: Representation and Colonialism* (1996). In successfully passing, the white subject inhabits the place of the other; the possibility of surveillance is expanded, exceeding the divisions imposed by time and space. Here, the act of passing is informed by a hegemonic white masculinity, the ability to be anywhere, at any time. Such a phantasy of 'going native', while threatening to some anthropological models of the other as always only the other, hence became a mechanism for the reconstitution of the other *through* the hegemonic self. Indeed, Low shows how the phantasy of 'going native' works as a theatrical display which, like fetishism, both affirms and disavows, the difference (1996: 203). The difference is disavowed in the assumption that the subject has assumed the place of the other; and yet in assuming the place of the other rather than simply being the other, the difference is perpetually re-affirmed. The phantasy, for example, seeks to uncover a glimpse of white skin beneath the native costume (1996: 203). Passing is here the phantasy of an ability (or a technique) to become without becoming. It is a form of appropriation of the place of the other in which the other cannot and does not speak. And yet, the uncanny difference which is glimpsed cannot be maintained in the passing through of one to the other. The process of fixation where identities are adopted through dress and manner, also involves the threatening potential of its own unfixability. It is this relation between fixation and loss that marks the risk of passing.

Passing for black as a white man can to this extent demonstrate the labour involved in the assumption of a white, masculine identity. It puts on display the other within the face of the same in order to manage and contain that other (= the domestication of the other). Through adopting or taking on signifiers of the subordinated other, passing becomes a mechanism for reconstituting or reproducing the other as the 'not-I' *within* rather than *beyond* the structure of the 'I'. Hence, when Griffin looks in the mirror he can say with conviction, 'he in no way resembles me'. The split between the 'he' and 'I' is seeable within the mirror image of the face. Passing for black as a white man can hence be understood as an 'ability' insofar as it is a technique; it is a set of practices through which 'knowledges' of the other become reproduced to affirm a white, masculine identity (to affirm the structure of the white face).

Significantly, with the shifts in form of racism towards a fetishizing of cultural rather than biological difference (Balibar, 1991: 22), passing for black becomes an increasingly powerful individual and national phantasy. Passing for black is enabled by 'adopting' elements of black culture, a process of adoption which then fixes and freezes those elements as indicators of what it means to be black. In Sunderland's sympathetic account of white women who pass as black, she emphasizes how those women imagine and project what it means to 'be black'. To quote from one of her interviewees: 'And I find that very much about Black people. You know I think, um. I just find the warmth there' (Sunderland, 1997: 40). While Sunderland clearly supports this re-presentation of the white self through claiming a filiation with black culture – for her this indicates a shift towards a recognition of mixed identities (1997: 53) – we can be more cautious. Not only is there a fetishizing and exoticizing of blackness as the Other at stake. We also have the re-creation of the white subject as the one *who knows the difference*, even if that difference is no longer seen as external to the self and community. Here, the white feminine subject becomes re-created through her *sympathy* for the Other (the Other's warmth). The Other becomes a mechanism which allows her *to know herself* (as black), by providing what is lacking in her self. Passing for black is a technique of knowledge insofar as it remains tied to the narrativization of the white female subject's knowledge of herself through her sympathetic incorporation of others (by assuming an image of blackness, it becomes known as that which is lacking in the white self).

Here, *the narrativization of hybrid and mixed identities expands the force of mastery as beyond the limitations of the singular face*: the face of the dominant self and nation expands through hybridity it expands by passing for what it is not (hence allowing the other to exist within the face). Indeed, one can consider how such individuated acts of passing legitimate the national phantasy of multiculturalism, in which one can pass for others by adopting or assuming *their style*. In this sense, multicultural national spaces also involve the assimilation of differences: difference becomes a matter of style that the white face can put on and take off. Passing as black is here a technique which confirms the nation's ability to 'be itself' by incorporating others (the 'we' of the nation becomes affirmed through difference, rather than against it).

The link between ability and technique is important when considering the practices around passing for white. One often talks of *being able to* pass for white (I mentioned earlier, that in Larsen's *Passing*, Irene *can* pass for white, but chooses not to). It is here, for example, that a link between mixed-raceness and passing is often assumed. The mixed-race subject can pass for white given that the mixed-race subject does not fully inhabit blackness – by not quite, being black. Of course, only some mixed-race subjects *can* pass, and some black subjects *can* pass. To conflate mixed-raceness and passing, is to imply that blackness pre-exists as a singular racial identity, as a recognizable or already read face.[4] The link then between mixed-raceness and passing is only partly determined; it is a question of histories of identification that do not fully grasp and fix their subject. The question of ability is undercut by this refusal of passing to be fully determined as belonging to a specific racial (non-)identity. Who is able to pass as white? The mulatto who does not look black due to the partial presence of whiteness? The assumption then of an ability to pass which is fully determined by the skin which is determined by race (or racial confusion) is a false one. Passing is not so much an ability, which is only available to certain subjects, but a technique. This technique is exclusive and exclusionary – it is not available to all subjects – as it depends on the relation between subjects and structures of identification where the subject sees itself, or is seen by others, as not quite fitting.

Considering passing in terms of 'ability' does not then involve assuming that the 'real' or 'natural' body determines the encounter, but demonstrates that encounters between others construct and reconstruct the body as a signifier of difference. The ability to pass for white involves a technique of the self: the projection of a bodily image (say, through the alterations of speech, hair, fashion and gestures) which is seen to be conflatable with whiteness. Bodies become reconstructed through techniques which serve to approximate an image. That bodily image takes on the life of the fetish; it perpetually re-creates itself as a signifier of desire through affirming and disavowing the difference.

This 'ability' to reconstruct the body through fetishism (which is not necessarily an intentional act) can involve forms of access to knowledge. In the event discussed earlier, my ability to pass for white was also informed by my middle-class background where my 'way of speaking', as a form of self-presentation which is clearly determined by a prior history of identification, could be conflated with respectability and hence whiteness (Skeggs, 1997; Twine, 1996: 201–10). This demonstrates how passing for any particular other identity brings into play contingent, complex and antagonistic identifications. The link between passing for black and access to knowledges and power is more clear and determined within a particular structure of identification. Here, the very technique of passing for black is informed by access to cultural capital and knowledges embedded in whiteness and colonial privilege where the other is assumed to be both knowable, seeable and hence be-able.

Passing and Community

Passing for a white woman as a black woman does not always involve a strategic or intentional act. In Sally Morgan's *My Place* (1995), passing occurs through the lack or absence of any knowledge that there is any difference. *My Place* is an autobiographical account of the discovery of Aboriginal identity; the attempt to retrace the past that was lost through the 'not telling' (or the erasure) of the past by others. Sally as a young girl is unaware of any difference, either in relation to herself or others. Her sense of comfort and ease suggests she is positioned as a white person who passes for white. Her assumption of whiteness involves an unconscious passing in relation to herself. She passes as white, not in relation to the gaze of the other, but in relation to her own gaze. It is the gaze of the other which challenges this luxury of passing, of literally assuming whiteness: she is asked where she is from by friends at school. She asks her mother who tells her she is Indian. Aboriginality is concealed as a dangerous knowledge. She then passes as an Indian woman.

Sally's 'discovery' of Aboriginality does not involve simply assuming the identity which was already hers prior to passing (reclaiming something that was stolen, reclaiming herself from the false or inauthentic assumption). Passing becomes a way of reinterpreting the past; it becomes a way of recognizing the mis-recognition that structured her subjectivity. Such a reclaiming takes place through looking at the face of her grandmother: 'For the first time in my fifteen years, I was conscious of Nan's colouring. She was right, she wasn't white. Well, I thought logically, if she wasn't white, then neither were we. What did that make us? What did that make me? I had never thought of myself as Black before' (1995: 97). Yet she still has to 'find out' what it means to be Aboriginal. This narrative of discovery of a past which is absent from the surface involves a community. It involves speaking to her family who tell her their stories. Sally becomes the subject of the text as an Aboriginal woman only through hearing others speak and retracing their partial and fractured stories. The story of assuming a lost Aboriginality in this sense involves a collective memory which forms the materiality of the text itself. Passing as a white woman who passes as Indian who becomes (or passes as) Aboriginal does not then simply involve the progressive and individuated movement towards the 'truth' or the 'kernel' of herself. The act of remembering through engagement with others creates the present identification as one that lives for the future of a displaced community.

The act of passing becomes then a story not of truth but of love. The process of remembering involves forms of closeness and proximity to each other in order to deal with the tragedy of 'the stolen generation', the generation of half-caste Aboriginal children who were taken away from their mothers and introduced into white communities as part of a policy of assimilation. This policy involved the assumption that eventually all traces of Aboriginality (as blackness) would be erased from the faces of Australia. In speaking to each other about the history of enforced separation, the generation of women in *My Place* resist their silencing and refuse to endorse this history of passing for white. But it is a painful process:

> It took several months to work through Mum's story and, during that time, many tears were shed. We became very close.
>
> Although she'd finally shared her story with me, she still couldn't tell my brothers and sisters. Consequently, I found myself communicating it to them in bits and pieces as it seemed appropriate. It was, and still is, upsetting for us all. We'd lived in a cocoon of sorts for so long that we found it difficult to come to terms with the experiences Mum had been through. (1995: 307)

Here, the sharing of stories is like the breaking out of a cocoon of assumed whiteness. Passing for white cannot be read then as simply Sally's individual story (a story of her 'I'). Rather, it is the re-forming and trans-forming story of a 'we' which had been made impossible, which had become erased from the surface of any living community. Passing for white was an enforced policy against Aboriginal people which divided generations of mothers and daughters from each other. Resistance to passing for white is enacted through the very proximity of speaking to each other about the pain of this passing. That proximity, that love, joins Sally's 'I' to others, forming a tenuous but creative 'we'. The 'we' doesn't constitute the smoothness of the narrative. The narrative becomes increasingly disjointed as it attempts to forge the links of a new community. Sally, as a narrator, self-consciously speaks of writing an alternative history of Australia. She wants other members of her family to tell their side of the story. We then have incorporated into her narrative *My Place*, the stories of these other 'I's', told in the first person singular. The 'I's' within her 'I' do not emerge through appropriation or absorption. The reader gains a sense of the discontinuities between subjectivities that informs the force of the community. Through narrating the act of speaking to each other, the reader is reminded that the 'we' itself is unnarratable beyond the disjointed patching of 'I's' whose status in the narrative cannot be rendered equivalent. The community lives through this impossibility; it becomes a force through a recognition of *that which cannot merge into one*. So here, in the unspeakable gaps between the stories, Aboriginality gets reconstructed as a politics of resistance, a politics based not on a concealment, but a revelation that there is 'more than one' (story) that opens up the future. Passing for Aboriginal involves a re-creation of the possibility of community and collectivity through the pain and hope of speaking to each other, of desiring to hear each other's stories.

At one level, *My Place* could be read as a text which moves from passing (the inauthentic identities of white/Indian) to being and identity (Aboriginality). However, the narrative is much more complex than this. Passing becomes narratable not as something that has to be sacrificed by a politics of identity, *but as something which becomes displaced into different and collective forms of identification*. As a form of critical knowledge, this passing 'joins' the individual subject to a marginal community through stories and partial memories, a joining which does not suture a gap, but makes visible its inevitability through active engagement (through the necessity and impossibility of speaking to each other). Passing as an Aboriginal involves in this sense 'giving' Aboriginality the meaning not simply of survival but of resistance; it means reiterating Aboriginality in affirmative and positive ways which challenge the enunciative authority of official histories.[5] It is here that passing, the making visible of the violent histories behind identity as self-presence (the histories of racial antagonism which are concealed by Sally, and other 'half-caste' Aboriginal subjects, passing as white) can become the basis for a transformative and collective politics.

Notes

1. See my article, 'Animated Borders: Skin, Colour and Tanning' (1998) for an analysis of the role of skin in forms of racial identification.

2. I have written extensively about this event which involves other aspects that I cannot mention here. For a fuller account see Ahmed (1996). For a consideration of this event in relation to autobiography see Ahmed (1997).

3. For an interesting analysis of the way in which mixed-race subjects are constantly being forced to identify themselves in social encounters by being asked question about 'Where are you from?' or 'What are you?' see Williams (1996).

4. Again, this reminds us of the importance of not theorizing mixed-raceness as a 'special case'. As Caroline Streeter suggests, representing the mixed or multi-racial subject in this way confirms the phantasy that there is a mono-racial identity (1996: 307).

5. One must note here how the reading of *My Place* within white Australia has authorized a discourse of appropriate(d) otherness. The fact that *My Place*, has been accommodated within white Australian literary self-representation, and 'Sally Morgan' has been individuated as the acceptable face of Aboriginality, needs to be addressed. Rather than dismissing *My Place* itself, we need to recognize the potential and irreducible danger of such reading practices in which the figuring of the author as an individual and autonomous hero, enables the radical contingency

of the textual relation to be effaced. Here, the other can be domesticated and appropriated, precisely insofar as it is assumed to be known or read *in the text*.

References

Ahmed, Sara (1996) 'Identifications, Gender and Racial Difference: Moving Beyond a Psychoanalytical Account of Subjectivity', pp. 359–86 in Renuka Sharma (ed.) *Representations of Gender, Democracy and Identity Politics in Relation to South Asia*. Delhi: Indian Book Centre.

Ahmed, Sara (1997) *It's Just a Sun Tan, Isn't It?': Auto-biography as an Identificatory Practice*, pp. 153–67 in Heidi Mirza (ed.) *Black British Feminism*. London: Routledge.

Ahmed, Sara (1998) 'Animated Borders: Skin, Colour and Tanning', pp. 45–65 in Margrit Shildrick and Janet Price (eds) *Vital Signs: Feminist Reconfigurations of the Bio/logical Body*. Edinburgh: Edinburgh University Press.

Balibar, Etienne (1991) 'Is There a "Neo-Racism"?', pp. 17–28 in Etienne Balibar and Immanuel Wallerstein (eds) *Race, Nation and Class: Ambiguous Identities*. London: Verso.

Bhabha, Homi (1994) *The Location of Culture*. London and New York: Routledge.

Brinks, Ellen (1995) ' "Who's Been in my Closet?": Mimetic Identification and the Psychosis of Class Transvestism in *Single White Female*', pp. 3–12 in Stanlie M. James and Abena P.A. Busia (eds) *Cruising the Performative: Interventions into the Representation of Ethnicity, Nationality and Sexuality*. Bloomington: Indiana University Press.

Butler, Judith (1990) *Gender Trouble: Feminism and the Subversion of Identity*. London: Routledge.

Butler, Judith (1993) *Bodies that Matter: On the Discursive Limits of 'Sex'*. London: Routledge.

Garber, Marjorie (1992) *Vested Interests*. New York: Routledge.

Griffin, John Howard (1970) *Black Like Me*. London: Panther Modern Society.

Ifekwunigwe, Jayne O. (1997) 'Diaspora's Daughters, Africa's Orphans?: On Lineage, Authenticity and Mixed-Race "Identity" ', pp. 127–52 in Heidi Mirza (ed.) *Black British Feminism*. London: Routledge.

Lacan, Jacques (1977) *Écrits: A Selection*. London: Tavistock.

Larsen, Nella (1994) *Quicksand and Passing*. New Brunswick, NJ: Rutgers University Press.

Low, Gail Ching-Liang (1996) *White Skins/Black Masks: Representation and Colonialism*. London: Routledge.

Morgan, Sally (1995) *My Place*. London: Virago Press.

Mullen, Harryette (1994) 'Optic White: Blackness and the Production of Whiteness', *Diacritics* 24(2–4): 71–89.

Skeggs, Beverley (1997) *Formations of Class and Gender: Becoming Respectable*. London: Sage.

Streeter, Caroline A. (1996) 'Ambiguous Bodies: Locating Black/White Women in Cultural Representations', pp. 305–22 in Maria P.P. Root (ed.) *The Multiracial Experience: Racial Borders as the New Frontier*. Thousand Oaks, CA: Sage.

Sunderland, P.L. (1997) '"You May not Know it, But I'm Black": White Women's Self-Identification as Black', *Ethnos* 62(1–2): 32–58.

Twine, France Winddance (1996) 'Brown-Skinned White Girls: Class, Culture and the Construction of White Identity in Suburban Communities', *Gender, Place and Culture* 3(2): 205–24.

Tyler, Carole Anne (1994) 'Passing: Narcissism, Identity and Difference', *Differences* 6: 212–48.

Williams, Teresa Kay (1996) 'Race as Process: Reassessing the "What Are You" Encounters of Bi-Racial Individuals', pp. 199–210 in Maria P.P. Root (ed.) *The Multiracial Experience: Racial Borders as the New Frontier*. Thousand Oaks, CA: Sage.

Young, Lola (1996) *Fear of the Dark: 'Race', Gender and Sexuality in the Cinema*. London: Routledge.

Sara Ahmed is a lecturer at the Institute for Women's Studies at Lancaster University. She has published articles on black feminism, post-colonial theory, postmodernism, deconstruction and psychoanalysis in journals including *Social & Legal Studies*, *Australian Feminist Studies*, *Hypatia*, *Oxford Literary Review*, *New Formations* and *European Journal of Cultural Studies*. Her first book, *Differences that Matter: Feminist Theory and Postmodernism*, was published by Cambridge University Press in 1998. She is working on a new book titled *Strange Encounters: Embodied Others in Post-Coloniality* (Routledge, forthcoming).

Classing Queer
Politics in Competition

Mariam Fraser

> [I]f the genealogical critique of the subject is the interrogation of those constitutive and exclusionary relations of power through which contemporary discursive resources are formed, then it follows that the critique of the queer subject is crucial to the continuing *democratization* of queer politics. (Judith Butler, *Bodies that Matter: On the Discursive Limits of 'Sex'*)

Introduction

ALTHOUGH IT is generally accepted that ethnicity, gender, sexuality and class are not 'separable' from each other (as in an 'additive' model of identity), it remains the case that they are frequently distinguished for the purpose of different kinds of identity politics. I want to explore the grounds on which such distinctions are often drawn, and consider, tentatively, some of the implications of those distinctions in the light of what I think are some of Judith Butler's most interesting questions. Towards the end of *Bodies that Matter* Butler suggests that it is necessary to continually interrogate for whom 'outness' is 'a historically available and affordable option'; that it is important always to ask: 'Who is represented by *which* use of the term [queer], and who is excluded? (Butler, 1993: 227).

The politics that Butler's own theory of performativity implies has itself been hotly debated in the context of who is or is not excluded from queer. In *Feminist Contentions* for example, Nancy Fraser argues that Butler's analysis of performativity is 'not well suited to the crucial work of articulation, contextualization, and provisional totalization. It does not, for example, help us to map the links among various discrete discursive regimes and thus to theorize the construction of hegemony' (N. Fraser, 1995: 163). In short, she argues that a theory of performatively constituted identities, while useful in some respects, cannot explain – or offer much in

▪ *Theory, Culture & Society* 1999 (SAGE, London, Thousand Oaks and New Delhi),
Vol. 16(2): 107–131
[0263-2764(199904)16:2;107–131;008258]

the way of changing – what Butler herself calls 'large-scale' issues of economic and social (in)justices (Butler, 1995a: 141), injustices which might include among them inequalities of class. Reiterating this point in slightly different terms more recently, Fraser argues that it is 'historicization', rather than 'destabilization or deconstruction', which best allows the social theorist to 'appreciate the social-structurally differentiated and historically specific character of contemporary capitalist society' (N. Fraser, 1998: 149). Accordingly, in the light of the 'multiple contradictory interpellations of social subjects' (N. Fraser, 1998: 149) which characterizes contemporary Western capitalist societies, Fraser distinguishes between 'injustices of distribution' and 'injustices of recognition' (N. Fraser, 1998: 141–2). The former refers to injustices of class, the latter to injustices of status and, in particular, to the status of 'women, racialized peoples, and/or gays and lesbians' (N. Fraser, 1998: 144).[1] Although Fraser argues that injustices of status are no less fundamental, and no less material, than injustices of distribution,[2] Butler nevertheless objects to this distinction on the basis that it implicitly renders 'questions of race and sexuality secondary to the "real" business of politics' (Butler, 1998: 36) (the 'real' business being, presumably, the politics of class). Further, unlike the 'real' business of politics, she argues, the *cultural* politics associated with struggles around race and sexuality are construed as 'factionalizing, identitarian, and particularistic' (Butler, 1998: 33).

This debate illustrates, first, that not only do distinctions between the identities of gender, sexuality, 'race' and class continue to be drawn, but that they acquire a specific potency in relation to different kinds of (identity) politics. It is with the (contested) relations between these identities, and in particular with their implications for a politics of performativity, that this article will be concerned. It is not my intention however, either to argue that Butler's theory of performativity – extended, as it recently has been, to Bourdieu's notion of the habitus – is not *relevant* to analyses of classed subjectivities (it is, as I will illustrate), nor is it to make a plea for some kind of totalizing inclusivity, to reinscribe 'common ideals' or 'to restore the universal' (Butler, 1998: 36). Indeed, I am in agreement with Butler when she argues that it is a mistake to locate 'the problem of difference as that which emerges *between* one identity and another' (Butler, 1998: 37). Instead, difference may be understood as 'the condition of possibility of identity, or rather, its constitutive limit: what makes it possible [is] at the same time what makes any final or closed articulation possible' (Butler, 1998: 37). It is precisely the 'constitutive limit' of queer, and some kinds of queer politics, that I want to explore here. I will argue that what is often taken to be the key site of much queer theory and activism – that is, the reappropriation of signifiers of difference – is problematic in the light of a close analysis of subjectivities which are informed by 'race', gender *and* class. More specifically, it may be that struggles which are frequently linked to issues of visibility are problematic in the context of subjectivities – class subjectivities – that are both enabled and constrained by a particular, and a particularly uneasy, relation to recognition and representation.[3]

Two Rallies

June Jordan speaks at two rallies in two days, both of which take place on the same Plaza at Berkeley. The first is a rally against racism; the second, a rally for bisexual, gay and lesbian rights. Her response is that to have two rallies is: 'disgraceful! There should have been just one rally. One rally: Freedom is indivisible' (Jordan, 1996: 13).

Jordan suggests that the reason for the division between race and sexuality, in this context, goes (at its most reductive) something like this:

> . . . the bottom line about gay or lesbian or bisexual identity is that you can conceal it whenever necessary and, so, therefore, why don't you do just that? Why don't you keep your deviant sexuality in the closet and let the rest of us – we who suffer oppressions for reasons of our ineradicable and always visible components of our personhood such as race and gender – get on with our more necessary, our more beleaguered struggle to survive? (Jordan, 1996: 12)

Jordan's rhetoric parodies those who pit the assumed 'visibility' of race and gender against the 'invisibility' of sexuality. The implication here is that gender is written on the body and is therefore visible in a way that sexual identities and activities are not. Similarly, black and white are immediately available to be accessed by sight. Such things are self-evident – the body stands as evidence for the black or white self – unless they are disguised by design. By contrast, homosexuality is not inscribed on the body and heterosexuality might not be 'seeable' (although the compulsoriness of heterosexuality [Rich, 1983] assumes us all to be so until we prove that we are not). In short, unlike the 'ineradicable' visible marks which declare one's gender and race, the signs of sexuality can be 'separated' from the self. As such, it can be 'closeted'. This is a politics of race and gender which, in June Jordan's experience, is in competition with a politics of sexuality.

Recent social and cultural theories, and especially feminist and queer theories, have sought to illustrate how common perceptions of identity are often, and usually implicitly, informed either by spatial or by temporal metaphors. In Jordan's example for instance, the 'sexed' and 'raced' body is understood to carry visible signs on its surface, on the skin.[4] In this respect identity is situated in space: the body is the *site*, or place, where the 'truth' of an identity is revealed. These signs of identity are somehow oblivious to time: a 'visibly' black body might age, might change in any number of ways, but what will remain steadfast, against the vagaries of time, is the colour of skin itself.[5] Black, white, male, female: these are identities which appear to be 'given' (at birth?) and to exist 'on' the body for *all time*. Sexuality, by contrast, is assumed to develop *over* time. Indeed, even if it is perceived to be an inherent 'essence', something one is 'born' with, sexuality is often considered to develop into full 'maturity' only over a period of years (for example, through puberty and adolescence). The relation between temporality and developmentalism is especially clear in a heterosexist culture where homosexuality, unlike heterosexuality, is frequently construed as an 'immature' state or is seen to be a temporary straying from the path of heterosexuality (such that homosexuality appears as narrative 'cul-de-sac', as it were). Thus where the narratives of heterosexuality, masquerading as 'the totality of Romance' (Sedgwick, 1994: 11), are authoritative and usually taken for granted, those of homosexuality are called into question:

> . . . questions of authority and evidence can be the first to arise. 'How do you know you're really gay? Why be in such a hurry to jump to conclusions? After all, what you're saying is only based on a few feelings, not real actions (*or alternatively*: on a few actions, not necessarily on your real feelings).' (Sedgwick, 1991: 79)

Evidence over time – don't 'hurry to jump to conclusions' – is required where visual 'proof' is perceived to be lacking. One would be surprised to hear of the colour white, for example, that: 'It's a temporary phase. You'll get over it'. A gay, lesbian or bisexual[6] narrative identity is often only grudgingly conferred when, to quote Paul Ricoeur's theory of narrative identity, 'a certain constancy of ... dispositions' and a 'kind of fidelity to the self' (Ricoeur, 1991: 192) can be demonstrated throughout the course of a lifetime. Without visual co-ordinates, narrative continuity – that which 'equates the present with the past, the actual with the potential' (Ricoeur, 1980: 186) – becomes the required evidence to support a sexual identity.

What makes these understandings of identity especially convincing, theorists have argued, is the certainty which often accompanies the visible identification of the 'truth' (of identity), a certainty which may at least partly be explained by the well-established link between 'what we see and what we know' (Berger, 1972: 7) in Western culture. Although the relation between seeing and knowing is contested, Western discourses have been largely guided by a visual paradigm (Jay, 1992, 1993). This long tradition, wherein the desire to see is likened to the will-to-knowledge, is played out today, for example, in the biotechnical universe, where echograms and echography, Rosi Braidotti argues, have scaled new heights in making the 'invisible' (such as the origins of life, tissues and cells) visible: 'the scopic drive is reaching a paroxysm; as if the basic principle of visibility had shifted into a mirage of absolute transparency, as if *everything* could be seen' (Braidotti, 1994: 49).[7] This is the 'triumph' of the visual image and visual representation, which functions as though 'the scopic ... were indeed the most adequate way of re-presenting the act of knowledge' (Braidotti, 1994: 49). Not only scientific culture, but contemporary Western popular culture too, Braidotti argues, rests 'on the fantasy that visibility and truth work together' (Braidotti, 1994: 69). It is the force of this tradition which ensures that material bodies, encoded with the seeable signs of identity, are assumed to carry their 'truth', overtly and irrefutably, on the surface of the skin. Given, by contrast, the assumed 'invisibility' of sexuality, it is no accident that its central metaphor, the 'closet', implies a place where things are hidden from view.

The Time it Takes . . .

It is into the heart of the presupposition that identities such as race and gender are somehow fixedly visible, and fixed for all time, that Judith Butler's theory of performativity intervenes. *Bodies that Matter* (1993) asserts that material bodies – 'real' bodies, including those which appear to be irrevocably marked by 'their' identities – have a temporal as well as a spatial dimension. 'Matter' will no longer be conceived 'purely' as a site or a surface, a space on which signs are available to be read by those who might 'master', empirically, the visual field (Tyler, 1994: 219). Instead, matter is understood to be *a process* of materialization which itself constitutes the static 'matter' of bodies. Crucially, as a process, materialization must, necessarily, be temporal. Matter does not 'exist', in and of itself, outside or beyond discourse, but is rather repeatedly produced through performativity, that which 'brings into being or enacts that which it names' (Butler, 1995a: 134). Performativity is never singular; the subject is 'subjected and produced time and again' (Butler, 1995b: 47).[8] Thus while it might seem certain that 'I am a woman', this identity is never given, and is always unstable. The subject might *appear* to have 'an identity', an identity which is resolutely written on the body, but this is only because reiteration 'conceals or dissimulates the conventions of which it is a repetition' (Butler, 1993: 12). In short, while the visual evidence might point to the inert and unchanging stasis of matter, matter is instead a discursive construction which 'not only takes place *in* time, but is itself a temporal process' (Butler, 1993: 10).

Recent work on the visibility, or invisibility, of ethnicity also seeks, in different ways, to destabilize the empiricism attributed to the visual field. Sara Ahmed argues that the reduction of race to skin colour ('chromotism') involves *investing* skin colour 'with the meaning of racial difference', a difference which 'may fix the object of the gaze into a logic of inclusion (you are white like me) or exclusion (you are black like them)' (Ahmed, 1996: 10). Black and white thus become the vehicles through which subject and object, self and other, are established. However, the boundaries between 'the "me" and the "not-me" ' (Gutman, 1988: 107) are not always transparent. Ahmed has herself been identified by white policemen as first Aboriginal (black like them) and then sun tanned (white like me). Passing as tanned, her body also passes as 'safe' (as opposed to 'criminal') because its colour is temporary, 'literally a detachable signifier, a "mask" that can be put on and taken off, inessential to the subject, and hence acceptable' (Ahmed, 1996: 17). This split between 'natural' or 'essential' black and 'inessential' tan also, Ahmed argues, shapes the differences between black and white femininities. The black woman's skin is perceived to be 'not pliable' (it is 'given', for all time) and, as such, is a sign of racial otherness, an always already sexualized femininity (Pettman in Ahmed, 1996: 18). The white woman's tan, by contrast, is a sign of class privilege; demonstrating a proper 'care for the self', it is an adornment which 'appropriates and domesticates the hyper-sexuality which is signified by black skin, rendering the presence of colour a temporary aberration which confirms the proper sexual order based on her protection from black men by white men' (Ahmed, 1996: 18). Identifying herself as *both* black *and* tanned, Ahmed will 'question [her reader's] construction of either' (Ahmed, 1996: 21).

Ahmed exploits the 'uncertain' colour of skin to destabilize the relations (and the assumed autonomy) between self and other, colour and race and white and black femininities. By contrast, the performance artist Adrian Piper prefers to assertively identify herself as black, handing out 'calling cards', which state her racial identity, to those who would attempt to 'pass her [as white] without her consent' (Phelan, 1993: 98):

> By appropriating the tight square of the business/calling card, Piper suggests that the *business* of politicizing racial difference involves marking its *disappearance*. . . . Piper's card then establishes, simultaneously, the failure of racial difference to appear within the narrow range of the visible and registers her refusal to let the visual field *fail* to secure it. The card itself ruptures the given to be seen and exposes the normative force of everyday blindness: if no one looks black, everyone is white. (Phelan, 1993: 98)

Piper's experiences illustrate Lisa Walker's point that 'subjects who can "pass" exceed the categories of visibility that establish identity' (Walker, 1993: 868). Her performance also indicates that those identities which are rendered 'invisible' might be absorbed into the authoritative 'norm' – if no one looks black, everyone is white.[9] That Piper is passed off as white illustrates the unmarked – and therefore assumed – nature of whiteness.[10] Richard Dyer (1988, 1997) argues that this is precisely where the power of whiteness lies; not in its representation as superiority, but rather as 'normality'. He seeks therefore, to render white itself 'visible' such that it is no longer perceived to be the normative 'blank' backdrop against which other identities and skin colours are measured.

Another way of challenging the 'self-evidence' of the visual field has been to highlight the role of narrative in the construction of identities. As John Berger suggests: '"I am" includes all that has made me so. It is more than a statement of immediate fact: it is already an explanation, a justification, a demand – it is already autobiographical' (Berger quoted in Probyn, 1993: 117). Vikki Bell illustrates how the visible (i.e. the seeable) is not 'given' and self-evident but is rather intertwined with narratives. 'Vision matters', she writes, 'and makes matter, but it is not autonomous in its phenomenality' (Bell, 1996: 231). Using the figure of 'Golden' in Toni Morrison's novel *Jazz*, Bell argues that the disclosure of ethnicity requires

– rather like the disclosure of sexuality is assumed to require – narratives that 'tell' what the body will not necessarily 'show'. Golden, who passes as white (his father is black), comes to learn 'that if one wants to "show" one's genealogy in the materiality of the body and to have a relationship based upon it, one has to embrace stories of blood, of history' (Bell, 1996: 225). In this respect, narratives call into question the forceful assumption that 'everyone is white unless they look black'. Similarly, Corinne Squire argues that Oprah Winfrey, when she said on a recent talk show that 'a lot of you all white people in this country is black and didn't know it. And it's shaking some people up, let me tell you ' (Winfrey in Squire, 1997: 242), is implicitly drawing attention to the instability of visible signifiers of identity. The show, called 'Family Secrets', included interviews with 'white' people who had recently discovered that one of their biological parents was black.[11] Although acknowledging that these shows often either 'whit[e] [African Americans and Hispanics] out or reduc[e] them to stereotypes' (Squire, 1997: 243), Squire also argues that miscegenation can be understood 'as a moment of utopian possibility':

> It is as if talk shows have heard Adrian Piper's rhetorical injunction ... to declare yourself black if your ancestry is even slightly nonwhite, and are in their own way responding.... you can see in [talk shows] an unnamed but significant color that is rarely visible elsewhere, a less than sparkling white. (Squire, 1997: 248)

The 'moment of utopian possibility', for Squire, is the moment when the boundaries between black and white are challenged, and when whiteness is 'compromise[d] ... by even the least trace of nonwhiteness' (Squire, 1997: 248). Significantly, it is narrative which, in this particular context, compromises 'pristine' whiteness and which may, in its turn, change the way colour is 'seen' and 'race' understood. Bell, who argues for the continued political value of terms such as 'mixed race' or 'hybridity' makes a similar point: 'as a categorization "mixed" cannot be presented visually, for it requires a narrative. For that reason, not for any new vanguardism, it may be a place, one place, to begin to prise open a complex that elides colour and "race"' (Bell, 1996: 235).

In each of the examples I have drawn on here, identity is revealed to be irreducible to the matter on which it is *seen* to be inscribed. In particular, the reminder of the role of temporality – be it in analyses of performativity or narrative – in the production of what is frequently understood to be an unequivocally visible 'matter' calls that spatial location into question. Temporal and spatial processes of identification are shown to be inseparable.

Theatrics

While contemporary theory often seeks to emphasize the role of temporal as well as spatial processes in the production of identities,[12] political campaigns and strategies are frequently informed by an accent on the 'object-in-space', the *visible* material body.[13] In her article entitled 'How to Recognise a Lesbian: The Cultural Politics of Looking Like What You Are', Lisa Walker notes that: 'Privileging visibility has become a tactic of late twentieth-century identity politics, in which participants often symbolize their demands for social justice by celebrating visual signifiers of difference that have historically targeted them for discrimination' (Walker, 1993: 868). The accent on visibility politics since the 1960s – encapsulated in slogans such as 'Out and Proud' or 'Black is Beautiful' – bears witness to the belief that visibility is a source of power.[14] Recently, a number of bisexuals have claimed that 'invisibility is . . . how we experience oppression' (Baker, 1992: 266). The catchword 'VisiBIlity', printed on T-shirts and badges at the 11th National Bisexual Conference in Britain, captures the investment in visible representation in a word. While this suggests that sexuality may also, like gender and race, suffer a metonymic reduction wherein the visible signifiers of an identity are conflated with the signified identity (Walker, 1993: 883), it is also the case that the ability to capture a complex system of signs in a single (usually visible) trope may be a powerful political weapon.[15] Walker argues, for example, that one of the reasons that the figure of the butch is 'glorified' as an 'authentic' lesbian is because her '"blatant" representation of sexual deviance' (Walker, 1993: 882) stands in stark contrast to the 'assimilation or the imitation of heterosexual stereotypes for the purpose of camouflage, that is, closetry, being "in the closet"' (Grahn quoted in Walker, 1993: 882). The butch lesbian renders her sexuality visible (through clothes, gestures, perhaps through bodily physique) by putting it on 'display'. She, like the drag artists that Butler analyses in *Gender Trouble* (1990), destabilizes the inside/outside binary that is productive of coherent gender identities. That is, drag is a double inversion of the assumption that the 'outer' male or female body is an expression of the 'inner' masculine or feminine self.[16]

Queer activism, and particularly the emphasis on the queer body, may be seen to be continuing this tradition of 'making visible'. At the 'die-ins' enacted by ACT UP for instance, the theatrical performance of death serves a political aim: it politicizes the division between the public and the private sphere in order that AIDS become a highly visible concern for everyone, rather than a stigmatized and private affair. Indeed, the account of agency offered by Butler's theory of performativity appears to lend itself to an accent on the visible queer body. For Butler, it is into the instability wrought by the discursive necessity of reiteration, that the (materiality of the) signifier might be reworked. Thus queer, as a site of collective contestation: 'is, in the present, never fully owned, but always and only redeployed, twisted, queered from prior usage and in the direction of urgent and expanding political purposes' (Butler, 1993: 228). Butler lists occasions of queer contestation:

> . . . cross-dressing, drag balls, street walking, butch-femme spectacles, the sliding between the 'march' (New York City) and the parade (San Francisco);

> die-ins by ACT UP, kiss-ins by Queer Nation; drag performance benefits for AIDS ... the convergence of theatrical work with theatrical activism; performing excessive lesbian sexuality and iconography that effectively counters the desexualization of the lesbian; tactical interruptions of public forums by lesbian and gay activists in favor of drawing attention and outrage to the failure of government funding of AIDS research and outreach.... (Butler, 1993: 233)

In each of these examples the visibility of the queer body itself assumes a political value wherein the theatrical is not *opposed* to the political but rather draws attention to 'the increasing politicization *of* theatricality' (Butler, 1993: 233).

One of the issues that has recently been raised by the theatrical performances of queer is the extent to which its campaigns have been complicated by high-profile identity projects which also assume the form of what might loosely be called 'aesthetic' lifestyles (Featherstone, 1991), but which are often based on a rather different agenda. The debate over the political efficacy of 'lipstick lesbianism' and whether homosexuals are accepted as consuming rather than social subjects (Clark, 1991: 192) is a pertinent example here (see also O'Sullivan, 1994 and (charles), 1993 who implicitly suggests that Queer is a brand name). Michel Maffesoli argues that such lifestyles – and a parallel can be drawn here with queer – represent 'a synergy between the ethical and the aesthetic' (Maffesoli, 1991: 18). He goes on:

> Whether trendy exercises in sensory isolation, or various forms of body-building, or jogging, or Eastern techniques of one sort or another, the body is being constructed as a value ... even in its most private aspects, *the body is being constructed only in order to be seen*; it is theatralized to the highest degree. Within advertising, fashion, dance, the body is adorned only to be made into a spectacle. (Maffesoli, 1991: 18-19, my emphasis)

At one level, the reappropriation of queer into, and by queer of, spectacular society may be understood to be a consequence of the historical context in which it is situated (the emergence of queer among a proliferation of lifestyles). From this perspective, queer activists exploit the very 'problem' of a media-saturated consumer culture itself. Thomas Yingling for example, following Baudrillard's lead, suggests that:

> AIDS activism has not been coopted into the great institutional machinery of culture that currently recodes sign value as use value ... but instead insists upon forcing spectacle itself into political use – hence the resurrection of agit-prop, street theater, poster art, etc. (Yingling, 1991: 296)

Yingling appears to be situating AIDS activism in the tradition of the avant-garde – the Dada, the Surrealists and the Situationist Internationalists for example – which has attempted to cross the boundaries between art, politics and everyday life. Rosemary Hennessey however, argues that the avant-garde itself should be considered in relation to 'the more general aestheticization of everyday life in consumer capitalism' (Hennessey, 1995: 164) and that queer theory and politics, as the latest participant in this trajectory, should explore in more detail the way that the emphasis on aestheticization obscures the social relations that make it possible. She writes: 'often trouble-making takes the form of a cultural politics that relies on concepts of the social, of resistance, and of pleasure that keep invisible the violent social relations new urban identities depend on' (Hennessey, 1995: 146–7). In this respect, the 'problem' of the emphasis on the visible and the aesthetic – and its *dependence* upon a very specific context (which Hennessey suggests is 'the new bourgeois professional class' (Hennessey, 1995: 150)) – is integral to queer. At its most general, Hennessey is concerned that queer theory and activism are relevant only to a privileged minority who can afford to turn their lives into a 'work of art'.

Hennessey's doubts about queer political campaigns and theories are twofold. With respect to political strategies, she objects to the emphasis on the commodity as part of a campaign for queer visibility. The intimate relation between Queer Nation, for example, and consumer culture is clear in the names its affinity groups have adopted. These include SHOP (Suburban Homosexual Outreach Program), QUEST (Queers Undertaking Exquisite and Symbolic Transformation) and United Colors (which focuses on queers of colour) (Hennessey, 1995: 159). The aim of these groups, Hennessey acknowledges, is not only to market positive images of queers, but also to tap into consumer desire and disrupt the heterosexual presuppositions on which this desire rests. Their tactics include 'rewriting the trademarks of corporations that appropriate gay street styles (changing the "p" in GAP ads to "y")' and 'parading into suburban shopping spaces dressed in full gay regalia, holding hands, or handing out flyers' in order to 'insert gay spectacle into the centers of straight consumption' (Hennessey, 1995: 160).

Reworking Marx's concept of commodity fetishism, Hennessey suggests that although Queer Nation exposes the hidden heterosexual meanings invested in commodities, this strategy rests on the illusion that the value of the commodity resides in the physical object itself – its signification, meaning or its role in the production of identity – rather than in the human labour that goes into producing it: 'When the commodity is fetishized, the labor that has gone into its production is rendered invisible' (Hennessey, 1995: 162). In other words, a 'bourgeois way of seeing', which rests on the notion of an autonomous aesthetic perception, disguises a story of class inequality which precedes and is productive of the object that seems to have appeared as if 'by magic'.[17]

Hennessey argues that queer theory too, like queer activism, reduces the question of social change to that of cultural representation.[18] For her, queer does not 'historicize' the signifier 'queer' so much as (merely) place it in a historical context. The work of historicizing, she suggests, requires establishing and tracing connections between social life on a number of different levels (rather than on the discursive level alone). She writes of Butler's analysis of drag for example, that:

> To historicize the meaning of drag among the urban middle class in the United States at the turn of the twenty-first century would be to link it as a discursive practice to the social relations that make it possible and in so doing situate practices specific to a particular social formation in the United States within the larger frame of late capitalism's geopolitics and multinational economy. (Hennessey, 1995: 150)

Hennessey argues that Butler's focus on 'the specific and the local (à la Foucault)' (Hennessey, 1995: 150) disallows this broader historicizing. And without this, the conception of identities as performative significations is brought perilously close to the notion of identity as self-fashioning (Hennessey, 1995: 167), a self-fashioning which Peggy Phelan similarly argues befits the 'fundamental aspiration of the American mythos' (Phelan, 1993: 105) which centres on the (entrepreneurial) invention and reinvention of identity.[19] Interestingly, Phelan uses Jenny Livingston's film *Paris is Burning*, which Butler herself analyses at some length in *Bodies that Matter*, to illustrate her point. She writes:

> Part of the appeal of *Paris* for a white, straight audience is its ability to absorb and tame the so-called Otherness of this part of Black and Latino gay male culture. The dreams of economic success, fame, and security articulated by the performers are exactly the same dreams of 'most American men'. The means by which these dreams are realized – self-invention, hard work, and ingenuity – are the same methods celebrated in the careers of Ragged Rick and *Rocky I* through *V*. (Phelan, 1993: 106)

To draw attention to the points of resonance between queer and self-fashioned, consumer-oriented and often 'entrepreneurial-style' lifestyles, is not to collapse them, nor to diminish the politics of queer. Unlike the self-fashioned lifestyles described above, Butler displaces any notion of individual intentionality. In *Gender Trouble* she explicitly states that her analysis does not represent 'a return to an existential theory of the self as constituted through its acts, for the existential theory maintains a pre-discursive structure for both the self and the acts' (Butler, 1990: 142). Theatricality too, she writes, 'need not be conflated with self-display or self-creation' (Butler, 1993: 232). I do, however, want to emphasize the complex context in which queer is situated. Insofar as both queer activism and lifestylization have a tendency to be concentrated within the field of visibility, and because they are based around the theatre of 'identity', an equivalence may be forced between them whereby their political intentions and effects cannot be distinguished. Theorists of the spectacle (Debord, 1977; Plant, 1992) might argue not only that each represents *a* spectacle, but also that they are absorbed, without differentiation, into the fleeting whims of *the* spectacle. Some have questioned, for example, ACT UP's 'obsessive relationship with its own image in the media' (Saalfield and Navarro, 1991: 362) and asked whether the queer aesthetic represents any more than an exercise in conspicuous 'lifestyle' consumption: 'Is going to an ACT UP demo like buying Calvin Klein underwear?' (Saalfield and Navarro, 1991: 362). This is an important question because, as Lois McNay puts it:

> . . . in a society in which the behaviour of individuals is often governed by an incitement to consumption, it may be necessary to determine the point at which the construction of one's life as a work of art ceases to be an act of conspicuous consumption – or in Bourdieu's terms a sign of 'distinction' – and becomes a gesture of resistance. (McNay, 1994: 155)

It is perhaps no accident that McNay makes reference, in the context of the aestheticization of the self,[20] to Bourdieu's notion of distinction, a term which is closely associated with his analysis of class. The ramifications for, and perhaps amplification of, class inequalities, McNay implies, should be considered when exploring the political efficacy of the aestheticization – or, one might add, the theatricalization – of politics, and especially the self. As Steph Lawler notes, the 'aesthetic' arena is not equally available to all. Also drawing on Bourdieu and, in particular, Bourdieu's notion of the habitus,[21] Lawler argues that it is the tastes and dispositions of the middle-classes *specifically* which are 'coded as *inherently* "right", *inherently* "tasteful"' (Lawler, 1997: 2). Taste, and being in possession of what is recognized and legitimized as 'good taste', is not understood as something which is acquired (over time), but is rather constituted as 'an *intrinsic* feature of the self' (Lawler, 1997: 11, my emphasis) (it is perceived to be 'given'). Significantly, the inability to inhabit particular forms of aesthetic lifestyles may mark 'the self itself . . . as "wrong" (or right) as pretentious (or authentic)' (Lawler, 1997: 16). What is important here is that the 'aesthetic' is understood 'not [as] a matter of inequality in legitimated forms of knowledges and aesthetics, but, precisely, [as] knowledge and aesthetics themselves' (Lawler, 1997: 2).[22]

It is possible to infer from both Hennessey's and Lawler's arguments that the 'politicization *of* theatricality' (Butler, 1993: 233), which Hennessey suggests is related to a more general aestheticization of everyday life, has implications which pertain to class and, specifically, to class inequalities. According to Hennessey, queer disguises the very relations – unequal class relations – that make that politics possible; for Lawler, it is the notion of the aesthetic itself which is problematic, informed as it is by class distinctions. In their different ways, both imply that the privileging of representation, as *the* domain where political battles are to be waged, requires a more thorough analysis, and one which is sensitive to the production not only of 'raced' and gendered identities, but identities which are 'raced', gendered and classed as well. Perhaps ironically, given the criticisms outlined above, I want to draw on Butler's work to illustrate this point,[23] work which, to return to this theme again, is a reminder that spatial and temporal processes of identification are inseparable from each other.

Contentions

Although, in *Feminist Contentions*, Butler concedes that understanding the production of subjectivity 'is not the only goal, and that there are questions of social and economic justice which are not primarily concerned with questions of subject-formation' (Butler, 1995a: 141), in her article 'Merely Cultural' (1998) and in *Excitable Speech* (1997) she does go some way to bringing those questions of 'social and economic justice' together with an analysis of subjectification. Her use of Bourdieu's notion of the habitus in the last chapter of *Excitable Speech* is particularly telling, because the habitus is often invoked to illustrate precisely *why* it is that issues of subject-formation and cultural representation cannot necessarily be divided from questions of social and economic (in)justices, and *how* it is that 'class formation operates between abstract structures and concrete specifics of everyday life' (Skeggs, 1997: 8).

Beverley Skeggs uses Bourdieu's work to show how the body, for instance, is a site where the perceived 'truth' of the self – a self that is classed, 'raced' and gendered – is rendered visible. For Bourdieu:

> ... bodily dimensions (volume, height, weight); bodily shapes (round or square, stiff or supple, straight or curved) and bodily forms (expressed through treating it, caring for it, feeding it and maintaining it) reveal the deepest dispositions of class, gender and race.... The surface of [the body] is the site upon which distinctions can be drawn. (Skeggs, 1997: 84)

While Bourdieu illustrates that class differences are played out through the material and the visible – the physical manifestation, in space, of class distinctions – they are also something which, significantly, materialize over time: 'The habitus – embodied history, internalized as a second nature and so forgotten as history – is the active presence of the whole past of which it is the product' (Bourdieu quoted in Lawler, 1997: 10). It is precisely the insistence on the 'obviousness' (Butler, 1997: 152), or 'inherent-ness' of the habitus (rather like the perceived 'given-ness' of visible identities) which disguises the temporality of class identifications and conceals the extent to which the habitus is 'inculcated from birth, [and] derives from one's position in a particular family form ... as well as within systems of education' (Lawler, 1997: 10). And it is this in particular, perhaps not surprisingly, which so impresses Butler. She writes:

> Bourdieu underscores the place of the body ... as the site for the reconstitution of a practical sense without which social reality would not be constituted as such. The practical sense is carried by the body, where the body is not a mere positive datum, but the repository or *the site of an incorporated history*. (Butler, 1997: 152, my emphasis)

Again, Butler stresses that Bourdieu's understanding of the habitus includes both spatial and temporal processes of identification, 'the *habitus* is formed, but it is also *formative*' (Butler, 1997: 155). To repeat: identification is never fully achieved; the (classed) subject is 'subjected and produced time and again' (Butler, 1995b: 47). In short, class inequalities, which might be thought of as 'large-scale' issues of social and economic justice (or injustice), give rise to 'real' social effects, one of the effects of which is classed subjectivities.

Butler does take issue with Bourdieu, however, arguing that his account of the habitus does not address the possibilities of agency. It is partly for this reason that she brings the theory of performativity (which Bourdieu considers elsewhere) to his analysis of the habitus. According to her, Bourdieu assumes that performative utterances 'are only effective when they are spoken by those who are (already) in a position of social power to exercise words as deeds' (Butler, 1997: 156). By contrast, Butler suggests that 'authorization and entitlement' are themselves performatively constituted (in other words, they do not reside in social structures which are external to discourse) and come from 'various and diffuse quarters that do not always operate as "official" discourse' (Butler, 1997: 157). Such quarters might include, for example, the arenas of taste, knowledge and aesthetics which, as Lawler illustrates, constitute the classed subject but do so without being an 'official' discourse which is associated with the state. However, Butler argues that the 'improper' use of the performative – for example by those who are not 'authorized' to speak – may have the effect of revealing, and thereby contesting, the 'prevailing forms of authority and the exclusions by which they proceed' (Butler, 1997: 158). The examples that she gives are the reappropriation of the signs 'queer', 'black' and 'women' (Butler, 1997: 158) and, indeed, persuasive cases can be made for the successful reappropriation of these terms in particular contexts.

It is notable, however, even startling, that while her analysis can be used to explain the processes by which class subjectivities are produced, Butler does not seriously interrogate the possibilities that the expropriation of the performative might offer those who would rally under a class banner. It is notable also, that where Lawler's argument, perhaps like Bourdieu's, is somewhat pessimistic and does not directly account for the issue of agency (the story is not a happy one, as she says herself), Butler's extension of Bourdieu's work injects a certain optimism into it. Rosemary Hennessey might suggest that this political optimism is possible only because queer evades the issue of class inequalities and, indeed, that it actively contributes to the invisibilization of such inequalities. However, even if it is the case that queer draws attention away from unequal class relations, it cannot be said that class *identities* are always invisible. Like the political movements based on the identities of sexuality, race and gender, struggles around class are also struggles around representation. Working-class men in particular, Skeggs argues, have been able to deploy class as a means of 'including themselves in a positively valorized social category' (Skeggs, 1997: 74). The 'Angry Young Men of 1950s popular representations', which are not dissimilar to 'the heroic males of Willis's (1977) [academic] study' (Skeggs, 1997: 79), provide an example here.[24] It is arguable then, that in this context class struggles are neither 'beyond' a politics of representation nor, relatedly, one of performativity. It is in her analysis of white working class *women* however, that Skeggs provides a sharp reminder that representations cannot be collapsed with, and are not the same as, dispositions.

One Rally?

At the start of this article I noted June Jordan's objection to attending two rallies, one on race, the other on sexuality. 'Freedom is indivisible' (Jordan, 1996: 13), she contends, which I understand to mean that the politics of sexuality, race and gender are inseparable from each other because the processes of identification which give rise to sexed, 'raced' and gendered selves are themselves inseparable. Although this point is frequently reiterated in contemporary, especially feminist, theory (see, for example, Ahmed, 1996), I want to call attention to it again here, in the light of Beverley Skeggs' work on white working-class women. Skeggs highlights a specific, historical, relation between the production of the identity 'White, working-class women' and representation, a relation which may have implications for the kinds of politics that working-class women might choose, or choose not, to engage in.[25] Importantly, Skeggs notes that when she imposes the categories 'White and working class' on the women she interviewed, she is not identifying their subjectivities, but rather the 'economic, social and discursive relations' (Skeggs, 1997: 165) in which they are positioned. That the women may or *may not* choose to recognize, or identify with, this discursive positioning is a key point and central to my argument here.

Representations, Skeggs argues, are 'symbolic appearances produced as a result of struggles over cultural capital' (Skeggs, 1997: 87). Historically, appearance has been problematic for both black and white working-class women. The appearance of the body in particular, 'the only tangible manifestation of the person' (Skeggs, 1997: 102), was collapsed in the 18th and 19th centuries with an 'ideal' of femininity which was also white and middle class: 'the visual became the site where values were allocated to groups of women and the construction of appearance as a sign of value became established. White middle-class femininity was defined as the ideal' (Skeggs, 1997: 102). For white and black working-class women, however, the signs of femininity did not, and do not today, always 'fit': 'coded as inherently healthy, hardy and robust' (Skeggs, 1997: 99), for example, working-class women were distanced from femininity. This in itself illustrates that the sign of femininity, although deceptively static, is temporal and thus: 'cannot guarantee a take-up. It will not and cannot be constantly occupied' (Skeggs, 1997: 106).[26] Not only the appearance but also the behaviour of working-class women is distanced from femininity:

> Femininity requires the display of classed dispositions, of forms of conduct and behaviour, different forms of cultural capital, which are not a part of [working-class women's] cultural baggage: they are unlikely to display 'divine composure', which includes the components of femininity as silent, static, invisible and composed. (Skeggs, 1997: 100)

Skeggs's analysis of classed *and* gendered subjectivities persuasively illustrates that 'representations are not dispositions' (Skeggs, 1997: 86). To secure the sign of 'respectable' middle-class femininity requires more than the appearance of femininity alone; it is also a way of behaving and a manner of conduct. Yet the behaviour of working-class women has been, and continues to be, pathologized. Lawler's work on the regulation and discipline of white working-class mothering specifically illustrates this point (Lawler, 1999). More broadly, a number of theorists have noted that 'the working class have been (through representation) continually demonized, pathologized and held responsible for social problems . . . [t]he negativity associated with the working class is ubiquitous' (Skeggs, 1997: 76).

While black working-class women have 'forged models of womanhood that continually and dramatically challenge prevailing notions of femininity' (Skeggs, 1997: 100), white working-class women, Skeggs argues, are more likely to disidentify themselves from an identity which has so many negative associations and connotations. Hence, unlike black working-class women, who may have access to a positive identity conferred by race, the white working-class women in her study were keen *not* to be recognized as working class:

> Class was central to the young women's subjectivities. It was not spoken of in the traditional sense of recognition – I am working class – but rather, was displayed in their multitudinous efforts *not to be* recognized as working class. They disidentified and they dissimulated. *Theirs was a refusal of recognition rather than a claim for the right to be recognized.* (Skeggs, 1997: 74, first italics in the original, second italics mine)[27]

Skeggs notes that: '[r]ecognition had to occur for identifications to be made' (Skeggs, 1997: 74). I would add, by extension, that recognition also has to occur for *re*-identifications to be made and that it is this in particular which casts recent queer theory and politics in a problematic light.

For Butler, it is the (usually public) reiteration of signifiers of difference that recontextualizes those signifiers:

> . . . the subject who is 'queered' into public discourse through homophobic interpellations of various kinds *takes up* or *cites* that very term as the discursive basis for an opposition. This kind of citation will emerge as *theatrical* to the extent that it *mimes and renders hyperbolic* the discursive convention that it also *reverses*. (Butler, 1993: 232)

Citation and mimesis are not necessarily an invitation to visibility politics, and theatricality, as Butler argues, does not have to be collapsed with self-display (Butler, 1993: 232). Nevertheless, the examples of 'theatrical rage' (Butler, 1993: 233) that Butler lists (see above) do tend to involve an '"acting out"' which, she writes, seeks 'to shatter the epistemic blindness to an increasingly graphic and public homosexuality' (Butler, 1993: 232). This notion of a 'graphic and public homosexuality' suggests that publicity is politically desirable and in this respect, although differently nuanced, queer can be understood to be continuing a tradition of 'making visible' identities which are discriminated against. This is witnessed, for instance, in the accent on the body in much of queer, a body which, as noted above, comes to assume a political value. The queer body, however, might be one 'which occupies social space and which is able to move through it in very different ways' (Skeggs, 1997: 163) to those of the women, for example, that Skeggs worked with. As Skeggs notes: 'Many theories of subjectivity [are] designed for a different body in different circumstances'; the women she interviewed 'did not assume that their bodies were valuable, that they had entitlements or that they were even interesting' (Skeggs, 1997: 163). The relation between these women and their bodies then, is historically very different from, and may not sit easily with what Butler identifies as a history of the 'politicization *of* theatricality' and the 'theatricalization of political rage' (Butler, 1993: 233).

Walker, Piper and Dyer too, who I have also referred to above, seek in their different ways to make visible that which is invisibilized by 'epistemic blindness'.[28] Lisa Walker for example, who is concerned with 'women of color who can "pass" for white and femme lesbians who can pass for straight' (Walker, 1993: 869), implicitly assumes that those who pass (by choice or not) should be given every opportunity to make themselves visible (Walker, 1993: 888). Yet the women that Skeggs interviewed were more likely to *refuse* rather than to *claim* the right to be recognized and they were more likely to disidentify *from* than to identify *with* working-class identities. This suggests that the problem with passing, in the context of white working-class women, is not that one may be passed against one's will, not that one may be passed off or passed over, but rather that 'someone may catch you out' (Skeggs, 1997: 86). Instead of 'taking up' or 'citing' the terms that (negatively) constitute the identity of 'White, working-class women', and – through mimesis – reversing that discursive convention, the women's dissimulations often had the effect of confirming the legitimacy of authoritative middle-class discourses:

> Their passing does not involve ironic mimicry (as has been suggested in Black passing attempts: see Bhabha, 1994) because it wants to be taken seriously; because it speaks from a position of powerlessness and insecurity. In this sense their attempts to pass are not a form of insubordination; rather they are dissimulations, performances of a desire not to be, a desire not to be shamed but a desire to be legitimated. They do not displace the middle class

> as normalized in a way that gay and lesbian passing may displace heterosexuality. Nor can they gain any pleasure from the passing as they could with sexual masquerade and gendered masquerade. (Skeggs, 1997: 87)

These dissimulations support and maintain the very discourses which contribute to the production of the (working-class) identities that the women seek to reject. Performativity in this context, as Butler argues in relation to drag, is clearly 'not unproblematically subversive' (Butler, 1993: 231).

My point, however, is *not* that these women have failed to be subversive, as working-class women are so often accused of (Walkerdine, 1990). Rather, it is that the privileged role conferred on the reappropriation of signifiers of identity (in the production and reproduction of identities) might be one place to start to address that which is potentially schismatic in much contemporary identity politics and, especially, in the theatrical politics of performativity. When the 'irreducible complexity', as Jordan puts it, of identity is thoroughly examined, a politics which is organized around recognition and (re)identification may be seen to exclude those who 'either d[o] not recognize themselves or d[o] not want to recognize themselves as the categories of identification that [are] available to them' (Skeggs, 1997: 164).

Conclusion

Judith Butler writes that:

> . . . the genealogical critique of the queer subject will be central to queer politics to the extent that it constitutes a self-critical dimension within activism, a persistent reminder to take the time to consider the exclusionary force of one's activism's most treasured contemporary premises. (Butler, 1993: 227)

Given the close association between seeing and knowing in Western culture, the forms of politics which are literally – 'seeably' – materialized 'in space' appear to have an advantage. In the argument that Jordan describes (and denounces), and that I began this article with, it is visible signs *specifically* which enable the identities of race and gender to gain a privileged position in what Lisa Walker calls a 'hierarchy of oppressions' (Walker, 1993: 872). Walker argues that, where visibility and authenticity are conjoined, 'members of a given population who do not bear that signifier of difference or who bear visible signs of another identity are rendered invisible and are marginalized within an already marginalized community' (Walker, 1993: 888). But I think it is also important to consider those who choose *not* to be (made) seeable and who may therefore be excluded from a politics that lends itself to visibility. Moreover, even if shattering 'epistemic blindness' does not *necessarily* require a visibility politics, and even if reappropriation does not *have* to be preceded by identification (as Skeggs says, subjectivity and identity are not the same) it does, presumably, require recognition. Partly owing to the historical relation between white working-class women and representation, for them, recognition is frequently problematic and often undesirable: '[White working-class women] spend more time either not recognizing the identifications which it is assumed that they make (e.g. class, femininity or heterosexuality) or disidentifying' (Skeggs, 1997: 164).

Annette Khun argues that '[t]o be working-classed ... generates a constant fear of never having "got it right" ' (Skeggs, 1997: 6) and, indeed, recent work on class illustrates that some people may not be able to 'get it "right" because they do not have access to the requisite amounts of knowledge and history which would enable them to know what getting it right really means' (Skeggs, 1997: 87). What I have suggested here is that, although the reappropriation of signifiers of difference might be 'right' in some instances, if (even) recognition of a particular identity is problematic, then it cannot be 'right' in all circumstances. This is illustrated insofar as the political and theoretical tools of analysis which are deployed in one context, may have very different, even inverse, implications when applied elsewhere. The analysis of the relation between white working-class women and the representations (of femininity in this example) that in part constitute them *as* 'white working-class women' both enables – as Butler's work on the habitus can be used to show – and constrains the use of the theory and politics of performativity. One way to begin to address these constraints would be not only to explore in detail the specific processes, both spatial and temporal, which are productive of subjectivities which are gendered, 'raced' *and* classed but to take that interrogation seriously, especially as it constitutes, to cite Butler again, 'a self-critical dimension within activism' (Butler, 1993: 227).

Notes

Thanks to the anonymous reviewers, to Natalie Fenton, Celia Lury, Angela McRobbie and also to the Women's Studies Research Group at Loughborough University, for their challenging comments on earlier drafts of this article. Special thanks to Vikki Bell and Steph Lawler.

1. Fraser notes that while 'a status injury ... is analytically distinct from, and conceptually irreducible to, the injustice of maldistribution ... it *may* be accompanied by the latter' (N. Fraser, 1998: 141).
2. And that, therefore, '[o]pponents of heterosexism' for example, should not be required to 'labour to translate claims of sexual status injury into claims of class deprivation in order to vindicate the former' (N. Fraser, 1998: 142).
3. It is important to acknowledge at the outset the different political and theoretical traditions which have informed analyses of class in Britain and in America. It is arguable that British scholarship, for example, has historically been influenced to a greater degree by Marxism than has American work on class. Similarly, it is notable that the queer politics to which Butler refers takes place almost entirely in the United States and that Beverley Skeggs's study, which I will be drawing on below as a means with which to explore that politics and theory, is based on white

working-class *British* women. Although there are many cultural differences between the two countries, differences which will give rise to different kinds of politics, I would argue that it is nevertheless important to examine the implications of queer theory and politics in a British context since it is so often referred to and used in British, especially feminist, theories of identity (see for example, recent bisexual theories and political strategies).

4. As Jackie Stacey notes: 'the skin [is] a particularly significant part of the body in its role as interface between inside and outside; [Kristeva] writes of the skin that it is "the essential if not the initial boundary of biological and psychic individuation"' (Stacey, 1997: 254n).

5. Although even those who have an investment in the notion that race is 'ineradicably' inscribed on the body (as colour and features) will have had to think twice recently. The change in Michael Jackson's skin colour is an extreme example. The Benetton magazine *Colors* also offers (less dramatic) ways to change one's skin colour – rather in the way that one might change the colour of one's jumper (Lury, 1997).

6. It is arguable that a bisexual-narrative-identity is particularly difficult to 'prove'. For details on the complexities of this, see for example Hemmings (1997: 17–18) and M. Fraser (1999).

7. Ironically, the increasing capacity of technology to represent the 'unrepresentable' has resulted in the invisibilization of the female body *as a whole*. Braidotti, among other feminists, has argued thus that medical technology obliterates, rather than dominates, the female body which is transformed into no more than a 'vehicle for scientific information' (Kember, 1995: 107).

8. Although neither power nor the subject 'acts'. Instead there is 'only a reiterated acting that is power in its persistence and instability' (Butler, 1993: 9).

9. Although Carole-Anne Tyler argues that Piper herself falls prey to the assumptions she seeks to critique. While Piper's performance 'very cannily attacks the narcissism of the white self by calling into question that subject's mastery of the visual field – empiricism itself' (Tyler, 1994: 219), Tyler suggests that in handing out calling cards to those she *assumes* are white, Piper not only interpellates those others as white, but also inverts the relation that has erased her own racial identity. Now, Piper assumes that everyone who is not black is white.

10. Similarly, Peggy Phelan notes that passing as heterosexual (by choice or not) is 'easy' because heterosexuality is assumed. Passing in this context, she argues, makes visible 'the unmarked nature of heterosexual identity. The one who passes then does not "erase" the mark of difference, rather the passer highlights the invisibility of the mark of the Same' (Phelan, 1993: 96).

11. The reverse of these 'White child/Black biological parent revelations' have recently been seen on British television and film. Elaine, one of the characters on *Brookside*, is black and has a white mother. In Mike Leigh's film *Secrets and Lies* the narrative revolves around a black (middle-class) woman finding and developing a relationship with her white (working-class) mother.

12. Indeed, Celia Lury (1998) suggests that analyses of narrative, for example, have taken precedence over analyses of the relation between seeing and self-knowledge which remains theoretically underdeveloped and is often absorbed and/or subsumed into debates around postmodernism. Her study of prosthetic culture goes some way to redress this balance, focusing specifically on the role of the

photographic image in creating 'novel configurations of personhood, self-knowledge and truth' (Lury, 1998: 2).

13. Which is not to suggest that the spatial is reducible to the visible, or that identity politics are entirely without narratives. Clearly, the making 'visible' of gay and lesbian sexualities often occurs through coming out stories. These narratives have a high profile, not least because they quite literally capture the movement from private to public, from the dark and enclosed 'closet' to the bright light where everyone can 'see'. Some argue that the linear trajectory that informs narrative, as well as its accent on 'origins and finalities and [the disclosure of] an original identity' (Moi, 1994: 7), is becoming increasingly problematic/problematized in late modernity (Plummer, 1995: 57).

14. Peggy Phelan notes that not only what she calls 'progressives' or 'the Left' (Phelan, 1993: 2) but the New Right too have revealed (and increased) their investment in visibility politics. An example here is the anti-abortionist's campaign Operation Rescue which centres around photographs of foetuses (Phelan, 1993: 130–7). I have argued elsewhere that to be visible is also to be more tightly bound to power/knowledge regimes (see M. Fraser, 1999).

15. Eve Sedgwick however, argues that the complexities of disclosure ensure that 'no one person can take control over all the multiple, often contradictory codes by which information about sexual identity and activity can seem to be conveyed' (Sedgwick, 1991: 79). Thus identities may be communicated not only without what are often perceived to be 'straightforward' visual cues, and/or without visual cues at all, but also without explicit narratives.

16. Despite this radical disjunction which Butler claims disrupts the heterosexual matrix, Walker points out that: 'Butler's expectation of coherence between (outer) sexual style and (inner) sexual consciousness puts her back within the framework of culturally intelligible identities that she seeks to destabilize. In the process of illustrating how the sexual styles of drag queens and butches visually denaturalize the categories of sex and gender by producing signs of their nonconformity to heterosexual norms on the body, Butler establishes them as coherent subjects in terms of political rather than gender intelligibility' (Walker, 1993: 885). Arguably, this political coherence has been complicated by the emergence of 'lipstick lesbianism' and the like (Cottingham, 1996).

17. This indicates that the physical, tangible, 'seeable' object does not constitute the whole of the material. Drawing on Marx, Hennessey argues that the material refers also to the human labour that is 'materially embodied in [commodities, but which] . . . is not visible in the objects themselves as a physical property' (Hennessey, 1995: 161). Thus the material is not reducible to the 'seeable', but rather exceeds it.

18. To this extent she seems to share the belief that queer, as Butler puts it, is 'merely cultural' (Butler, 1998: 36). Butler claims not only that new social movements, like queer, are often 'relegate[d] to the sphere of the cultural' (Butler, 1998: 33), but that this cultural focus is condemned on the grounds that it 'substitutes a self-centred and trivial form of politics that focuses on transient events, practices, and objects rather than offering a more robust, serious and comprehensive vision of the systematic interrelatedness of social and economic conditions' (Butler, 1998: 34).

19. The 'American mythos' sits particularly well with lifestylization insofar as both imply that there is no aspect of the self which cannot in some way be altered or 'overcome' if the subject chooses. Interestingly, Dana Clark, in her analysis of the commodification of gay identities, suggests that (life)stylization 'promotes a liberal discourse of choice that separates sexuality from politics and connects them both to consumerism' (Clark, 1991: 193–4). Hence anti-essentialist positions – here promoted perhaps unexpectedly by the media in its focus on 'lifestyle lesbianism' – are not in themselves inherently desirable. As Eve Sedgwick notes, the notion that we can choose whatever sexual identity we want to be has facilitated the right-wing prescription that 'gays who wish to share in human rights and dignities must (and *can*) make the free-market choice of becoming *ex*-gays' (Sedgwick, 1994: 226).

20. McNay's argument is concerned specifically with Foucault's arts of existence.

21. The habitus refers to the non-conscious system of dispositions which derive from the subject's economic, cultural and symbolic capital. Bourdieu makes explicit how, although all classes acquire or inherit forms of capital, only some of those capitals can be capitalized upon: 'Analysing access and legitimation of cultural formations enables us to see how cultural capital is or is not converted into symbolic capital and hence how inequalities are generated and systematic disempowerment engendered. Symbolic capital is powerful capital: it brings power with it. If one's cultural capital is delegitimated then it cannot be traded as an asset; it cannot be capitalized upon (although it may retain significance and meaning to the individual) and its power is limited' (Skeggs, 1997: 10).

22. This is especially significant given that knowledges of taste, style and aesthetics are assumed to be a property of the individual, an individual who is constrained or enabled *only* by their own personal 'choices'. The accent on the individual thus serves to conceal the specific *class* character of lifestylization. I do not mean to suggest however that: '"Aesthetics" is simply an existing, historically specific discipline; "aesthetic experience" is explicable in terms of ideology and political values; and "aesthetic evaluation" is nothing but a function of one's class or other interests' (Wolff, 1983: 31). There is surely more to the issue of aesthetics, although it is not my intention to explore this question here.

23. Although it may be ironic to do so, it is also productive, since it is not my intention here to reinforce the division between class identities (and an analysis of social and economic conditions) on the one hand, and the identities of 'race', gender and sexuality (and a politics of performativity) on the other.

24. One is also reminded of recent British films like *The Full Monty* and *Brassed Off*. As Steph Lawler points out, these representations rely on some sort of notion of 'the Noble Worker' (personal correspondence).

25. Although Skeggs discusses the production of the identity 'White working-class women' across a range of different contexts, for the sake of brevity, and because the links between representation and femininity are already well established (see for example Nead, 1993; Williamson, 1983), I will be referring mainly to her analysis of the constitutive role that femininity plays in this context.

26. That there is always already a distance between working-class women and ideal femininity, suggests, Skeggs argues, that not only is 'the ideal of femininity a bourgeois sign but the attempts to subvert femininity [witnessed, for example, in theories of masquerade] are locked within the same range of projections' (Skeggs, 1997: 105).

27. Although, importantly, this is not to imply that the women Skeggs interviewed necessarily wanted to identify as middle-class either. They did not. 'What the women desire is to be valued, not pathologized' (Skeggs, 1997: 94).

28. Although there is an important difference between these theorists: Walker and Piper are concerned to make visible 'marginal' identities, while Dyer argues that the contemporary focus (both academic and otherwise) on images of those 'defined as oppressed, marginal or subordinate' serves to reproduce the 'sense of the oddness' of these groups. He writes: 'Looking, with such passion and single-mindedness, at non-dominant groups has had the effect of reproducing the sense of the oddness, differentness, exceptionality of these groups, the feeling that they are departures from the norm. Meanwhile the norm has carried on as if it is the natural, inevitable, ordinary way of being human' (Dyer, 1988: 44). It is for this reason that Dyer seeks to make white visible.

References

Ahmed, S. (1996) 'Tanning the Body: Skin, Colour and Gender', paper presented at Lancaster Women's Studies Dayschool on 'Passing'.

Baker, K. (1992) 'Bisexual Feminist Politics: Because Bisexuality is not Enough' in E.R. Weise (ed.) *Closer to Home: Bisexuality and Feminism.* Seattle: Seal.

Bell, V. (1996) 'Show and Tell: Passing and Narrative in Toni Morrison's *Jazz*', *Social Identities* 2(2): 221–36.

Berger, J. (1972) *Ways of Seeing.* London: BBC and Penguin.

Braidotti, R. (1994) *Nomadic Subjects: Embodiment and Sexual Difference in Contemporary Feminist Theory.* New York: Columbia University Press.

Butler, J. (1990) *Gender Trouble: Feminism and the Subversion of Identity.* New York: Routledge.

Butler, J. (1993) *Bodies that Matter: On the Discursive Limits of 'Sex'.* New York: Routledge.

Butler, J. (1995a) 'For a Careful Reading', in L. Nicholson (ed.) *Feminist Contentions: A Philosophical Exchange.* New York: Routledge.

Butler, J. (1995b) 'Contingent Foundations: Feminism and the Question of "Postmodernism"', in L. Nicholson (ed.) *Feminist Contentions: A Philosophical Exchange.* New York: Routledge.

Butler, J. (1997) *Excitable Speech: A Politics of the Performative.* London: Routledge.

Butler, J. (1998) 'Merely Cultural', *New Left Review* 227: 33–44.

(charles), H. (1993) '"Queer nigger": Theorising "White" Activism', in J. Bristow and A. Wilson (eds) *Activating Theory: Lesbian, Gay and Bisexual Politics.* London: Lawrence and Wishart.

Clark, D. (1991) 'Commodity Lesbianism', *Camera Obscura* 25–6: 181–201.

Cottingham, L. (1996) *Lesbians Are So Chic … That We're not Really Lesbians at All.* London: Cassell.

Debord, G. (1977) *Society of the Spectacle.* Detroit: Black and Red.

Dyer, R. (1988) 'White', *Screen* 29(4): 44–64.

Dyer, R. (1997) *White.* London: Routledge.

Featherstone, M. (1991) *Consumer Culture and Postmodernism.* London: Sage.

Fraser, M. (1999) *Identity Without Selfhood.* Cambridge: Cambridge University Press.

Fraser, N. (1995) 'Pragmatism, Feminism, and the Linguistic Turn', in L. Nicholson (ed.) *Feminist Contentions: A Philosophical Exchange.* New York: Routledge.

Fraser, N. (1998) 'Heterosexism, Misrecognition and Capitalism: A Response to Judith Butler', *New Left Review* 228: 140–50.

Gutman, H. (1988) 'Rousseau's *Confessions*: A Technology of the Self'. in L.H. Martin, H. Gutman and P.H. Hutton (eds) *Technologies of the Self: A Seminar with Michel Foucault.* London: Tavistock.

Hemmings, C. (1997) 'Bisexual Theoretical Perspectives: Emergent and Contingent Relationships', in Bi Academic Intervention (eds) *The Bisexual Imaginary: Representation, Identity and Desire.* London: Cassell.

Hennessey, R. (1995) 'Queer Visibility in Commodity Culture', in L. Nicholson and S. Seidman (eds) *Social Postmodernism: Beyond Identity Politics.* Cambridge: Cambridge University Press.

Jay, M. (1992) 'Scopic Regimes of Modernity', in S. Lash and J. Friedman (eds) *Modernity and Identity.* Oxford: Blackwell.

Jay, M. (1993) *Force Fields: Between Intellectual History and Cultural Critique.* London: Routledge.

Jordan, J. (1996) 'A New Politics of Sexuality', in S. Rose and C. Stevens et al. (eds) *Bisexual Horizons: Politics, Histories, Lives.* London: Lawrence and Wishart.

Kember, S. (1995) 'Medicine's New Vision?', in M. Lister (ed.) *The Photographic Image in Digital Culture.* London: Routledge.

Lawler, S. (1997) '"Getting Out and Getting Away": Women's Narratives of Class Mobility', paper presented to the Women's Studies Research Group, Loughborough University.

Lawler, S. (1999) *Mothering the Self.* London: Routledge.

Lury, C. (1997) *Consumer Culture.* London: Routledge.

Lury, C. (1998) *Prosthetic Culture: Photography, Memory and Identity.* London: Routledge.

McNay, L. (1994) *Foucault: A Critical Introduction.* Cambridge: Polity.

Maffesoli, M. (1991) 'The Ethic of Aesthetics', *Theory, Culture & Society* 8: 7–21.

Moi, T. (1994) *Simone de Beauvoir: The Making of an Intellectual Woman.* Oxford: Blackwell.

Nead, L. (1993) *The Female Nude: Art, Obscenity and Sexuality.* London: Routledge.

O'Sullivan, S. (1994) 'Girls who Kiss Girls and Who Cares?', in D. Hamer and B. Budge (eds) *The Good, the Bad and the Gorgeous.* London: Pandora.

Phelan, P. (1993) *Unmarked: The Politics of Performance.* London: Routledge.

Plant, S. (1992) *The Most Radical Gesture: The Situationist International in a Postmodern Age.* London: Routledge.

Plummer, K. (1995) *Telling Sexual Stories: Power, Change and Social Worlds.* London: Routledge.

Probyn, E. (1993) *Sexing the Self: Gendered Positions in Cultural Studies.* London: Routledge.

Rich, A. (1983) 'Compulsory Heterosexuality and Lesbian Existence', in E. Abel and E.K. Abel (eds) *The Signs Reader.* Chicago: University of Chicago Press.

Ricoeur, P. (1980) 'Narrative Time', *Critical Inquiry* 7(1): 169–90.

Ricoeur, P. (1991) 'Narrative Identity', in D. Wood (ed.) *On Paul Ricoeur: Narrative and Interpretation.* London: Routledge.

Saalfield, C. and Navarro, R. (1991) 'Shocking Pink Praxis: Race and Gender on the ACT UP Frontlines', in D. Fuss (ed.) *Inside/Out: Lesbian Theories, Gay Theories.* New York: Routledge.

Sedgwick, E.K. (1991) *The Epistemology of the Closet.* Hemel Hempstead: Harvester Wheatsheaf.

Sedgwick, E.K. (1994) *Tendencies.* London: Routledge.

Skeggs, B. (1997) *Formations of Class and Gender.* London: Sage.

Squire, C. (1997) 'Who's White?: Television Talk Shows and Representations of Whiteness', in M. Fine, L. Weiss, L.C. Powell, L. Mun Wong (eds) *Off-White: Readings on Race, Power and Society.* London: Routledge.

Stacey, J. (1997) *Teratologies: A Cultural Study of Cancer.* London: Routledge.

Tyler, C.-A. (1994) 'Passing: Narcissism, Identity, and Difference', *differences: A Journal of Feminist Cultural Studies* 6(2–3): 212–48.

Walker, L. (1993) 'How to Recognize a Lesbian: The Cultural Politics of Looking Like What You Are', *Signs: Journal of Women in Culture and Society* 18(4): 866–91.

Walkerdine, V. (1990) *Schoolgirl Fictions.* London: Verso.

Williamson, J. (1983) 'Images of "Woman": The Photography of Cindy Sherman', *Screen* 24(6).

Wolff, J. (1983) *Aesthetics and the Sociology of Art.* London: Allen and Unwin.

Yingling, T. (1991) 'AIDS in America: Postmodern Governance, Identity and Experience', in D. Fuss (ed.) *Inside/Out: Lesbian Theories, Gay Theories.* New York: Routledge.

Mariam Fraser teaches at the Department of Social Sciences at Loughborough University. Her book, *Identity without Selfhood*, will be published by Cambridge University Press in March 1999.

Mimesis as Cultural Survival

Judith Butler and Anti-Semitism

Vikki Bell

> Wittig understands gender as the workings of 'sex', where 'sex' is an obligatory injunction for the body to become a cultural sign, to materialise itself in obedience to a historically delimited possibility, and to do this, not once or twice, but as a sustained and repeated corporeal project. The notion of a 'project', however, suggests the originating force of a radical will, and because gender is a project that has cultural survival as its end, the term strategy better suggests the situation of duress under which gender performance always and variously occurs. (Judith Butler, 1990: 139)

WHY IS it that, as we exit the 20th century, we 'feminist scholars' are engaged in projects that emphasize performativity, and debating ways of understanding what a commitment to anti-essentialism leaves us with? If an emphasis on performativity aids us in comprehending our gendered subjectivities, does it also reveal something about our historical positionality? In this article I want to begin from the observation that this 'century of women' has also been the century whose political visions have been sadly and brutally challenged by the need to understand the reproduction and tenacity of essentialist forms of belonging. In addressing the genealogy of a particular concept – mimesis – that has become popular within feminist theorizing of identity, I mean to imply that the popularity of 'the mimetic' within contemporary feminist thought has much to do with the way in which the conception of identity as the 'stylised repetition of acts' (Butler, 1993) offers the opportunity to conceive identity 'beyond essentialism' and thus to be a part of the demand that this century close with its intellectuals engaged in an optimism that responsibly remembers.

I want to illustrate here the sense in which 'mimesis' has an intellec-

▪ *Theory, Culture & Society* 1999 (SAGE, London, Thousand Oaks and New Delhi), Vol. 16(2): 133–161
[0263-2764(199904)16:2;133–161;008259]

tual heritage, or what I would term a 'specific genealogy', that was moulded by the events of the 20th century, a social-theoretical history that has centrally involved grappling with racism and, of particular concern here, with anti-Semitism. I focus on Judith Butler's highly influential work on gender (1990, 1993, 1997a, 1997b) in order to suggest that it reveals a certain feminist inheritance of an emphasis on mimesis and imitation that resonates with the ways in which theoreticians responded to the calamitous events of essentialist politics and versions of belonging that were central to the political vision of Hitler's National Socialism and to the events of the Second World War. In her writings, Butler offers a certain trajectory of her work, and explicitly calls upon her intellectual heritage, one that is headed in name by Nietzsche and in attitude by genealogy, but that also includes significant psychoanalytic, deconstructionist and existentialist inheritances. Rather than rehearse that trajectory, my intention is to point to this other trajectory, to the ways in which her attempts to think gender non-essentially have a specific relation to attempts to theorize anti-Semitism. This is to give Butler's work a genealogy that traces the notion of mimesis back into work which employed the concept within socio-theoretical responses to anti-Semitism.

I am treading a specific path through this ambitious argument, one that illuminates certain important thinkers at the expense of others. I begin by introducing Butler's arguments through her indebtedness to De Beauvoir, before emphasizing the role that the concept of mimesis takes in Butler's work. In the next section I take a cue from the work of Jonathan Boyarin, who highlights the underplayed notion of cultural survival in Butler's work, in order to shift focus on to the history of mimesis in socio-theoretical thinking about anti-Semitism. That section therefore addresses the influential text of Adorno and Horkheimer, *Dialectic of Enlightenment* (1986), where the concept of mimesis was employed, rather differently, in their attempts to comprehend anti-Semitic fascism in the context of the unfolding of capitalist 'civilization', as well as in the important, if highly criticized, work of Jean-Paul Sartre, *Anti-Semite and Jew* (1965). This tracing is presented not in order to replace that which is more visible in Butler's work, but in order to supplement it with a particular concern in mind. Nor is the article intended as a critique of Butler's position; indeed it applauds Butler's position, and is intended as a certain form of defence, by seeking to give it a specific genealogy in this way. My concern is to answer the critiques which regard the attention to performativity and mimesis as ahistorical and apolitical, as 'obsessive' about 'the subject', by illustrating and to some extent reorienting the debate. Within that reorientation the idea of 'cultural survival' will be crucial, since it ties Butler's work on gender explicitly with this work on ethnicity and racism and forces attention to the specific historical and political context within which mimetic behaviour and identity performance takes place.

Butler, Mimesis and Imitation: Carrying on Gender

In *Gender Trouble* Simone De Beauvoir is the source of a series of questions for Butler, centring on the notion of 'becoming a woman':

> The phrase is odd, even nonsensical, for how can one become a woman if one wasn't a woman all along? And who is this 'one' who does the becoming? Is there some human who becomes its gender at some point in time? Is it fair to assume that this human was not its gender before it became its gender? . . . And, perhaps most pertinently, when does this mechanism arrive on the cultural scene to transform the human subject into a gendered subject? (1990: 111)

Butler pushes De Beauvoir's thesis to its extreme position, suggesting that De Beauvoir invites further questioning on the relationship between sex and gender, ones that the latter herself did not pursue. First, if one is not born, but 'becomes' a woman, the distinction between sex and gender allows one to interrogate further the cultural construction of sexes and genders: 'it does not follow that to be a given sex is to become a given gender; in other words, "woman" need not be the cultural construction of the female body, and "man" need not interpret male bodies' (1990: 112). For De Beauvoir there *is* an anatomical factor in the causality of 'becoming', since she argues that there is a psychic interpretation of the anatomy, whereby the boy has the ability to assume an 'attitude of subjectivity' because he has – through the psychic interpretation of the penis – an 'alter ego', a point by which to compare himself with his companions. The girl, by contrast, cannot 'incarnate herself in any part of herself', such that she has a diffuse and inward-looking attitude, and this is, De Beauvoir contends, the function of the doll, with which the girl identifies, enabling her to act towards 'herself' (1993: 292–3). Thus masculinity, for De Beauvoir, is indeed tied to the male body, and feminine behaviour to the female, albeit in a negative sense in the latter case. Taking a cue from Foucault's *History of Sexuality, Volume One* (1981), Butler refuses to make the sexed body the anchor for a discussion of gender *tout court*, for, as Foucault suggested:

> . . . it is precisely this idea of sex in itself that we cannot accept without examination. Is 'sex' really the anchorage point that supports the manifestations of sexuality, or is it not rather a complex idea that was formed inside the deployment of sexuality? In any case, one could show how this idea of sex took form in the different strategies of power and the definite role it played therein. (1981: 152)

In emphasizing this point, Butler pursues a line of questioning that leads from De Beauvoir on towards her own thesis. Perhaps, Butler posits, *contra* De Beauvoir, there are 'genders, ways of culturally interpreting the sexed body, that are in no way restricted to the apparent duality of sex' (1990: 112). The apparent duality of sex may be the effect, she argues, of the deployment of compulsory heterosexuality. Moreover, De Beauvoir's use of the term 'becoming' leads Butler to wonder further that:

> . . . if gender is something that one becomes – but can never be – then gender is itself a kind of becoming or activity, and that gender ought not to be conceived as a noun or a substantial thing or a static cultural marker, but rather as an incessant and repeated action of some sort. (1990: 112)

Butler employs De Beauvoir as part of the build-up to her own position, which is one that continually questions the cultural conflation of gender and sex, and their production within compulsory heterosexuality, emphasizing instead the performative aspects of gender. In a Foucauldian (and Nietzschean) manoeuvre, Butler questions the way in which the performance of gender produces the *effect* of an organizing principle – an identity – that appears to *cause* the behaviour. Gender is 'performative', constituted by the various acts of gender, a 'construction that conceals its own genesis', such that 'the tacit collective agreement to perform, produce and sustain discrete and polar genders as cultural fictions is obscured by the credibility of those productions' (1990: 140). There is thus a 'trope of interiority' whenever the body (or the sexed body) is regarded as *causing* gender. Although gender is generally understood to be interior, stable and causative, it is better interrogated, Butler is suggesting, as a cultural fiction, as a way of producing the effect of 'identity', and therefore, as the exterior, contingent resultant of repeated 'acts, gestures, enactments' which are:

> . . . performative in the sense that the essence or identity that they otherwise purport to express are *fabrications* manufactured and sustained through corporeal signs and other discursive means. That the gendered body is performative suggests that it has no ontological status apart from the various acts which constitute its reality. This also suggests that if that reality is fabricated as an interior essence, that very interiority is *an effect and function of a decidedly public and social discourse*, the public regulation of fantasy through the surface politics of the body, the gender border control that differentiates inner from outer and so institutes the 'integrity' of the subject. (1990: 136, emphasis added)

I want to focus on the argument that gender is a 'truth effect' of a public and social discourse; for Butler's argument here is that gender is *imitative*. What does Butler mean when she argues that gender is imitative? In her reply to other contributors in the volume *Feminist Contentions* Butler states that femininity is 'an impossible ideal, on which compels *a daily mime* that can, by definition, never succeed in its effort to approximate that ideal' (Benhabib et al., 1995: 142, emphasis added). Here, she gives her position a trajectory that is somewhat different from that gleaned from *Gender Trouble*, in that she highlights the role of linguistics in the development of her thesis.[1] She emphasizes that, from linguistics, one learns that the performative act is one that brings into being or enacts what it names;

and that, further, any sense of a prior agency is the effect of the utterance. The subject, although seemingly the source of the utterance – the 'doer behind the deed' – is in this way performatively constituted. From this, Butler argues that one can also think of gender as involving an ensemble of performative acts which draw upon conventions that the acts 'cite' and by which they are understood (Benhabib et al., 1995: 134). The 'public and social discourse' of the above quotation can be thought of, as Butler refines it in *Excitable Speech* as historically sedimented linguistic conventions that have a 'sedimented iterability'. Gender is, as it were, an embodied citing of sedimented ideals. Gender is an embodied performativity that attempts to mime the impossible ideals of the public and social discourse, the historically sedimented conventions that demand one displays a gendered subjectivity.

Where lesbian sexuality is derided as a fake or bad copy (of heterosexual relations), Butler's position redirects attention on to the assumptions that result in the privileging of heterosexuality as the original which homosexuality is then said to copy (Butler, 1991: 17). Heterosexuality, too, her argument runs, involves a process of mimicry, where the ideals that are mimed are the publicly and socially reiterated norms. The use of the notion of imitation in Butler, then, is one that attacks the thinking that would imply that lesbianism is a kind of miming, and argues that 'all gendering is a kind of impersonation and approximation' (1991: 21). The imitation that is gender is one that produces the notion of the original as its effect: 'the naturalistic effects of heterosexualised genders are produced through imitative strategies; what they imitate is a phantasmatic ideal of heterosexual identity, one that is produced by the imitation as its effect' (1991: 21). The project of heterosexual identity is an endless repetition of itself, a compulsive production or mimicry, of its impossible ideals.

In contrast to other understandings of mimesis, there is no judgement of mimesis in Butler's work, and no judgement of one who participates in mimetic behaviour since all individuals are involved in imitation. There is, similarly, no attempt to place mimesis on either side of the dichotomies good/bad, natural/unnatural. Hegemonic heterosexuality involves all in mimesis, and yet the ideals that are being mimed are *impossible* to mime completely. They are impossible to occupy in terms of their own logic, for hegemonic ideals are never truly separate from that they would exclude. The ideals remain discursively tied to one another, and those who live amidst them are necessarily engaged in performances which, once interrogated, reveal the sense in which the purported identity and the excluded identity are also profoundly tied to one another at the level of the psyche.

Butler argues that the maintenance of ideals of masculinity and femininity involves the performance or repetition of a heterosexual matrix which is inherently unstable. Heterosexuality offers subject positions (ideals) which can only be 'taken up' (mimed) by the subject through a process of repression or renunciation. Butler states: 'no "subject" comes into existence as a speaking being except through the repression of certain possibilities of speech (this is the significance of psychosis as impossible speech)' (1991: 139). For the order of heterosexuality to reign, and, in turn, its related gendered positions to be comprehended, there is a repression of forbidden impulses or desires, such that particular ways of naming the self become unviable. 'Oppression works', she writes, 'not merely through acts of overt prohibition, but covertly, through the constitution of viable subjects and through the corollary constitution of a domain of unviable (un)subjects – *abjects* we might call them – who are neither named nor prohibited within the economy of the law' (1991: 20). As Butler argues in *Gender Trouble*, there is, with respect to gendered heterosexuality, a psychic process which can be likened to melancholia, whereby the lost (the forbidden) loved object is carried within the ego, forming part of it. Heterosexual ideals demand that the very possibility of homosexuality be refused by the subject: it is the forbidden path. The possibility that is repressed and refused is to be *continually* refused, and the homosexual becomes thereby 'encrypted' within the heterosexual:

> There are structures of psychic homosexuality within heterosexual relations, and structures of psychic heterosexuality within gay and lesbian sexuality and relationships ... the ideal of a coherent heterosexuality that Wittig describes as the norm and standard of the heterosexual contract is an impossible ideal, a 'fetish' ... (1990: 121–2)

This encrypting is melancholic in that it carries the lost or 'forbidden' object with it in a way which elsewhere Butler likens to the way that Melanie Klein saw guilt operating 'as a way of preserving the object of love from one's own obliterating violence' (in Butler, 1997b: 25). It is exactly this psychic carrying *with* that makes heterosexuality an anxious project – heterosexuality is 'consistently haunted by that domain of sexual possibility that must be excluded for heterosexualized gender to reproduce itself' (1993: 125). The fear of difference that this focus on mimesis reveals is not that which it is common for campaigners for queer rights to point to – that between heterosexuals and homosexuals – but that between the performance, the ideal and the necessary excluded (see Girard, 1978, on this point). When the 'gaps' are illuminated, and made seeable, the exposure of gender as performative threatens the very idea of identity in the sense of a fit between mind and body. This is exactly why Butler returns to the example of drag, which reflects the imitative structure of hegemonic gender, disputing the claim that bodies and genders 'fit', and that heterosexuality is natural and original:

> To claim that all gender is like drag, or is drag, is to suggest that 'imitation' is at the heart of the *heterosexual* project and its gender binarisms, that drag is not a secondary imitation that presupposes a prior and original gender, but that hegemonic heterosexuality is itself a constant and repeated effort to imitate its own idealisations. (1993: 125, original emphasis)

It is at this point that Butler comes closest to Irigaray's argument that mimesis might become a strategy. For Irigaray mimesis is a strategy that has the potential to reveal the construction of Woman by illuminating through 'playful repetition' what is supposed to remain invisible. She writes:

> To play with mimesis is thus, for a woman, to try to recover the place of her exploitation by discourse, without allowing herself to be simply reduced to it. It means to resubmit herself – in as much as she is on the side of the 'perceptible', of 'matter' – to 'ideas', in particular to ideas about herself, that are elaborated in/by a masculine logic, but so as to make 'visible' by an effect of playful repetition, what was supposed to remain invisible: the cover up of a possible operation of the feminine in language. (Irigaray, 1985: 76)

Irigaray's focus is different from Butler's insofar as Irigaray believes there is something one can term 'the feminine' in language which masculine logic has attempted to exclude. Mimesis is used differently by the two writers because, for Irigaray, mimesis is on the level of strategy – one that reveals through its repetition of ideas about women – and not of constitution, as it is for Butler. However, Butler also sees in the mimetic nature of gender, as she understands it, the possibility of disruption, and comes close to Irigaray if only in the sense that Butler often uses a language of revealing the unseen relation between discursive and hegemonic ideals, on the one hand, and the constitution of the subject, on the other.[2]

Butler implies that heterosexuality remains hegemonic because it produces the idea of homosexuality whilst simultaneously disallowing its articulation as an identity, as owned in the same way that heterosexuality is 'owned'. But because of its reliance upon a simultaneous renunciation, Butler suggests – and this is the window of hope – there is a 'promising ambivalence of the norm' (1997a: 91) in the sense that there is the possibility of exposing the alterity within the norm, and the failure therefore of 'the norm to effect the universal reach for which it stands' (1997a: 91). What in *Excitable Speech* Butler terms the authorized and the 'deauthorised', elsewhere the viable and the (allegedly) abject, are sites of enunciation or 'identities', that are created at the very same moment.

It seems that Butler's refusal to judge mimesis per se is coupled with a sense in which the possibility of miming differently is held out as an *illuminating* possibility, due to the instability of heterosexuality and its attendant genders, and the possibility of showing the alterity within the norm is regarded as '*promising*'. This might imply, and some have indeed taken it to imply, that the refusal to mimic hegemonic ideals is the implied 'solution' to the division of gender and sexuality, and the inequities that rely upon these divisions. And yet there is also a sense in which Butler implies that mimicry as a strategy of resistance or subversion – either in Irigaray's sense, or in the sense of attempting to mime the 'wrong' ideals, to flout the hegemonic relations between bodies, identities and performance – might frequently be one that would simply entail too many *risks*. Hence the importance of the term *hegemony* in Butler. That heterosexual matrices and gender ideals are hegemonic implies not simply that they are held up as normal, but also that the boundaries are *policed* so that the traversing of these boundaries entail various judgements, even punishments. Butler refuses to go so far as to actually *advocate* the crossing of boundaries – even if she speaks of performativity as open to 're-signification' (in Benhabib et al., 1995: 135) – remaining instead 'merely' the astute analyst of situations where the illumination of 'the gaps' occurs. Just as those who transgress are not elevated into heroines, so those who perform and thus maintain hegemonic ideals and norms are not to be automatically judged negatively. It is to these *risks* and the *policing* of gender that I now turn, in order to focus on the importance of placing mimesis in the context, and especially in terms of the power relations, in which it takes place.

Cultural Survival

Towards the end of *Gender Trouble* Butler argues that 'gender is a project that has cultural survival as its end' (1990: 139). The notion of cultural survival, to which Boyarin (1995: 1322) has drawn attention, makes Butler's work sound much more ominous than the playful way it is often presented. What Butler talks about in terms of resignification (or in her earlier terms of parody and subversion), is rendered dangerous in this phrase, which implies that compliance with the 'sedimented norms' must be seen within the context of the risk involved in behaving otherwise. She continues the point: '[so that] the term strategy better suggests the situation of duress under which gender performance always and variously occurs' (1990: 139).

The category of mimicry as Butler employs it in her work is one that I would argue carries with it a sense of sadness, both of forfeiting (possibilities of being otherwise) and of resignation to 'carrying on' under duress. There is no playful repetition here. Gender performance is regarded as a strategy of *survival*, formed within a heterosexual matrix which, while not compulsory, is hegemonic, such that the psychic structures it deploys are analogous to melancholia, in which the lost object is incorporated into psychic life as part of the ego, object of ambivalence, i.e. both loved and hated. Moreover, wherever a performance is situated on the 'outside', in a non-hegemonic position, it is frequently named by the terms which reincorporate it to the 'inside'. There may be times when such enunciations illuminate the 'gap' between ideals and performances, but there is no necessary connection there. Most of the time, gender is performed, and (presumably) 'read' or seen, because there is an issue of *survival* at stake.

Jonathan Boyarin (1995) makes an intriguing intervention into the debate around Butler's work within which he begins a rumination on the place of Jewish communities in relation to the arguments in *Gender Trouble*, and how her arguments would translate into a Jewish context. One of the themes of his article is that of cultural survival, in terms of how persistently *non-hegemonic* identities are figured by Butler. Non-hegemonic identities, he explains, would be those that persistently resist the hegemonic epistemic regime that Butler is exploring in relation to gender; these might 'not only be Jews in a Christian or post-Christian society, but "religious" Jews in a secular Jewish society' (1995: 1318). Boyarin's purpose is to bring the performativity of identity into an account of cultural genealogy, to expose a sense in which a Jewish political subject can be thought as founded upon 'generational connection and its attendant anamnestic responsibilities and pleasures' (Boyarin and Boyarin, 1993: 701) making possible a maintenance of cultural identity thought through notions of generation and diaspora in such a way that highlights the Jewish embrace of the idea that there is no pure originality, that all subjective action takes place through at least a moment of imitation (Boyarin and Boyarin, 1995b: 29). In the tradition of rabbinic Judaism, Boyarin and Boyarin write, 'discovering that something has already been said by someone greater is no diminution, but an enhancement, and there is an explicit value attached to citation' (1995: 29). Thus Boyarin and Boyarin suggest a reading of mimicry – that is, of citation and embodied performativity – as a project of survival that can be both a *healthy* sustenance of a culturally given and temporally sustained identity as well as the site of a politics of interruption.

In this manner, the work of Jonathan Boyarin and Daniel Boyarin offers a way of reading Butler's emphasis on the mimicry of ideals as a way of producing the effect of identity through a Jewish tradition, so as to connect her thesis of mimesis to a notion of *generational* mimicry and non-hegemonic identities as projects or strategies of survival. In what follows I also wish to move the context within which Butler is read, and to suggest that there is a tradition of thinking mimicry within a history of thought around anti-Semitism.[3] Before elaborating the implications of placing cultural survival more strongly to the fore, I wish to draw out the relationship of Butler's mode of theorizing to some key figures in the theorization of anti-Semitism. I do so in order to argue that it is not simply a case of regarding Butler's as requiring translation into a different context; in tracing this specific genealogy of the concept of mimesis, I mean to suggest a stronger argument which is that Butler's work already has, in its intellectual heritage, a connection with these attempts to comprehend anti-Semitism and anti-Semitic fascism. The connections will then allow a further set of questions to be asked about the relationship of Butler's feminist theory to differing usages of the concept of mimesis.

Judaism, Anti-Semitism and Mimesis

The classic text of Adorno and Horkheimer, *Dialectic of Enlightenment*, is an important forerunner to the work of Boyarin and Boyarin. In response to the events of the Second World War, Adorno and Horkheimer felt obliged to surrender the 'innocence of philosophy' as they attempted to understand the 'indefatigable self-destructiveness of enlightenment' (1986: xi). Read as setting the context for later social-theoretical responses to anti-Semitism, this work offers a place from which to embark upon the specific route for thinking about more recent debates concerning identity and mimesis.

Dialectic of Enlightenment gave a crucial role to the concept of mimesis, but one which was very different from that which both Butler and Boyarin and Boyarin would later present. The idea of mimesis was utilized by Adorno and Horkheimer, within their historical context and with their specific theoretical inflections, in order to make an argument about anti-Semitism and fascism.[4] Their concept of mimesis is not easily assimilable to the post-Derridean understanding, for it is employed to name a natural process. Although natural, however, it is also susceptible to control. In their writings they mean to illuminate the historical and socio-economic contexts in which mimetic processes took place, and, in particular, to understand the fascistic attempts to denigrate and repress mimetic behaviour. They wrote:

> . . . anti-Semitism is based upon a false projection. It is the counterpart of true mimesis, and fundamentally related to the repressed form; in fact, it is probably the morbid expression of repressed mimesis. Mimesis imitates the environment, but false projection makes the environment like itself. For mimesis the outside world is a model which the inner world must try to conform to: the alien must become familiar; but false projection confuses the inner and outer world and defines the most intimate experiences as hostile. (1986: 187)

In contrast to the way in which Butler uses the notion of mimicry as copy (of a hegemonic norm) mimesis was described by Adorno and Horkheimer as a mode of adaptation, part of a healthy assimilation and accommodation of the environment within which one moves. Such a conception is indebted to psychoanalytic ideas of identification, by which Adorno and Horkheimer were profoundly influenced. Its fundamental assumption, which is not necessarily in itself a psychoanalytic one, is that the infant naturally imitates the environment around it, responding to the gestures of first contact. However, civilization has attempted to control human physical adaptation to nature, replacing:

> . . . organic adaptation to others and mimetic behaviour proper, by organised control of mimesis, in the magical phase; and finally, by rational practice, by work, in the historical phase. Uncontrolled mimesis is outlawed. (1986: 180)

Thus Adorno and Horkheimer argue that the reflection of nature that mimesis involves has been suppressed, and is suppressed in each generation, in order for humans to fit into the capitalist schema which holds up other modes of being as necessary for its particular order of things. Where mimesis appears *qua* mimesis, including the forms of magical and religious rituals, it is suspect and disallowed. Only activity – rational practice – is allowed.

Mimesis is described by Adorno and Horkheimer as both a positive natural response to adaptation, and as an activity that social interests – here, capitalist ones – are involved in attempting to control. Yet, like all suppressed inclinations, mimetic behaviour is never completely destroyed, and reappears. Even though capitalistic civilizations would wish to be rid of mimesis – to individuate and make humans merely 'human', as it were – this is an impossible desire. Those 'blinded by civilisation', Adorno and Horkheimer argue, experience 'their own tabooed mimetic features' in the behaviours and gestures of others, and they respond to them as old-fashioned, embarrassing and fearful remnants that survive in the rational environment of civilization (1986: 181–2). Any expressiveness is experienced as an exaggeration in a civilization where only an 'unmoving and unmoved countenance' is acceptable. For the anti-Semite, it is the Jews who are seen to engage in expressive mimetic behaviour, responding to natural impulses and ignoring the requirements of civilization in which a 'fit' between individuals and the socio-economic system has been elevated above that between individuals and human nature. This would be a point at which Boyarin and Boyarin would be curiously in accord with Adorno and Horkheimer, insofar as they argue that rabbinic traditions allow, even encourage, a mimesis. The difference, of course, would be that for the former, this mimesis is a mode of continuance of tradition in the name of cultural and generational reproduction – the project of survival – whereas Adorno and Horkheimer suggest that in the minds of the anti-Semites, the mimesis is not of cultural traditions, but of natural, emotional inclinations, inclinations which should, according to their repressive (and repressed) logic, be controlled in the name of civilization.

In anti-Semitic fascism, however, a certain form of mimesis *was* allowed, Adorno and Horkheimer argue, which can be thought as a second level of mimesis. Anti-Semites both blame the Jew for engaging in forbidden mimetic behaviour – of flouting the demands of civilization that one should avoid giving in to suppressed emotive expressivity – and at the same time, engage *themselves* in a form of mimicry of 'the Jew', that is, the image which anti-Semitism presents of the Jew. Anti-Semites imitate their image of the Jew, in a false version of natural response to others, and are thereby themselves able to enjoy an activity forbidden by civilization:

> There is no anti-Semite who does not basically want to imitate his mental image of a Jew, which is composed of mimetic cyphers: the argumentative movement of a hand, the musical voice painting a vivid picture of things and feelings irrespective of the real content of what is said, and the nose – the physiognomic *principium individuationis*. . . . Anti-Semites gather together to celebrate the moment when authority permits what is usually forbidden, and become collective only in that common purpose. Their rantings are organised laughter. (1986: 184)

This is the mimesis of mimesis, then, in which it matters little whether Jews really do have the mimetic features that the anti-Semite sees there, because anti-Semitism is based on a *projection*, whereby 'impulses which the subject will not admit as his own even though they are most assuredly so, are attributed to the object – the prospective victim' (1986: 187). The mimesis of mimesis is a process in which the subject mimes because s/he longs for the other, desires in some way what s/he imagines the other to be. This sense of mimesis is also that which Sartre describes in *Anti-Semite and Jew*, where the anti-Semite gives himself[5] the pleasure of ranting, reporting and voicing evils which he attributes to the Jews:

> He [the anti-Semite] can thus glut himself to the point of obsession with the recital of and criminal actions which excite and satisfy his perverse leanings; but since at the same time he attributes them to those infamous Jews on whom he heaps his scorn, he satisfies himself without being compromised. (1965: 46)

The recitation that is taking place here, therefore, is one which gives the speaker pleasure, and is a mimicry that is 'a basic sadism' (1965: 46). For Sartre, this mimesis is based on fear, not of the Jews, but of the anti-Semite's own situation, a fear of 'himself, of his own consciousness, of his liberty, of his instincts, of his responsibilities, of solitariness, of change, of society, and of the world' (1965: 53). The ambivalence towards liberty is similarly important in the argument of Adorno and Horkheimer, for whom anti-Semitic fascism has to be viewed in the context of a frustration that is the gap that yawns between the potential that civilization's discourse of liberty holds up for people, and its actuality.

The psychic processes involved in repressed mimesis are to be understood, Adorno and Horkheimer argued, in the context of the mockery that the masses had suffered insofar as they had had to repeatedly suppress the longing for happiness which liberalism and capitalism had promised them. The hatred felt by the anti-Semites was directed at an image of that happiness, which they perceived the Jews as having achieved despite the fact that the latter did not have any real access to power (1986: 172). Through this argument, Adorno and Horkheimer dovetail their analysis of anti-Semitism with a critique of capitalism, arguing that instead of pointing to the real villains of the new mercantile industrial age, the anti-Semite points to the scapegoat, the population who had seemingly created their own happiness, wealth and community within but despite the capitalist structures with which they, the masses, had been obliged to live. Fascism is the crystallization of a general condition in which it becomes superfluous for man to plan his own happiness because in a world where repression and a capitalist mentality reign, all responsibility is to the apparatus and reflective thought is anathema. Thus 'the dialectic of Enlightenment is transformed objectively into delusion' (1986: 204).

Sartre's work had a different route of philosophical indebtedness from Adorno and Horkheimer's, one that speaks less of capitalism and its inequities in its attempt to comprehend anti-Semitism, and more of intersubjective economies. There is for Sartre an investment in anti-Semitism as an attachment to a tradition and a community: 'The phrase, "I hate the Jews" is one that is uttered in chorus; in pronouncing it, one attaches himself to a tradition and to a community – the tradition and community of the mediocre' (1965: 22). The citation of what would be termed 'hate speech' in contemporary America, was thus for Sartre, as it is for Butler, a citation that keeps alive a discourse which at the same time as it excludes, creates a community of same-thinking speakers. The community network of anti-Semites, Sartre wrote, binds in anger those whom other hierarchies would disaggregate (1965: 30). It is in this bonding quality of anti-Semitism that Sartre sees the anti-Semite attaching himself to a tradition formed in relation to the pretext of the Jew. Although there were particular reasons why it was the Jews who were chosen as objects of revulsion, elsewhere it might be 'the Negro or the man of yellow skin' (1965: 54). The Jew would be invented by the anti-Semite did he not exist, writes Sartre (1965: 13), since, one surmises, the Jew fulfils a necessary function for the anti-Semite, to 'stifle his anxieties at their inception by persuading himself that his place in the world has been marked out in advance' (1965: 54).

Insofar as Sartre's work posed anti-Semitism as an imagined remembrance through repetition, and despite its functionalist structure, it is an argument that prefigures Boyarin and Boyarin's position on the maintenance of Jewish traditions themselves, with the important difference, of course, that there is a disparity between the two cases in terms of the nature of the subject's reflection on their embodied reminiscence of tradition. That is, there is a difference between the way that Sartre implies that the anti-Semite 'remembers' and the way that Judaism is remembered according to Boyarin and Boyarin. This concerns the nature of reflection.

Sartre's argument was that the anti-Semite was unreflective, a man who had chosen 'to live entirely outside himself, never to look within' (1965: 21). As such, Sartre echoes the argument of Adorno and Horkheimer, who, trying to understand the psychological state of the anti-Semite within a Europe which had attached itself to a narrative of liberalism and enlightenment, asserted that anti-Semitism was a projection that was not a problem because it was projection as such – since for them projection is present in all perception – but because of 'the absence from it of reflection' (1986: 189). Anti-Semitism involves a process which projects on to the world without taking in what is given back to the subject, such that projection makes the world a void; just as with the paranoiac, so with the anti-Semite, there is no limit to the ego's projections, no information that causes the ego to reflect upon itself (1986: 189–90).

For Sartre, the Jews in an anti-Semitic society, in contrast to the anti-Semite, are forced to be overly self-reflective – there is 'the necessity imposed upon the Jew of subjecting himself to endless self examination' so that he assumes a 'phantom personality' (1965: 78–9). The existential situation overdetermines the Jew, Sartre argues, for there is nothing determinate about the synthesis of characteristics (psychical and physical, anatomical, social, religious) that make up 'the Jew'. The bond between Jews is the shared experience of being placed as a Jew:

> It is neither their past, their religion, nor their soil that unites the sons of Israel. If they have a bond, if all of them deserve the name of Jew, it is because they have in common the situation of a Jew, that is, they live in a community which takes them for Jews. (1965: 67)

The mimicry that the Jew is obliged to participate in is one that Sartre bases in the concepts of authenticity and inauthenticity. The authentic path is to live within the situation, to be conscious of it, and to assume its responsibilities and risks (1965: 89). But authenticity requires one to live in a situation which 'is quite simply that of a martyr' (1965: 91). The inauthentic situation must be more tempting, reasons Sartre. But it is exactly the inauthentic Jew whom the anti-Semite focuses upon, that is, the one who attempts to 'pass'. The avenues of flight that characterize the route of the inauthentic Jew are collected into the 'monstrous portrait' that is made to stand for the 'Jew in general' (1965: 94). While Sartre argues that inauthenticity implies no moral blame, he does suggest that the assimilating Jew is acting in bad faith (1965: 99) and that he has 'allowed himself to be persuaded by the anti-Semites' (1965: 94), even that he makes himself anti-Semitic wherever he sees the traits that he denies in himself in other Jews (1965: 106). Furthermore, Sartre implies that there is a felt moral responsibility to the extent that the Jew sees authenticity as continuing a tradition and keeping open the possibility of being Jewish:

> To be a Jew is to be thrown into – to be *abandoned to* – the situation of a Jew; and at the same time it is to be responsible in and through one's own person for the destiny and the very nature of the Jewish people. For, whatever the Jew says or does, and whether he have a clear or vague conception of his responsibilities, it is as if all his acts were subject to a Kantian imperative, as if he had to ask himself before each act: 'If all Jews acted as I am going to do, what would happen to Jewish life? (1965: 89-90)

Thus the theme of cultural survival has a place in Sartre's arguments too, in the form of an obligation to continuance, a theme which is also present in Levinas' later reflections on National Socialism and anti-Semitism in which he argued that after Auschwitz there is a 'commandment to faithfulness', an obligation to live and remain Jews. For Levinas, however, this becomes also a commandment to defend the state of Israel:

> To renounce after Auschwitz this God absent from Auschwitz – no longer to assure the continuation of Israel – would amount to finishing the criminal enterprise of National Socialism, which aimed at the annihilation of Israel and the forgetting of the ethical message of the Bible, which Judaism bears, and whose multi-millennial history is concretely prolonged by Israel's existence as a people. . . . The Jew, after Auschwitz, is pledged to his faithfulness to Judaism and to the material and even political conditions of its existence. (1988: 162–3)

The situation of 'remaining Jewish', however, is not a straightforward one in Sartre's argument, for the Jew, even and especially the authentic Jew, attempting to live the situation in which he is taken for a Jew, is in danger of denying the possibility of Jewish existence. Forced to observe himself through the eyes of others, he becomes simultaneously a witness and an object, such that, for Jews, wishing to know the Jew through introspection is also to deny him ('the Jew') (1965: 97). In making himself subject, he makes himself object.

Boyarin and Boyarin would dispute Sartre's position, finding the language of authenticity and inauthenticity objectionable and restricting, so that even as they would share, I believe, the broad political impulse behind the work, they would differ on the manoeuvres that Sartre's philosophical position obliges him to take. For although Boyarin and Boyarin also would wish to rethink the bonds that make up a 'Jewish community', they would argue that being 'taken for a Jew' does not *constitute* that community, such that the focus is less on the perception of Jews from without, and more on the continuance of various practices that internally, as it were, constitute Jewish traditions. They would maintain that there is a place for a non-essentialist but genealogical, non-biological *performative* sense of continuity, where questions of authenticity are inappropriate. Sartre's existentialism places him in a position where there is a privileging only of the present, only of the *situation* within which human actors meet, and of judging their behaviour at that moment. Tradition in Sartre is demoted to the status of a self-pitying lie:

> If it is true, as Hegel says, that a community is historical to the degree that it remembers its history, then the Jewish community is the least historical of all, for it keeps a memory of nothing but a long martyrdom, that is, of a long passivity. (1965: 66–7)

The questions of continuing remembered traditions are more active and crucial than this for Boyarin and Boyarin, but not as an impulse to Zionism. Levinas entwined a pledge to faithfulness to Judaism with the question of land, i.e. the continuation of the state of Israel. Boyarin and Boyarin refuse the presumptive link between tradition and land as a dangerous one, and distance themselves from it. I will now focus upon the arguments of Boyarin and Boyarin as a route to thinking mimesis in a way that brings Butler's thesis back into this discussion.

As I have mentioned above, Jonathan Boyarin considers how Butler's work would position Judaism, and would translate into a Jewish context (1995), a line of questioning that focuses on a notion of cultural survival. Via an emphasis on cultural survival, the Boyarins' purpose is to link the notion of performativity with an account of cultural genealogy, to expose a sense in which a Jewish political subject can be thought as founded upon generational connection and embodied practices (Boyarin and Boyarin 1993: 701). If one accepts that Judaism values imitation *qua* citation, there is a way of reading Butler's emphasis on the mimicry of ideals as producing the effect of identity in a way that connects her thesis to a notion of *generational* mimicry and non-hegemonic identities as projects or strategies of survival. As both a sustenance of a culturally given and temporally sustained identity as well as the site of a politics of interruption, mimicry can be understood as an alternative theoretical framework for considering embodied performativity, one that avoids the negative associations of genealogical ways of thinking ethnicity, which have often been associated with racism. The embodied citational practices of Judaism in a diasporic context, may have, Boyarin and Boyarin suggest, a particular contribution to make to this politico-theoretical manoeuvre.

In an influential article published in 1993 – 'Diaspora: Generation and the Ground of Identity' – Boyarin and Boyarin argue that scholars of identity have inherited a tendency to refute genealogical ways of thinking about group identity from the attack that was launched at the very beginnings of Christendom in the Letters of Paul, where coming together in spirit was elevated above any genealogical bodily connection between people. But, they point out, there has been a sustained Jewish counterdiscourse to this position. They wish to propose a notion of critically grounded identity as a way to confront those forms of 'pure theory' (1993: 694) that, in line with Pauline tradition, make 'things of the body . . . less important than things of the spirit', and in which the physical connection of common descent from Abraham and the embodied practices with which that genealogy is marked off as difference are rejected in favour of a connection between people based on 'individual re-creation and entry de novo into a community of common belief' (1993: 695).

Thus in Paul was made a move toward wholeness and unity that despite itself unintentionally devalued what could be seen as the mimetic nature of Jewish practice so that: 'to stand for anything other than what the apostle stands for is to articulate for oneself a place of difference, which has already implicitly been associated with discord and disorder' (1993: 696). The drive to sameness in Pauline discourse can also, Boyarin and Boyarin argue, be seen in the politics of group relations. As Paul became source of Christianity *tout court* the 'coercive move toward sameness' became directed to the Jews: 'the place of difference increasingly became the Jewish place and the Jew the sign of discord and disorder in the Christian polity' (1993: 697). This is despite the fact that Paul intended to include the Jews, and in an important sense, saw his position as the fulfilment of Judaism.

Boyarin and Boyarin argue that the right to remain different has to be kept at the level of practice and descent, for otherwise the Jew risks becoming an ideal which works to deprive Jews of their difference. Their position is one that attempts to avoid the idealization of difference, and rejects, for the same reasons, those well-intentioned theoretical positions that regard as always and necessarily pernicious those communities that uphold their specialness (1993: 698).[6] Their purpose, then, is to articulate a modern, but non-Zionist, Jewish subject:

> We suggest that a Jewish subject position founded on generational connection and its attendant anamnestic responsibilities and pleasures affords the possibility of a flexible and nonhermetic critical Jewish identity. (1993: 701)

No doubt Sartre's *Anti-Semite and Jew* would be cast from such a position as one of the attempts to idealize Jewishness, not in the sense of valorizing Jews, but in the sense of diluting difference through an attempt to avoid adopting a position which feels too close to that of the racist or anti-Semite. Sartre's repeated attempt to employ existentialist concepts in such a way that continually denies grounds of difference, is a means to avoid anti-Semitism, but comes perilously close to the Pauline form of idealization. Thus his work would be situated in what Boyarin and Boyarin would see as a Platonic mode of claiming (spiritual) equivalence between human subjects: 'the valorisation of any kind of elective and affective connection between people over against the claims of physical kinship is deeply embedded in the Platonic value system Europe has largely inherited from Paul.' But genealogical ways of thinking about identity, the Boyarins are suggesting, need not be immediately saddled with the baggage of racist discourse. Indeed:

> The insistence on the value of bodily connection and embodied practice that is emblematic of Judaism since Paul thus has significant critical power vis a vis the isolating and disembodying direction of Western idealist philosophies. (1993: 705–6)

For Boyarin and Boyarin, therefore, one needs to think about the generational forms of mimicry that take place within all the complexities and contingencies of the diaspora. Their position shares an affinity with Butler's emphasis on performativity and the mimicry of ideals, but the contextualization is different. This is due, in part, I believe, to the differences between thinking about gender and sexuality as performed identities, and thinking about religious and ethnic identities. It seems that feminist theory is entering a stage in which the difficult work of thinking the relationship and differences *between* different modes of difference – class, 'race', sexuality, ethnicity – demands to be thought as a central issue, so that the list does not substitute for the complexities of engagement. The recent debate between Butler (1998) and Nancy Fraser (1998) in the journal *New Left Review* is in part about the possibility of thinking through the construction and relationships between differences (here, between class and sexuality), and, indeed, the debate between Rita Felski and other feminist scholars in the journal *Signs* (1997) on the topic of difference, similarly suggests this is a new agenda for feminist thought. In the next section I will pursue these questions in relation to my specific genealogy of Butler's use of mimesis.

Mimesis in a New Agenda

How does this discussion of mimesis in relation to thinking anti-Semitism and Judaism give a context in which to return to Butler's work? Reversing the manoeuvre of the Boyarins we are now in a position to ask, what does this revisiting tell us about gender and mimesis? The notion of cultural survival is highlighted, I think rightly, by these discussions. For both Adorno and Horkheimer, and for Sartre, this was also a very real issue at stake, as they pondered how recovery from the atrocities of the Second World War was to take place. The way in which Butler thinks cultural survival is less overt, but, nevertheless, it is a place from which to think about the role of several key turns and distinctions in her work. In pursuing this term, however, I think it is important to give some consideration to the different domains that have been brought together in the above discussion. How similar is the use of the term mimesis in the various authors? Can the term 'cultural survival' smooth over any differences in the ways these writers are using the term?

There are several ways in which Butler's use of the term mimicry parts company with Adorno and Horkheimer, not least because of the naturalization of mimesis in the latter's work. For Adorno and Horkheimer, mimesis is posited as a foundational and natural process. For them, mimetic behaviour is positioned as almost equivalent to a notion of accommodation such as one finds in Piagetian developmental psychology, a *natural* mode of human adaptation to being in the world. In the context of capitalism, however, and this is their contribution, this natural developmental process is suppressed, and where it erupts it takes on a distorted form with potentially fascistic qualities. But whereas, in Adorno and Horkheimer, repressed mimesis is the eruption of a natural process suppressed by the socio-economic order, in Butler there is nothing 'natural' about the process of mimicking either 'the norms' or 'the other'.

A second reason why one would expect a different twist in the concept of mimesis in Adorno and Horkheimer from its usage in Butler is because of the different theoretical inheritances of each, and in particular the different understandings of power that these entail. Adorno and Horkheimer write within their Frankfurt School context, premised on beliefs and utilizing terms that would be anathema to Butler's Foucauldian persuasion. In Butler, economic contexts are downplayed, if not altogether absent,[7] but it is certainly the case that although the socio-economic context does not suppress a *natural* behaviour, certain modes of mimicry either uphold or deviate from the contexts in which they are performed. In this sense, Butler is interested in processes of domination, just as Adorno and Horkheimer were. Moreover, the notion of cultural survival points to the importance of hegemony in Butler's thesis, and this in itself is instructive. Butler speaks of hegemonic norms which are mimed in the process of subjectification and identification, and implies that the mimesis of these norms is difficult – if not impossible – to avoid. The leftist framework is betrayed both by the term hegemony, and by Butler's usage of the Althusserian notion of interpellation. More than merely indicative of a sense of the power relations within which mimesis occurs, these terms, taken together with the argument that gender is oftentimes a matter of cultural survival within a 'situation of duress', imply that mimesis is a strategic mode of 'going on' with a specific socio-cultural context, in which other corporeal styles are abjected, foreclosed or simply too risky.[8] Within the hegemonic heterosexual project, subjects are produced that are engaged in a repeated endeavour to imitate the idealizations of that project (1993: 125); those whose desires take them outside that project are obliged to monitor the safety of the spaces they inhabit before corporeal styles and gender performances transgress or stretch the hegemonic regulatory norms.

The embodied repetition of hegemonic norms needs to be understood within the context of these power relations and their various modes of policing, because it needs to remain clear that Butler's account attends to the differing modes of survival for which mimetic behaviour occurs. Several factors can influence the degree to which heterosexualized genders are performed; these can concern perceptions of personal safety, for example, but they may also concern one's subjective need or desire to mark oneself as gendered. The embodied repetition of the non-hegemonic (in all countries bar Israel, and perhaps even there) identity – 'Jew' – of which Boyarin and Boyarin speak, resonates strongly with Butler's arguments, as they recognize, and in terms of religious ritualized bodily movements and markings this is especially the case. Jonathan Boyarin has illustrated how his own partaking in Jewish communal activities has had just this quality, that is, an embodied marking out, the performance of which can be more or less strongly marked according to one's response to changing situations and one's changing sense of requiring community bonds. Mimicry across a generational boundary is attractive, comforting even, but also, to differing degrees, and particularly as one reaches adulthood, a matter of felt need within contexts, a fact that becomes particularly apparent when one travels and reconnects to the 'community' in different locales (see Boyarin, 1996).

In this, there is a similarity between the work of Boyarin and Boyarin and Butler. There is, however, a sense in which the mimicry of which Boyarin and Boyarin speak approaches a functionalist sociological notion of cultural reproduction, and is related in turn to a notion of respect for one's ancestry, especially in terms of their sufferings, that manifests in an embodied remembrance of one's genealogically given positionality. The 'double mark of the male Jew', as they term it, involves embodied remembrance, both by altering the body (of one's sons), but also by displaying embodied difference (oneself); even if the marking practice of circumcision unites Jews in terms of numbers, they point out that it is the wearing of the *yarmulke*, the (relatively removable) headcovering, that marks the body of the Jew Jewish for spectators (Boyarin and Boyarin, 1995). In Butler, by contrast, gender performance is regarded less as a means of being faithful to gendered cultural inheritances, an obedience to traditions out of generational respect, and more in terms of the disciplinary mechanisms that surround divergence from those norms of performance: 'acting out of line with heterosexual norms brings with it ostracism, punishment and violence' (1991: 24). Cultural survival is not that which it is for the Boyarins, therefore – a form of re-membering and re-production borne out of a genealogically given selfhood, and a desire to remain faithful – but is presented in Butler as a more regulated mode of conformity, that is less conscious of its positivity and its need for reproduction, and more conscious of the shaming and punishments (and less often but sometimes, of the pleasures)[9] of deviating from those norms. It is a training, in the Foucauldian sense, that is disciplinary. In considering the ways in which cultural ideals of womanhood operate to discipline women's movement through space, the presentation of her body, and her use of facial expressions, Sandra Lee Bartky (1988) has argued the sense in which femininity is not an insignificant matter of sexual difference, but a matter of disciplinary power, in Foucault's sense that women become self-regulating subjected subjects, but also in the sense that performing differently carries regulative punishments, especially, in Bartky's examples, punishments relating to sexual availability and reputation.[10]

Although it might be attractive and even fruitful to think gender as a mode of belonging in which each socially designated female conforms out of generationally given respect for her maternal line (is it our mothers we would disappoint if we were able to 'give up' gender?), gender feels, from the point of view of this discussion, and paradoxically perhaps, much less 'in the family' than religious or ethnic affiliation. Moreover, while Judaism of course entails rules and regulations, as well as means for the casting out, disciplining and disowning, of those who do not conform, Boyarin and Boyarin are focusing upon the sense in which the maintenance of Jewish ways of life is a matter of the positive survival of Judaism within a diasporized context. In order for Jews to survive *qua* Jews, such repetition must occur. In Butler, by contrast, the survival is less that of a culture within another culture, and more the survival of the self within a (gender-regulated) culture. Taking up the abject position 'beyond' gender is at the linguistic level a complex manoeuvre, she suggests (hence the reference to psychotic speech, above),[11] whereas in our multi-faith world, one might imagine, altering one's religious affiliation, or moving in and out of an intensity of affect around it, is a *communicable* – if by no means trivial – matter.

It feels somewhat misguided to allow the discussion to move in such a direction, as if it were possible to compare either 'religious' or ethnic affiliation with gender allegiance. These authors are aware that the performance of ethnic or religious affiliation can be the site for gender performance (and vice versa) so that, for example, the Boyarins write: 'the marks we ground our selfhood in are only imposed on and available to *male* Jews – although in nonorthodox communities women are increasingly adopting the *yarmulke* – and hence they are inescapably inscriptions of hierarchising and reifying difference' (1995: 17, emphasis added). Moreover, there are evidently dangers and costs involved in the altering of ethnic and religious affiliation, as there are of gender. The point is not to criticize the authors' awareness of such complexities, but to suggest that the similarity that the Boyarins draw between their position and that of Butler's may be a little rushed. The mimicry of the norms of one's (persecuted) cultural allegiance is a matter of enabling the survival of one's genealogy throughout, at least, one's own generation. The 'citation' of gender(ing) norms, however, is not posited by Butler as a means of maintaining that which our maternal line has bequeathed us, for gender is not in itself *a* culture, but is, rather, a mode of distinction that is culturally constituted. This divergence in argumentation, subtle as it may be, becomes important as it highlights the need to avoid reproducing the tendency to think ethnicity and gender as parallel and comparable processes. Such a tendency falters because it refuses to think through the modes by which 'culture', including ethnic or religious cultures, 'transport' gender within themselves, and conversely, modes of gendering can 'transport' ethnicity.

There is a further worry that leads me via another route to argue that gender mimicry and generational ethnic mimicry need to be kept analytically separate, such that their simultaneity be better traced. This concerns the processes that Butler captures with her notion of encrypting. This relates to the use that Butler makes of Freud's writings on melancholia – in particular the way she employs a notion of encrypting the possibility of being otherwise as analogous with a melancholic encrypting of the other – which implies that in embarking upon a route of gender survival one cannot avoid encumbering a certain specific kind of psychic baggage. The performance of (either) heterosexualized gender 'carries' the abjected possibility of being the other (gender and sexuality) with it.

Interestingly, the encrypting of homosexuality within the psychic structures of heterosexuality is a process the effects of which might be likened to the role of repressed mimesis in Adorno and Horkheimer in a specific sense. It is perhaps taking liberties with the texts to suggest this connection, for there are several principles – particularly about subjectification and, relatedly, about how psyches operate within a socio-economic context – that I pass over to make this leap. Nevertheless, it would seem that one could liken the phenomena of drag as presented in Butler to the repressed mimesis of the anti-Semitic fascist in Adorno and Horkheimer. For just as in repressed mimesis the anti-Semite mimics the other in order to engage in forbidden mimetic behaviour that s/he mistakenly or otherwise projects on to 'the Jew', in drag men impersonate the qualities they impute to feminine performance in such as way that it matters little, as Sartre also said of the relation between the anti-Semite and the Jew, whether women do truly have those qualities. Where Butler points to drag she does so, as I have explained, in order to provide an analysis of what is illuminated there, i.e. crucially, the distance between sex, gender identity and gender performance. There is no *need* implied in Butler – that is, the men who impersonate women have no psychic need to engage in mimesis. Nevertheless, the notion of encrypting suggests there is a form of release – even if that release is a non-subjectively felt illumination of the heterosexual matrix. Although it is without the element of naturalized psychic need, therefore, there is an echo of repressed mimesis in drag, and, as with the rantings of the anti-Semite that mime mimesis, of the correlative sense of ambivalence toward the loved/hated object mimed.

That said, and to whatever extent one concedes this peculiar connection, my understanding is that the encrypting of the 'unviable' subject identity is fundamental to gender identity within the heterosexual matrix, principally because there is, currently, no available third sex (despite Monique Wittig's attempts to make 'lesbian' do this work). The structure of melancholia is such that the encrypting of what is 'given up' in order to mime the subject position of one's gender/sexuality, requires a 'knowledge' of that forbidden other as an integral part of the process of performing the 'chosen' identity (see Benjamin, 1997), even if that knowledge is a distorted form of knowledge such as arguably one finds in those instances of drag that refuse the heterogeneity of women by miming the exaggerated 'ideal', with all the ambivalence that that implies.

In the case of ethnicity, it is more difficult to assert that there is *an* encrypted other, a comparable 'knowledge', accurate or distorted, faithful or unfaithful, that is *required* for the identification to take place. If this is the case, it would be a reason why one has to be careful about moving too quickly from the analysis of gender to that of 'race' or ethnicity. For with Butler's stress on this encrypting, there is a sense in which, in the case of gender, mimicry is a process in which the 'other', the non-mimed, is nevertheless also 'known' and carried with the mime, encrypted, if not as its opposite exactly, as its limit. The performance of gender always involves the process of abjection, renunciation or differentiation; heterosexual femininity requires by definition a relation to masculinity (the desired) and homosexuality (the abjected), *as formational*. As Butler describes it, the constitution of gender is melancholic, impossible because it carries its alleged 'opposite' with it. However, in the Boyarins' notion of mimicry across generations, there is no *necessary* knowledge of 'the other' implied. Even in a multi-religious community one can be a practising Catholic, say, without the 'knowledge' of how, by which embodied citations, one would be a practising Jew. The mimicry of one's generationally given knowledge and practices requires knowledge of the prior generation and its practices, but the ethnic self does not seem to rely for its very *constitution* upon knowledge of 'other' ethnicities or religions, even if these religions themselves, historically and discursively defined themselves through the boundaries and connections they form with each other. The melancholias that may accompany the ethnic mimesis of which the Boyarins write, are therefore, *psychically* speaking, of a different order from those that concern gender, based as they are on generational reproduction of a faith and sense of *lineage* (be that more or less embodied) rather than on the reproduction or 'citation' of a *line of differentiation* (masculine/feminine) each side of which is defined by even as it rejects its opposite.

There is an important point that flows from these questions and which concerns the relationship between citation and self-constitution. The various writers brought together here do not lead one to regard every instance of mimesis as self-constitutional. Is it the case, for example, that the rantings that link the anti-Semite to a tradition of anti-Semitism, as Sartre describes, are as self-constitutive as the mimicry of gender citation? And how are these instances of mimesis to be understood in relation to the mimesis of one's own ethnic or religious genealogy?

Butler has a notion of citation that links her thesis explicitly with the maintenance of tradition, and that uses the philosophical perspective developed in relation to subjectification and gender to speak about racist speech. In an argument reminiscent of Sartre she writes in reference to racist speech:

> ... neither the law nor hate speech are uttered exclusively by a single subject. The racial slur is always cited from elsewhere, and in the speaking of it, one chimes in with a chorus of racists, producing at that moment the linguistic occasion for an imagined relation to an historically transmitted community of racists. (1997a: 80)

This form of citation, therefore, is one that provides a self-identity that is not singular but, due to its citational nature, a placing of the self within a racist community and tradition. In doing so, one positions others in order to construct and bolster one's own sense of superiority as a racialized subject: both those who have historically agreed and those of whom one speaks. Adorno and Horkheimer suggest something to this effect when they speak of the anti-Semite engaging in a mimesis of those whom he judges as anachronistically mimetic; when the anti-Semite, that is, gives in to a suppressed desire to engage in mimesis himself. The anti-Semite produces an image of the Other that enables a self-constitution as not-Other even at the very moment that he proceeds to enact that Other: 'they are so awful', he says, 'they are just like this, just as I am being now'. In Butler, however, racist citation is not given the self-constitutional role that is the citation of gender norms. The imagined relation to a tradition of racists may be a situating of the self, an aesthetics of existence, but its power emanates from the imagined community that gives one an imagined place amongst others, rather than the scenario with gender, where the subject is engaged in a performative constitution of oneself as a 'one'. It is, indeed, a source of political hope that this is the case; moving beyond racist speech is not about moving beyond linguistic resources that make one 'culturally intelligible'.[12] Although the hope for absolute non-repetition of racism, the dream of censorship, is not viable, for repetition will occur, Butler suggests, the question is is how that repetition can be different, or interrupted. The interruption of gender norms is similarly posited by Butler as a possibility;

indeed, her whole thesis is to stress the temporal, repeated and therefore interruptable nature of gender performativity (the question of 'agency' is for her about the possibility of resignification). However, even if such an interruption is 'visible' in certain cultural phenomena such as drag, it is not comparable to the way in which Butler speaks of interrupting racist hate speech. This is because the citation of the racist slur is not self-constitutional in the way that gender (currently) is in the sense that the discursive possibilities for moving 'beyond' gender are not as readily available as are those of moving beyond a racist enunciative mode.[13] This relates to the notion that becoming gendered is about being 'culturally intelligible'; that 'sex' is not what one has or is, but 'how "one" becomes viable at all' (see Butler, 1993: 2). The difference turns on the possibility of surviving outside that subject position. Again, the notion of 'cultural survival', together with the intentions and visions of the speaker, become all important. In each instance, therefore, it seems pertinent to enquire whether citations are self-constitutional, or whether they are 'merely' citations, for it is exactly the connection between subjectivities, embodiment and modes of affiliation through citation that these writers help illuminate.

It may be that I have set up these questions falsely here. Is it ever possible to think about gender outside the question of ethnicity? Hegemonic ideals must surely be simultaneously both 'about' gender and 'about' ethnicity, since the mimesis of hegemonic ideals, the 'style of the flesh' they involve, varies both within and between cultures. 'Masculinity' and 'femininity' do not exist 'without' or 'outside' or 'before' ethnicity. And yet it feels politically important for an anti-racist position to attempt to distinguish between self-constitutive mimesis and mimesis that is not related to subject-constitution. The political thrust of this work is to reach a point where one is able to contemplate how subjects are constituted in relation to notions of themselves and others, but more, how these are mobile and changing relations. But does this make the projects of anti-racism and feminism the same? Isn't there something different, presently at least, about attempting to resignify ethnicities in an anti-racist manner, as opposed to attempting to resignify gender differentiations?

Indeed, the importance of reading Butler with Boyarin and Boyarin against earlier work on mimesis and anti-Semitism revolves around the issue of thinking about subjectivities in relation to realigning political commitment and cultural identities. The work of Boyarin and Boyarin is crucially about how one might be able to think ethnic difference without falling into racism. They do so by arguing that it is possible to rescue the notion of personal genealogy from its racist overtones. The Boyarins pose their argument against, inter alia, that of Jean-Luc Nancy, whose work, they suggest, has as its political impulse the refusal of modes of argumentation that have fascistic potentialities, but whose argument leads him to repeat a Pauline utopia that poses the coming together of political groupings as a necessarily disembodied connection. In stressing the citational but embodied nature of identities, the Boyarins join Butler in positing a political hope that affiliations, genealogical or not, can be – and frequently, *are* – wrested from any associations of inscribed destiny.[14]

This sense of a joint purpose – between the feminism of Butler and the anti-racism of Boyarin and Boyarin – is undoubtedly important. Clearly, an attention to the constitution of identities and how they might be realigned or subverted links these authors' work. However, I am arguing that one might hesitate a little longer before endorsing the suggestion that the Boyarins make. That is, they argue that one might think of gender along the same lines as they speak of Jewish communities, as a sort of 'diasporised gender identity' (1993: 721):

> We suggest that a diasporised gender identity is both possible and positive. Being a woman is a special kind of being, and there are aspects of life and practice that insist on and celebrate that speciality. (1993: 721)

The impulse to make this connection is made clear; that is, the notion of diaspora in relation to gender emphasizes the unfixed nature of identity and bodies, and avoids dualisms, such that 'we can substitute partially Jewish, partially Greek, bodies that are sometimes gendered and sometimes not' (1993: 721). However, for the reasons discussed above, I would wish to resist this manoeuvre: the similarities in thinking embodied performances do not suffice. As the Boyarins themselves suggest, there is an issue of land or territory involved here. The notion of diaspora involves a notion of a remembered or promised land (Gilroy, 1993), and frequently an imagined 'homing' sentiment (Brah, 1996). The special position that Jewish communities have as models of thinking more flexibly about the term 'diaspora' (see e.g. Gilroy, 1996), is due to the way it can act as a model for prising open the 'deadly discourse' that couples 'race and space' (Boyarin and Boyarin, 1993: 714):

> Cultures, as well as identities, are constantly being re-made. While this is true of all cultures, diasporic Jewish culture lays it bare because of the impossibility of a natural association between this people and a particular land. (1993: 721)

While gender is indeed a marked or 'special' way of being, it does not have this association or even disassociation with a land. (For although the use of space is certainly gendered, there is not *a* place, or a land, that is mythically or otherwise, 'home' to all women.) It is preferable, therefore, to connect ethnicity and religion and gender on the lines of embodied performativity, watching how modes of mimicry and citation occur in the forms of embodiment that produce effective subjects, but without rushing to assimilate them. It is for this reason perhaps that Butler speaks, in the interview in this collection, of ways of thinking race and gender non-sequentially, in terms of how one may operate as the 'unmarked background' of the other.

Conclusion

Although mimesis as a concept has a history of marking a division between the real and the copy, the work that I have discussed breaks with this sense in order to point to the norms that govern people's modes of subjectification and affiliation. In this article I have argued that there is a way of resituating Butler's work as a feminist inheritance of attempts to theorize anti-Semitism in the post-Second World War period. This is not a straightforward trajectory, since although Sartre's work was clearly important for Butler's intellectual development, these would not be connections that she herself would emphasize, nor maybe even accept as important. Nevertheless, through the concept of mimesis, I have suggested that it is possible and fruitful to rethink Butler's position alongside those who employed the term in ways that are related but that involve crucially different assumptions. What has arisen from such an exercise is the importance of the issue of cultural survival, which throws a certain light on Butler's socio-political vision. Cultural survival is a concept which relates to Butler's retention of a notion of hegemony, such that the interpellation of subjects of which she speaks is not a process that is either natural or foreclosed in any given culture, but is a process which takes on the appearance of being both, because it takes place in a disciplinary context.

The texts considered here illustrate the sense in which mimesis is a concept that has been employed in different ways, such that although I have focused upon the concern to think non-essentialist identities in terms of embodied performativity that is shared by Butler and the recent work of Boyarin and Boyarin, I would also argue that the earlier texts of Adorno and Horkheimer and Sartre indicate the importance of clarifying just how these contemporary uses of the concept are to be related to former issues of the natural and the artificial, to repression and freedom, to authenticity and inauthenticity, as well as to questions of socio-economic context and cultural traditions.

The question of mimesis in this new agenda is significant, therefore, in its reutilization of the question of mimesis in a way that moves the focus away from assumptions of the repressed natural process that underpinned Adorno and Horkheimer's thesis, and towards the complex manoeuvres of continued performances and continued 'tradition', away from judgements of authenticity and towards the reasons why people maintain certain embodied subjectivities. Such a perspective raises the questions of generational relations, of foreclosed possibilities and of affective attachments to identity that reach beyond the Nietzschean sense of a wounded attachment. A focus on the responsibilities and pressures of 'cultural survival' seems fruitful as a guiding concept in this exploration of the connections between identification, affiliation and the power contexts within which mimesis, as a form of repetition or 'citation', occurs.

Notes

This article forms a chapter of my forthcoming book, *We, Feminists: Specific Genealogies in Feminist Thought*, Sage: London.

1. Butler mentions therefore J.L. Austin's *How to do Things with Words*, Derrida's 'Signature, Event, Context' in *Limited, Inc.* and Paul De Man's readings of Nietzsche in *Allegories of Reading*.

2. For Butler's own response to Irigaray, see the discussion in *Bodies that Matter* (1993: 36–55).

3. As there is a history of thinking racism in relation to the concept of mimesis, and which is the backdrop for much of the recent work on mimicry in relation to passing. See for example, Fanon (1986) or Bhabha (1994).

4. Adorno and Horkheimer also give a complex place to women in relation to mimesis, suggesting that gender has a differential relationship to the historical changes they chart in relation to mimesis. On the complexities of women, representation and the representation of women in their schema, see Hewitt (1994). I am aware that I am avoiding a discussion of these complexities because I wish to stress the use of their concept of mimesis in relation to anti-Semitism by way of drawing a continuity and a contrast with Butler's use of mimesis in relation to gender.

5. Sartre writes with the masculine pronoun.

6. Thus they criticize, for example, the work of Jean-Luc Nancy – especially *The Inoperative Community* – because he seems to suggest that since violence that has been done in the name of communities and solidarity, any already existing community is regulated beyond consideration by virtue of its existence to a world we have lost or which never existed.

7. In the *New Left Review* debate, mentioned above, Butler herself has turned attention to this question (1998) where she argues that the regulation of sexuality is central to the functioning of political economy. See also the reply by Nancy Fraser in the same volume.

8. These alternatives have different psychoanalytic implications. In the last the decision can be conscious risk assessment; foreclosure implies something more than repression, a situation where the alternatives could not be brought to consciousness because they do not reside in the psyche; with abjection, there may be the possibility of recovery of the alternative possibility from the unconscious.

9. The quotation referring to punishments for transgressing heterosexual norms continues 'not to mention the transgressive pleasures produced by those very prohibitions' (Butler, 1991: 24).

10. There would be another line of discussion to pursue here, that would take this feminist work on Foucault's concept of disciplinary power back into conversation with Adorno and Horkheimer's (1986) *Dialectic of Enlightenment* in order to pursue the argument there that women are included in the thesis presented there by virtue of their exclusion from philosophical discourse. As argued by Andrew Hewitt, 'women are instrumentalised as the representatives of the possibility of exclusion understood as an escape from the all-inclusive system of power . . . the initial – and damning – exclusion of women from the philosophical project is reworked as a potential exemption from the totality both of power as ontologised domination and of reason as a system of closure' (1994: 147). Hewitt's excellent article explores the

contradictions and potentials of attempting to think the place of women in relation to the argument of *Dialectic of Enlightenment*.

11. And despite the fact that gay communities do attempt to subvert these, using 'inappropriately' gendered pronouns, etc.

12. Except perhaps in the most racist of societies where – it is an empirical question – the possibility of 'moving beyond' is so tightly constricted that one is rendered unintelligible.

13. Note that this sentence concerns moving beyond a racist position, not moving beyond ethnic affiliations. Moving beyond ethnicity may be as difficult as moving beyond gender, and the questions are surely entwined on the personal level.

14. For this reason the idea of 'tradition' that Boyarin and Boyarin use needs to be repeatedly problematized. When 'tradition' in Boyarin and Boyarin is likened to the position of hegemonic norms in Butler, as this discussion implies it must be, it becomes perhaps more clear that any notion of 'tradition' needs always to be related to the mode of remembrance, and the circumstances of its citation and performance, in order to avoid a conservative position that simply sees traditions as that which has been repeated and passed on, and to keep an emphasis on the contingency and complexities of both memory and performance. Very often it is through the lens of present circumstances and situations that the repetition of past traditions is deemed important.

References

Adorno, T. and Horkheimer, M. (1986) *Dialectic of Enlightenment*. London: Verso. (First published 1944.)

Austin, J.L. (1962) *How to do Things With Words*. Cambridge, MA: Harvard University Press.

Bartky, S. (1988) 'Foucault, Feminism and the Modernisation of Patriarchal Power', in I. Diamond and L. Quinby (eds) *Feminism and Foucault: Reflections on Resistance*. Boston, MA: Northeastern University Press.

Bell, V. (forthcoming) *We, Feminists: Specific Genealogies in Feminist Theory*. London: Sage.

Benhabib, S., J. Butler, D. Cornell and N. Fraser (1995) *Feminist Contentions: A Philosophical Exchange*. New York: Routledge.

Benjamin, A. (1997) *Present Hope: Philosophy, Architecture, Judaism*. London: Routledge.

Bhabha, H. (1994) *The Location of Culture*. London: Routledge.

Boyarin, D. and Boyarin, J. (1993) 'Diaspora: Generation and the Ground of Jewish Identity', *Critical Inquiry* 19 (summer): 693–725.

Boyarin, J. (1995) 'Before the Law, There Stands a Woman: in *Re Taylor v. Butler* (with Court-Appointed Yiddish Translator)', *Cardozo Law Review* 16: 1303–23.

Boyarin, J. (1996) *Thinking in Jewish*. Chicago: University of Chicago Press.

Boyarin, J. and Boyarin, D. (1995) 'Self-Exposure as Theory: The Double Mark of the Male Jew', in D. Battaglia (ed.) *Rhetorics of Self-Making*. Berkeley and Los Angeles: University of California Press.

Brah, A. (1996) *Cartographies of Diaspora: Contesting Identities*. London: Routledge.

Butler, J. (1990) *Gender Trouble: Feminism and the Subversion of Identity*. New York: Routledge.

Butler, J. (1991) 'Imitation and Gender Insubordination', in D. Fuss (ed.) *Inside/Out: Lesbian and Gay Theories*. New York: Routledge.

Butler, J. (1993) *Bodies that Matter: On the Discursive Limits of 'Sex'*. New York: Routledge.

Butler, J. (1997a) *Excitable Speech*. New York: Routledge.

Butler, J. (1997b) *The Psychic Life of Power: Theories in Subjection*. Stanford, CA: Stanford University Press.

Butler, J. (1998) 'Merely Cultural', *New Left Review* Jan/Feb: 33–45.

De Beauvoir, S. (1993) *The Second Sex*. London: Everyman. (First published 1949.)

De Man, P. (1986) *Allegories of Reading*. New Haven, CT: Yale University Press.

Derrida, J. (1988) *Limited, Inc.*, trans. S. Weber and J. Mehlman. Evanston, IL: Northwestern University Press.

Fanon, F. (1986) *Black Skin, White Masks*. London: Pluto Press. (First published 1952.)

Felski, R. (1997) 'The Doxa of Difference', *Signs* 23: 1–21.

Foucault, M. (1981) *The History of Sexuality, Volume One*. Harmondsworth: Penguin.

Fraser, N. (1988) 'Heterosexism, Misrecognition and Capitalism: A Response to Judith Butler', *New Left Review* March/April: 51–61.

Gilroy, P. (1993) *The Black Atlantic: Modernity and Double Consciousness*. London: Verso.

Gilroy, P. (1996) 'Diaspora Crossings: Intercultural and Transnational Identities in the Black Atlantic', in A. Alund and R. Granqvist (eds) *Negotiating Identities*. Copenhagen: Studia Imago Logica.

Girard, R. (1978) 'Interview', *Diacritics* March: 31–54.

Hewitt, A. (1994) 'A Feminine Dialectic of Enlightenment? Horkheimer and Adorno Revisited', *New German Critique* 28: 143–70.

Irigaray, L. (1985) *This Sex Which is not One*, trans. C. Porter with C. Burke. Ithaca, NY: Cornell University Press.

Levinas, E. (1988) 'Useless Suffering', in L. Bernasconi and D. Wood (eds) *The Provo-cation of Levinas*. London: Routledge.

Nancy, J.-L. (1991) *The Inoperative Community*. Minneapolis: University of Minnesota Press.

Sartre, J.-P. (1965) *Anti-Semite and Jew*. New York: Schocken. (First published 1946.)

Vikki Bell is a lecturer in the Department of Sociology at Goldsmiths College, University of London. She is the author of *Interrogating Incest: Feminism, Foucault and the Law* (Routledge, 1993) and of *'We Feminists': Genealogies in Feminist Theory* (Sage, forthcoming 1999), as well as several articles on the thought of Michel Foucault, feminism and theories of difference.

On Speech, Race and Melancholia

An Interview with Judith Butler

Vikki Bell

JUDITH BUTLER'S work has been extremely influential in feminist theory and philosophy, and its influence is also beginning to be felt more widely within cultural studies. In this interview, I wanted to ask Judith Butler about her most recent work, especially *Excitable Speech* (1997) which had just been published at the time of the interview, in terms of how it represents a continuation of certain themes and how it represents moves into new terrains of debate. In particular, I wanted to give her the opportunity to address both possible critiques of her work, especially around the issue of the possibility of political visions and the attention to speech when theorizing subjectification, and, with an eye to the interview's incorporation in this *TCS* issue, to introduce some of the tensions that are of interest in this context. That is, just what is the possibility of using the same analytical framework to talk both about racializing and gendering processes? How useful is the concept of melan-cholia? How are textuality and visuality interconnected?

VB: I was interested to find out what was behind the move you make in *Excitable Speech* to the work of Austin – in combination with Althusser – in the first essay [of the book]: was that motivated by a need to answer some of the theoretical questions you were left with after using Foucault and Lacan more predominantly in the past? Or was it a response to the contemporary field of legal decisions that you are looking at explicitly [in the book]?

■ *Theory, Culture & Society* 1999 (SAGE, London, Thousand Oaks and New Delhi), Vol. 16(2): 163–174
[0263-2764(199904)16:2;163–174;008260]

JB: Well, I think that there were two problems. One is that I had made a set of fairly strong claims in both *Gender Trouble* and *Bodies that Matter* that the subject is constituted in discourse, and I received several criticisms and queries about that: what does it mean to be constituted as the subject only by discourse? What is the mechanism of that constitution? What do we mean when we say constitution? So I think *Bodies that Matter* sought to understand constitution through the notion of materialization. But then I was in a bit of a bind because I felt that the predominant Foucauldian frame that I had been using didn't give me a precise enough account of what it meant for a subject to be constituted in discourse given that a subject is only partially constituted, or is sometimes constituted in ways that can't quite be anticipated: how do I talk about the failure of subject constitution? How do I talk about its tenuousness or vulnerability? How do I talk about its unpredictability? People also wanted concrete instances – for me to give an example of what it meant – so it seemed to me that although the Althusserian frame relies upon this verbal address, this being hailed by another, at least it produces the possibility of a subject not answering, of a subject being constituted along certain kinds of fault lines. Althusser's work gave me a scene, as it were, with which to start to ask the question: what does it mean to appropriate the terms by which one is hailed or the discourse in which one is constituted? And sometimes in Foucault it just seems too unilateral. In *Discipline and Punish*, perhaps one of the places where the theory of subject constitution is too unilateral, it's clearly too unnuanced. It's as if the prisoner is simply made, it's as if somehow the prisoner is constituted almost mechanistically. The central chapters there about the body strike me as problematic because they can't accommodate a theory of the psyche, and they can't accommodate the vulnerability or the unpredictability of subject constitution. There's not enough give in *Discipline and Punish*. So I suppose that's why I was recalled to the Althusserian scene, so that I might meditate a bit about when and where the discourse through which one is constituted fails to hit its mark.

VB: There's a tension it seems to me in using Austin next to Althusser, given the different domains in which they were thinking. What happens, for example, to the Marxism of Althusser when you pull him on to the domain of Austin?

JB: I think that the only reason that Austin is interesting is that he gives us this distinction between the illocutionary and the perlocutionary. And he gives us a fantasy. He charts, without knowing it, a fantasy of sovereign power in speech. Mine is not a loyal use of Austin. I suppose the use of Austin became important because you know it is a theory of the performative, and this is a word that I've been using all along without quite dealing with him, which has already been somewhat scandalous. I think in *Gender Trouble* I actually took it from Derrida's essay on Kafka, 'Before the Law' which had Austin as its background but which I didn't bother to pursue. But more importantly, speech act theory has been used by a number of feminist scholars in the pornography and hate speech debates. I'd say that contemporary legal scholars in the US are very preoccupied with Austin, not just MacKinnon but the philosopher from Australia, Ray Langton, Frederick Schauer at Harvard and other First Amendment scholars are suddenly extremely interested in this. But they think that the speech act is something performed by a subject, performed on another subject, or part of an address that one subject makes to another. My interest is in the Althusserian problem of how, one might say, a speech act brings a subject into being, and then how that very subject comes to speak, reiterating the discursive conditions of its own emergence. So it seems to me that hate speech has to be located in both this first and second dimension. But the real task is to figure out how a subject who is constituted in and by discourse then recites that very same discourse but perhaps to another purpose. For me that's always been the question of how to find agency, the moment of that recitation or that replay of discourse that is the condition of one's own emergence. So I think I need Althusser and Austin. I think Althusser gives me interpellation, the discursive act by which subjects are constituted, and Austin gives me a way of understanding the speech acts of that subject.

VB: *Excitable Speech* is much more about the questions of speech act and sovereignty, as opposed to questions of discourse and genealogy. But there are some points in *Excitable Speech* in which those questions are raised again. I wanted to ask you in this context about a phrase that seems to be a favourite of yours, that comes up in *Bodies that Matter* and *Excitable Speech*, and it's this phrase from Foucault which is 'Discourse is not life, its time is not yours.' I wanted to ask about that phrase because it seems to pose a question which is about the responsibility of the speaker in terms of inheritance and citation, but also to have a sense of the future about it, in the sense that the way in which you contribute to a discourse might not be the way that you intend to, or that it might be used differently in the future. Could you say a bit about that phrase and what work you think it does for you? How does it fit into your vision? I'm pushing you toward an idea of some sort of politics of speech.

JB: I might need you to say more, but I'll just say this as a way of opening the discussion: I think there has been a somewhat sceptical response to Foucault and the question of discourse and agency in which people say that the life of the subject is simply discourse or that everything can be reduced to discourse, or reduced to what the subject says – a kind of collapse of discourse and enunciation – which is problematic. Maybe there is also a sort of logocentric idea to the effect that the subject comes into being through its speech and *is* only its speech in that quasi-Aristotelian way. What I find really interesting is that the subject in speech is always both more than itself and less than itself in any given speech act, that what it speaks is not simply its own speech but it speaks a life of discourse and it is installed, as it were, in a life of discourse that exceeds the subject's own temporality. This isn't the romantic idea that I speak and my words exceed me and immortalize me, or I write and my words exceed me and immortalize me through time, it's not so much that. It's actually about being, as it were, always already lost to or always already expropriated by a past of discourse that I do not control, and a future of discourse that I do not control; that the time of discourse exceeds the time of my life doesn't memorialize my agency. It's actually a certain principle of humility and a certain principle of historicity, of being installed in a historicity that is not my own, but which is the condition of my own. In that sense it's a historicity that exposes the limits of my autonomy but which I would also say is the condition of my autonomy, oddly enough. But a politics, you want me to move to the politics . . . [police car siren sounds] . . . there's politics . . . a state of emergency! . . . I want to say that there's a different notion of responsibility. I think in the US we go around trying to target people who say racist things, and indeed there are good reasons to do that, targeting people who say homophobic things, holding them responsible for their speech. I think there are all kinds of reasons to stop a person when they speak such things and say, for example, 'look, that's a racist act'. I think that's important. But I think a politics that begins and ends with that policing function is a mistake, because for me the question is how is that person, as it were, renewing and reinvigorating racist rituals of speech, and how do we think about those particular rituals and how do we exploit their ritual function in order to undermine it in a more thorough-going way, rather than just stopping it as it's spoken. What would it mean to restage it, take it, do something else with the ritual so that its revivability as a speech act is really seriously called into question.

VB: You say at one point that the question is how the repetition of an injurious statement or calling will occur and when, and you say that is the pain and the promise. That's the politics then, this opening up of the possibility [of repeating differently] – not the possibility of not repeating, but the possibilities concerning where and how. It seems to me that people are going to press you on the same issue of politics that they pressed you on around *Gender Trouble* – they want to know . . .

JB: . . . more concretely . . . like five suggestions on how to proceed.

VB: Is that a moment that you feel you should refuse, in the way that Foucault did?

JB: I don't know if I should refuse it, I think what's really funny – and this probably seems really odd considering the level of abstraction at which I work – is that I actually believe that politics has a character of contingency and context to it that cannot be predicted at the level of theory. And that when theory starts becoming programmatic, such as 'here are my five prescriptions', and I set up my typology, and my final chapter is called

'What is to be Done?', it pre-empts the whole problem of context and contingency, and I do think that political decisions are made in that lived moment and they can't be predicted from the level of theory – they can be sketched, they can be schematized, they can be prepared for, but I suppose I'm with Foucault on this. I'm willing to withstand the same criticisms he withstood. It seems like a noble tradition.

VB: You talk at some point about 'vain utopias', and yet you also talk about an alternative vision of democracy, or you suggest that you are coming from a broadly speaking democratic position. It seems that 'vain utopias' are linked in some way with identity politics. One of Foucault's favourite poets René Char once asked 'how can we live without the unknown in front of us?' [suggesting] that we need that sense of the contingency that you are talking about in order to go on. But there are certain things that you think are misguided around the question of identity politics, around setting up utopias?

JB: I can't remember where I talk about 'vain utopias', I can't remember what my reference is.

VB: It's mentioned in *Excitable Speech* I think. I was just thinking about Wendy Brown's work, where she talks about *ressentiment* [and feminist argumentation and politics]. Is there a chiming that's, unsurprisingly, going on there?

JB: Probably. She introduced me once at a talk as an ironic utopian.

VB: And you like that?

JB: Evidently. It was obviously an interpellation that worked! I recognized myself in it.

I do think that one cannot work with political theory without a sense of the unforseeable, without anticipating a break within the present regime that cannot be known in the present. I'm always searching for such breaks. I also think that what appears as a radical rupture usually turns out to have within it a trace of the past. That produces a certain irony in the end.

VB: OK. Can I move to a slightly different way in, and ask about issues around racialization, because your work seems to be increasingly to incorporate issues of racialization and racism since *Bodies that Matter*. Could you say something about the processes of subjectification that you term 'girling' and ... I don't know if you use the term racialization but you mention Kendal Thomas's work on being 'raced'? You want to distance yourself from the idea of 'double oppression' and that way of thinking about racism and sexism as structures that confer oppression. How then do you see those processes interacting or working together?

JB: I think that I'm less interested in theories of intersectionality, or in versions of multiculturalism that try to keep processes of gendering and racing radically distinct. I'm much more interested in how one becomes the condition of the other, or how one becomes the unmarked background for the action of the other so that, for instance, in the Anita Hill event, it became very interesting how the various analyses could either focus on the gendered aspects or focus on the racialized aspects of that public spectacle, but they could not quite see, most of them, how they worked together. There were a couple of pieces in that Toni Morrison (1993) volume on Clarence Thomas and Anita Hill that I felt did do that, and Morrison herself I think gestures towards it at the beginning. For me, it's not so much a double consciousness – gender and race as the two axes, as if they're determined only in relation to one another, I think that's a mistake – but I think the unmarked character of the one very often becomes the condition of the articulation of the other. Then the question is how to sustain an analysis that is able to shift perspectives sequentially in such a way that no one reading is actually adequate without the other. I'm not sure that what I want is a synthetic reading. I think what I want is a set of sequential readings that expose the partiality of each constitutive reading. So I like Kendall Thomas's work quite a bit. I think that it is the most rhetorically and philosophically interesting work in the legal theory of racialization that I know. His idea of what it is to be 'raced' is very much about the accumulation of speech acts. Speech acts don't always have to be explicit, verbal statements – it's not that one becomes raced as it were by being addressed explicitly. There are all sorts of implicit modes of address that structure institutions. I think what I don't like are structural accounts of racialization that refuse to understand the temporality of the structure, the fact that the structure must be reiterated again and again, and that it has a kind of ritual dimension and that its very temporal dimension is the condition of its subversion. I mean I suppose I've always thought that – it remains true of *Gender Trouble* and it remains true of this contemporary work. What is poststructural in my work is the fact that I want those subjectivating norms to be temporalized and open rather than fixed and determinate. I'm also wary of theories that seek to compartmentalize gender over here and race over here, and I'm wary of those that seek to synthesize them absolutely or set up analogies between them as if they are isomorphic in relation to one another. I think there is some interarticulation, which seems much more promising to me – what that means is that the theoretical means of describing that is going to have a narrative form and it's going to be sequential and it's not going to give or explain everything at once. I'm not sure I can do better than that right now.

VB: On the question of narrative that you raise there, I was thinking about the piece that you wrote about Rodney King and the LA riots, because there you are more focused on the use of the visual evidence and the politics of seeing. I was wondering whether you see a tension between the idea of the narrative, and the dominance of the idea of the text, in thinking through processes of subjectification [on the one hand], and the politics of visuality [on the other]? Do you agree that there is a tension given that the stuff about masquerade and mimicry is very much about the way in which people are categorized and placed visually, and then this work is more about the categorization through speech: can both senses or both forms be theorized through a similar theoretical frame?

JB: I think I'm actually trying to struggle free of a narrow version of textualism, quite frankly. I think for me the very fact that I am emphasizing speech in *Excitable Speech* is something that some of the more strictly Derridean friends of mine would be wary of, given the way in which speech is supposed to be secondary to writing so for me it's not as if there is some primary textuality of writing that I then find in the visual or verbal field. Obviously I take a lot from him and especially the theory of iterability. On the other hand I do think that there is a performativity to the gaze that is not simply the transposition of a textual model on to a visual one; that when we see Rodney King, when we see that video we are also reading and we are also constituting, and that the reading is a certain conjuring and a certain construction. How do we describe that? It seems to me that that is a modality of perfomativity, that it is racialization, that the kind of visual reading practice that goes into the viewing of the video is part of what I would mean by racialization, and part of what I would understand as the performativity of what it is 'to *race* something' or to be 'raced' by it. So I suppose that I'm interested in the modalities of performativity that take it out of its purely textualist context.

VB: Coming back to processes of subjectivization, I wanted to ask you what happened to the use of the analogy of melancholia that you use at the end of *Gender Trouble* to talk about how the melancholic structure of heterosexuality encrypts the homosexual. Is that an analogy that could be used in the field of 'race' as well?

JB: Absolutely. In fact I have several students who are working on melancholia and 'race'. Let me say two things. One, I have another book recently published with Stanford University Press called *The Psychic Life of Power* which has an extended discussion of melancholia and gender and sexuality, so I take that up there. It's an effort in a way to reconcile the Foucauldian perspective with the theory of the psyche which does involve this whole analysis. Second, I think that there is all kinds of interesting work to be done on melancholia and 'race' and in particular with the place of 'race' within diasporic culture in which as it were the origins of racialization are foreclosed – [there is] the impossibility of return to any pure notion of race, the impossibility of an historical return to the origins of racialization in say the US and slavery or in emigrations from Africa or the Afro-Caribbean, that kind of impossibility of return and yet a mindfulness of history and a desire for history that's never quite satisfiable. So to the extent that the history of race is linked to a history of diasporic displacement it seems to me that melancholia is there, that there is, as it were, inscribed in 'race' a lost and ungrievable origin, one might say, an impossibility of return, but also an impossibility of an essence. I think also that the history of miscegenation involves a history of melancholia in an interesting way, that to the extent that cross-racial sexual relations have been foreclosed – and I use that word specifically, i.e. not just prohibited but foreclosed – in the sense of unthinkable. Those forms of desire become ungrievable within available public discourse. There are certain kinds of love that are held not to be love, loss that is held not to be loss, that remain within this kind of unthinkable domain or in a kind of ontologically shadowy domain; it's not real, it's not real love, it's not real loss. So I think that can be linked with some of the work I've done on the unthinkability and the ungrievability of homosexual attachment.

VB: But it's a melancholia that's discursively given, as opposed to a more classical Freudian sense of melancholia?

JB: Yes, I suppose so. It's a love foreclosed by discourse.

VB: Is it an analogy or is it a 'real' melancholia?

JB: I think that there are cultural forms, culturally instituted forms of melancholia. I suppose by that I would also mean discursively in the broad sense of discourse. It's not a question of this ego not being able to love that person – it's not that model – it's rather what it means to have one's desire formed as it were through cultural norms that dictate in part what will and will not be a loveable object, what will and will not be a legitimate form of love. To the extent that there are racial foreclosures on the production of the field of love, I think that there is a culturally instituted melancholia because what that would mean is that there is a class of persons whom I could never love or for whom it would be unthinkable for me to love, and they are constituted essentially as the unthinkable, the unloveable, the ungrievable, and that then institutes a form of melancholia which is culturally pervasive, a strange ungrievability.

I also think that there is a lot of interesting work in the US on the problem of slavery and memory, and contemporary US scholars like Saidiya Hartman (1997) has written about what it means to try and grieve the losses of slavery. She actually tells the story of travelling to Africa, going back to the sites of slave trade under the sponsorship of US corporate travel plans for African Americans who want to find their roots – MacDonald's corporations sponsoring African Americans to go back to Libya to see exactly where the slave boats were launched from, to try and relive and re-experience that trauma, which of course is a money-making enterprise for these corporations and which produces the following situation. She returns to these sites in order ostensibly to re-enact or re-live that trauma, only to find herself interpellated into a commodity system – here are the tokens, the fetishism, the slave trade, buy them! Buy them, African American middle class of the United States, and help this capitalist enterprise! So she gets interpellated by capital at the very moment in which she returns to re-experience this loss, and it turns out that this loss actually cannot be found because it's a loss that is also covered over precisely through the commodity structure. So what she ends up confronting is the loss of the loss, in Hegel's sense, the impossibility of grieving a loss which is not only figured by this commodity system but covered over once again by it. So it becomes an impossible referent, it becomes an impossible object of grief. That strikes me as a highly melancholic situation. It's an ungrievable loss.

There's Deborah McDowell also in the US who has done some work on melancholia and race, talking about what it means to have repeated, endless images of black men who are murdered on the streets of urban US cities in the newspaper all the time. There is this numbing effect every time she gets the *Washington Post* in which there's this picture of another young black man who has died on the streets of Washington D.C. and his weeping mother. This has almost become an iconography of US journalism. She says that the way in which these deaths become figured is that all of these black men become interchangeable with one another, that there are infinite numbers of them, and that it's a scene that's produced again and again, that these lives are nameless and interchangeable with one another and 'lost' again in and through the journalistic representation. Then there's this figure of the grieving mother. But the question is is there any end to that grieving? Is there any possibility of a grieving that would actually work through that loss? Or is it the case that the sheer numbers and the sheer repetitive force of this iconography is such that there's no possibility of a completed grief, that it's actually an infinitely extended grief, which makes it into a candidate for melancholia. Her argument is that the public discourse that gives us these lives and gives it to us through that iconography institutes a kind of melancholia for the black community which can't be overcome. It makes melancholia into as it were a kind of constitutive condition of urban black culture. There's a kind of grieving that is limitless and without end.

VB: I wonder if I can use that to connect back with what you have argued about AIDS in your contribution – 'Sexual Inversions' – in the Hekman book, because it seems that you are arguing that AIDS has brought death into the deployment of sexuality in a way that Foucault didn't envisage, and that he depicted an older form of power which figured the link between sex and death as archaic, so it is constantly reiterated that there was an older form of power, that it *used* to be that sex and death were connected, but that now we are governed through a bio-political form which takes life as its object. It seemed to me that you were arguing that AIDS has brought death into the deployment of sexuality such that sex can be seen as an agent in itself, as causative, so that we might want to update Foucault's project in the first volume of *The History of Sexuality* to bring it forward in some way.

Would it be right to see you as involved in some ways in an updating of that project?

JB: Yes, but I think that Foucault probably updated himself. The shift between the first and second volumes is an under-read shift, and very often it is lamented, and readers think that the exuberance of the first volume is lost in what follows. But I actually think that what follows is very interesting, because the self-care emphasis is in a way an allegory for surviving with AIDS. It think it is much more self-consciously within the culture of AIDS, a project that resonates with what it means to cultivate life against death. I think there is an awareness of finitude and mortality in the subsequent volumes. I think in 'Sexual Inversions', what I found particularly ironic was that Foucault made this sort of blanket claim that plagues were over, and probably in the very moment in which he wrote that sentence he was HIV positive. It strikes me that he was not only blind to AIDS, as he would have had to have been in the late 1970s, but he was also clearly blind to plagues that are outside the purview of a narrow European perspective. It seems to me that he was really in the grips of a fantasy that somehow disease was fully controlled, that we'd somehow mastered the problem of mass scale dying that is the result of epidemics, and that we had now turned to more subtle forms of the culture and maintenance of human life forms. I think he was just wrong. My interest in AIDS, though, I think links up to this problem of melancholia in a different way. I think perhaps I mentioned it in that article (1996), but in the US there's been a series of these quasi-psychological articles in newspapers about gay men, in particular, who suffer from depression not because they have the virus but because they don't. It gets termed 'sur-vivor's guilt' and my sense is that the so-called depression actually has everything to do with living in a culture in which gay relationships don't get legitimated as real relationships, and hence when they dissolve, or when a partner dies, the loss isn't really legitimated as legitimate loss – hospitals don't release the body to the lover, courts don't accept the status of the partner, families do or do not convene to grieve the loss, places of employment struggle to accept whether this is equal to a spousal death, whether bereavement policies apply on airplanes, etc. – so I think there is a kind of cultural institution of denial on this issue that raises the question of whether this is a grievable loss.

VB: So the narratives are a form of this 'forced narrative' that you talk about, the narratives of these surviving men?

JB: Well I think that the question is whether one can survive without the possibility of grief – I think grief needs its public rituals. If there's a public foreclosure of the possibility of grief and the recognition of loss, then it's not that an individual fails to grieve, it's that there's a public foreclosure of the possibility of grief, instituting melancholia throughout that culture, and that is part of this depression that the newspapers are trying to psychologize.

VB: It would be interesting to see if you see a difference in Britain, the way that AIDS is debated in our public sphere. Yesterday in the *Guardian* there was a headline 'AIDS: No longer a death sentence?' as if there's an attempt to bring AIDS back into the realm of the administration of life, or, rather, to remove the association with death.

JB: Yes, and it's so quick. This happens in the US too. The very fact that there are protease inhibitors that prolong life for some, and only for those who have extraordinary amounts of money is quickly taken up as a sign that AIDS is no longer fatal, and that it's not linked with death any more. It's really been astonishing, how quickly and manically that conclusion has been drawn, and it's why people like Larry Kramer, for all of his excess, are really important because they just continue to disrupt that public mode of denial. I think that kind of interruption, that interruption of denial, that interruption of a kind of hallucinatory ease about all of this is crucial.

Interview conducted on 13 May 1997.

References

Butler, J. (1990) *Gender Trouble: Feminism and the Subversion of Identity*. New York: Routledge.

Butler, J. (1993) *Bodies that Matter: On the Discursive Limits of 'Sex'*. New York: Routledge.

Butler, J. (1996) 'Sexual Inversions', in S. Hekman (ed.) *Feminist Interpretations of Michel Foucault*. University Park: Pennsylvania State University Press.

Butler, J. (1997a) *Excitable Speech*. New York: Routledge.

Butler, J. (1997b) *The Psychic Life of Power: Theories in Subjection*. Stanford, CA: Stanford University Press.

Foucault, M. (1979) *Discipline and Punish*, trans. A.M. Sheridan. London: Penguin.

Foucault, M. (1981) *The History of Sexuality Volume 1: An Introduction*, trans. R. Hurley. Harmondsworth: Penguin.

Hartman, S. (1997) *Scenes of Subjection*. Oxford: Oxford University Press.

Morrison, T. (ed.) (1993) *Race-ing Justice, En-gendering Power: Essays on Anita Hill, Clarence Thomas and the Construction of Social Reality*. London: Chatto and Windus.

Judith Butler is a Professor in the Department of Rhetoric, University of California at Berkeley. She is the author of *Subjects of Desire* (Columbia University Press, 1987), *Gender Trouble* (Routledge, 1990), *Bodies that Matter* (Routledge, 1993), *The Psychic Life of Power* (Stanford University Press, 1997), *Excitable Speech* (Routledge, 1997), as well as numerous articles and contributions on philosophy, feminist and queer theory.

Vikki Bell is a lecturer in the Department of Sociology at Goldsmiths College, University of London. She is the author of *Interrogating Incest: Feminism, Foucault and the Law* (Routledge, 1993) and of *'We Feminists': Genealogies in Feminist Theory* (Sage, forthcoming 1999), as well as several articles on the thought of Michel Foucault, feminism and theories of difference.

Subject, Psyche and Agency
The Work of Judith Butler

Lois McNay

Introduction

THERE ARE perhaps three predominant theoretical trends in feminist thought on gender and sexuality: post-Lacanian psychoanalytic theory, theories of intersubjective communication derived from Habermas and post-Foucauldian theories of discursive construction. Within the Foucauldian tradition, it is the work of Judith Butler on the performative construction of gender that has had the most influential impact upon feminist understandings of gender identity, furthermore her work has also done much to bridge the over-polemicized gap between the psychoanalytic and constructivist perspectives.

In this article I consider two themes in Butler's work: the dialectic of subject formation, namely that the autonomous subject is instituted through constraint, and the question of the relation between the psyche and the social. Both these themes are given considerable attention in Butler's two recent works, *Excitable Speech* (1997a) and *The Psychic Life of Power* (1997b) which are the focus of this article. I argue that, perhaps more than any other feminist theorist, she has systematically elaborated a way of understanding gender identity as deeply entrenched but not immutable and has thereby pushed feminist theory beyond the polarities of the essentialist debate. At the same time, her thought has also dislodged attendant antitheses, notably those of determinism versus voluntarism and psyche versus the social. With regard to the former, the introduction of a notion of historicity into a conception of the symbolic yields a concept of agency that does much to unpack Foucault's rather elliptical remarks on how power breeds its own resistance. With regard to the second opposition, Butler manages to introduce the destabilizing force of the category of the

■ *Theory, Culture & Society* 1999 (SAGE, London, Thousand Oaks and New Delhi),
Vol. 16(2): 175–193
[0263-2764(199904)16:2;175–193;008764]

unconscious into the functionalist accounts of identity in which a constructivist perspective often results. However, by reconfiguring the psyche as an effect of the interiorization of social norms, she also manages to avoid the tendency towards ahistoricism that hampers psychoanalysis in order to maintain a sense of the social specificity of modalities of desire and gender.

It is difficult to overestimate the extent to which Butler's compelling reformulation of these theoretical impasses has succeeded in pushing feminist thought on gender identity on to new conceptual terrain. Nonetheless, I also draw attention to certain limitations with the theory of the performative which loosely revolve around placing what is an overwhelmingly symbolic account of identity formation in the context of the social and political relations that traverse it. I argue that the concept of agency that underlies Butler's notion of a politics of the performative remains abstract and lacking in social specificity. The idea of the performative provides a compelling account of the open temporality of structure that permits the emergence of autonomous action, but it does not really consider how this symbolic indeterminacy relates to other social structures and how it may catalyse or hinder change. There is no doubt that Butler's sociocentric reworking of the interconnection between psyche and social provides a nuanced account of gender identity, but it tends to result in a negative model of action as the displacement of constraining social norms. It is also important for a conception of agency to include an account of the creative dimensions of action where actors actively appropriate conflicting sociocultural values to institute new collective forms of identity. An understanding of the creative dimensions of action is important for an analysis of how a performative politics, based on the reshaping of gender and sexuality, is to transcend the private sphere in order to have a transformatory impact on collective values and identity norms.

The points to which I draw attention are often implied in Butler's account of the performative but not fully developed. My criticisms, therefore, are intended to be complementary to her thought and hopefully to continue thinking through, from a social theoretical perspective, the issues of stability and change within gender identity which her stimulating and bold thought has done so much to initiate.

Agency and the Performative

Butler's notion of the performative represents an attempt to get beyond an understanding of gender identity as a one-sided process of imposition or determination, without lapsing into a voluntarist model of the subject. Rather than thinking of gender as a quasi-permanent structure, it should be thought of as the *temporalized regulation* of socio-symbolic norms and practices where the idea of the performative expresses both the cultural arbitrariness or 'performed' nature of gender identity and also its deep inculcation in that every performance serves to reinscribe it upon the body. Performativity does not refer to a voluntarist process of performance so much as a 'forced reiteration of norms' in the sense of a compulsory and constraining heterosexuality that impels and sustains gender identity (Butler, 1993: 94). Although constraint is the condition of possibility of sexuality, this does not mean that the cultural imperative of heterosexual norms is inexorable. Change arises from the constitutive instability of the symbolic and discursive structures which invest the body with meaning. The cultural necessity for a performative reiteration of these symbolic norms highlights the extent to which they are not natural or inevitable and are, therefore, potentially open to change.

By emphasizing the historicity of structure, the concept of the performative highlights how constraint is constitutive but not fully determining of gender subjectivity, in other words, a theory of agency is outlined. Central to the idea of performative agency is an understanding of temporality not as a series of discrete, punctuated moments, but rather as a process of *materialization* in which the constraints of social structures are reproduced and partially transcended in the practices of agents: 'construction . . . is itself a temporal process which operates through the reiteration of norms; sex is both produced and destabilized in the course of this reiteration (1993: 10). Embodied gender identity, then, has a similar 'double historicity' (Bourdieu, 1992: 139). It is a sedimented effect of reiterative or ritualized practices; the repeated inscription of the symbolic norms of heterosexuality upon the body and the living through of those norms permits the emergence of a stable bodily ego (Butler, 1993: 14). The performative construction of gender identity is simultaneously constitutive of agency in that the identificatory processes through which norms are materialized enable the formation of a subject who is capable of resisting those norms. This process of resistance takes place at the boundaries of the corporeal norm, in the domains of 'excluded and delegitimated' sex (1993: 16). The partial and conflictual identifications made by those who are excluded from a heterosexual regime can result in a destabilizing process of *resignification* in which symbolic norms are subversively used to articulate homosexual identities evident, for example, in queer practices.

Butler's account of agency relies on Foucault's idea of 'subjectivation' which denotes the dialectical aspect of identity formation, that 'the subject is constituted through practices of subjection, or, in a more autonomous way, through practices of liberation, of liberty' (Foucault, 1988: 50). Despite this insight, Butler, along with others, notes that Foucault himself does not elaborate sufficiently on the specific mechanisms whereby the subject may be formed in submission but is not reducible to it (Butler, 1997b: 2). Indeed, it could be argued that, despite the dialectical idea of subjectivation, Foucault does not succeed in integrating systematically the two moments of submission and autonomy and this is illustrated in the oscillation of his thought between the determinism of the work on discipline and the voluntarism of the final work on ethics of the self (McNay, 1999). Butler's work represents a sustained attempt to overcome this aporia and its success is evident in the huge influence it has had on other areas of study. Yet, there is a sense in which the idea of the performative appears to replicate a weakness of Foucault's model, namely, that it provides an etiolated and rather formal account of agency which lacks a hermeneutic dimension; it is, as Fraser puts it 'deeply antihumanist' (Fraser, 1995: 67).[1] Butler's explanation of the indeterminacy of the symbolic process of materialization provides an abstract account of the structural conditions that give rise to agency, but it lacks a description of how the performative aspects of gender identity are lived by individuals in relation to the web of social practices in which they are enmeshed. In short, insofar as it appears to be primarily a capacity of symbolic structures rather than of individuals, Butler's idea of agency lacks social and historical specificity.[2]

An implication of this abstract account of subject formation is that an analysis of the political dimensions of agency – the capacity of individuals to engender change within the socio-cultural order – is not fully explored. On the whole, there is a tendency in Butler's work to confine discussion of the politics of the performative to a series of dualisms – signification versus resignification, norm versus abjection – which are far from adequate in capturing the complex dynamics of social change and how this impacts on identity formation. Thinkers including Selya Benhabib and Nancy Fraser have accused Butler of reducing gender politics to the relatively narrow arena of issues associated with the linguistic representation of sexuality (e.g. Benhabib, 1995; Fraser, 1995). In the next section, however, I examine how, in her most recent work, Butler takes on this problem of the conflation of the political with the symbolic through a re-elaboration of the notion of the performative in terms of speech-act theory. By demonstrating the mutual inherence but irreducibility of the realms of speech and conduct to each other, Butler offers a more precise formulation of her conception of the political efficacy of the performative and how it relates to institutionalized forms of political intervention.

Excitable Speech

Excitable Speech addresses the problem of the lack of socio-historical specificity in the idea of the performative by insisting on the importance of the distinction between the symbolic and practice – 'speech and conduct' – in order not to conflate the existence of hegemonic norms with the ways in which they may be taken up and modified in the practices of social actors. *Excitable Speech* offers a dazzling reworking of the notion of the performative in terms of speech-act theory and is based around the central thesis that speech is always, to some degree, out of control rendering it susceptible to processes of unauthorized appropriation and, hence, resignification. Recognition of this instability – the *excitability* of discourse – frees speech from the all-encompassing intentionality of the putative sovereign subject. A space is thereby opened for an alternative conception of agency in terms of a counter-discourse that acknowledges its emergence from and dependency upon structures of constraint: 'agency begins where sovereignty wanes. The one who acts ... acts precisely to the extent that he or she is constituted as an actor and, hence, operating within a linguistic field of enabling constraints from the outset' (1997a: 16).

This concept of agency underscores the indeterminacy inherent in even the most violent and oppressive forms of discourse or hate speech and is sustained through the distinction between illocutionary and perlocutionary performatives. The former are speech acts that enact what they are saying in the moment of saying whereas, in the latter, certain effects follow from, rather than being synchronous with the act of speech. Following Derrida's critique of Austin, Butler demonstrates the incoherence of understanding the illocutionary act as that which executes its deed at the moment of utterance by arguing that its performative power relies on forms of ceremonial, ritual and convention whose necessarily prior status undoes the idea of the single, self-contained moment of performance. The instantaneity of effect is undone by the existence of structures that pre-date and outlast the performative: 'The "moment" in ritual is a condensed historicity: it exceeds itself in past and future directions, an effect of prior and future invocations that constitute and escape the instance of utterance' (1997a: 3). In Butler's view, Austin's understanding of illocutionary force rests on an untenable conflation of utterance with effect or speech with conduct. Although it has corporeal effects, the injury of speech cannot be as immediate as that of physical assault, rather it operates through a process of temporal deferral where its repeated effects bring into being or materialize derogated subject positions. Interpellation of the subject is not an instantaneous act of subjection, but involves a process of cultural reiteration which engenders a somatic circuit of recognition. The process of temporal deferral where the original conditions of utterance cannot be indefinitely sustained points also to the possibility of the intentionality of the utterance going awry and producing unintended effects of subversion and counter-discourse. The open temporality of speech results in a dissemination of effects beyond the control of the speaking subject that may result in the possibility of resignification, or the subject's 'linguistic survival as well as, potentially, that subject's linguistic death' (1997a: 28).

Butler's work on the radical historicity of symbolic structures has important implications for feminist theory. To briefly note one; it suggests a revised formulation of the relation between symbolic, ideological and individual narratives of identity in terms other than those of dissimulation and misrecognition. The main problem with construing the symbolic construction of gender identity as the imposition of a patriarchal ideology, for example, is that the discontinuous nature and effects of representations of femininity are disregarded producing a coherent, unified feminine subject as a substrate of subordination (Adams, 1990: 107). The idea of the instability of speech, which renders it open to reappropriation, replaces simplified notions of misidentification with a more complex model of positionality with regard to conventional gender norms, suggested, for example, in Holloway's notion of investment (Holloway, 1984). Ideological images may momentarily stabilize meanings allowing individuals to identify with or against persons or situations. This is suggested in Winship's work on young women's magazines which, she claims, articulate visual codes of femininity in such a way as to offer readers a more assertive and confident sense of independent femininity (Winship, 1985). The expression of identity, no matter how marginal, cannot take place in isolation from dominant norms and pre-given ideological forms. For a narrative to be meaningful and to acquire a degree of social authority, it must draw to some extent on culturally dominant discourses of truth-telling and this involves inevitably a process of autonomization where a given narrative transcends relevance to its initial situation (e.g. Gilmore, 1994: 23–4).

Although it suggests a dialogical account of the subject's location with regard to dominant norms, it may appear that, rather than moving towards a more distinct understanding of political agency, the idea of the perlocutionary performative entrenches itself deeper within a primarily linguistic account of identity formation. Butler goes on, however, to draw out brilliantly some of the problematic political implications that a closing of the gap between speech and its effects has upon the political analysis of 'hate speech'. Catherine MacKinnon, for example, understands the effects of pornography in terms of the illocutionary performative, that is, that hate speech constitutes its addressee at the moment of utterance. Pornography does not reinforce patriarchal structures, it constructs women's social reality in the form of a visual imperative which compels a compliance with its demand: 'the image says, "do this", where the commanded act is an act of sexual subordination, and where, in the doing of that act, the social reality of woman is constructed precisely as the position of the sexually subordinate' (Butler, 1997a: 67). The problem with such an analysis is that it positions the objects of pornographic representation so unambiguously in the position of victim that it denies the agency of the oppressed. This is evident in MacKinnon's categorical refusal to recognize that lesbian and gay pornography does not simply replicate structures of victimization, but, in fact, has emancipatory implications for those whose sexuality is denied public expression. Furthermore, this collapsing of speech with its effects justifies strategies of state intervention, such as censorship, on behalf of those who are presumed to be unable to act for themselves. As Foucault has recognized, the intensification of juridical control in areas such as sexuality is used often against the very social movements and marginal groups it is meant to protect.

The insistence on the gap between speech and conduct, then, does not represent a retreat by Butler into abstruse linguistic theory, but rather broadens an understanding of political agency beyond institutional and juridical action, giving support to 'ways of restaging and resignifying speech in contexts that exceed those determined by the courts' (1997a: 23). In the next section, however, I argue that the relation between resignificatory practices and other social structures remains unexplored and, thus, the distinction between speech and conduct becomes blurred again. The symbolic comes to metonymically represent other social and political relations and Butler's idea of political agency remains, therefore, an abstract potentiality rather than the result of specific social practices.

Speech and Effect

Although an emphasis on the temporal gap between speech and conduct is central to Butler's notion of a subversive reworking of dominant forms, there is a sense in which the distinction is not maintained insofar as the primarily symbolic notion of resignification comes to replace a more sociocentric conception of agency. There remains a tendency to valorize the linguistic act of resignification per se as inherently subversive at the expense of a more sustained consideration of the extent to which attendant social relations are dislodged or reinforced by such an act (Fraser, 1995: 67–8). In other words, political agency is understood as a generalized potentiality connected to the distantiation of speech from its original conditions of utterance and not as a more variable phenomenon whose effects, subversive or otherwise, are contingent on a particular configuration of economic and social relations. This is not to deny the important political implications of the examples of resignification given by Butler, for example, in her discussion of the military's treatment of homosexuals. Nor is it to insist on a rigid division between socio-political practices and symbolic forms. Claude Lefort, for example, has demonstrated how the indeterminacy of hegemonic norms and values has important political effects in that it renders democratic systems open to contestation (Lefort, 1986; McNay, 1998). The primacy Butler's model accords to the process of symbolic identification results, however, in a disregard of the specificity of socio-political power relations and of the connections between the two spheres.

The extent to which Butler prioritizes the symbolic over the socio-political is evident in her discussion of Bourdieu's work in the final chapter of *Excitable Speech*. The engagement with his thought is, in certain respects, overdue; Butler's thematization of the performative through the ideas of temporality and reiteration bear close resemblance to Bourdieu's understanding of the interiorization of symbolic violence through the concepts of habitus and practice (McNay, 1999). Despite these affinities, Butler is critical of Bourdieu's notion of symbolic violence in that it ties the speech act too closely to its institutional context and misses the processes of temporal deferral and dissemination that are constitutive of the indeterminacy of the performative and of the potential for misappropriation. In this regard, Butler's remarks echo those of commentators who claim that Bourdieu's theory is so skewed towards explaining social reproduction that it is unable to offer an account of change or disruption within the social structure (e.g. Alexander, 1994). A similar lack of indeterminacy hampers Bourdieu's notion of habitus which, by stressing the extent to which there is an accommodation between dominant power relations and bodily dispositions, misses the extent to which the process of corporeal inculcation is never straightforward or complete. There is a residue, or bodily volatility, that renders strategies of domination vulnerable to displacement: 'This excess is what Bourdieu's account appears to miss or, perhaps, to suppress: the abiding incongruity of the speaking body, the way in which it exceeds its interpellation, and remains uncontained by any of its acts of speech' (Butler, 1997a: 155). By producing an account of power that is structurally committed to the status quo, Bourdieu forecloses the possibility of agency emerging from the margins. In contrast, the performative compels simultaneously institutionalized forms of recognition and a critical perspective on existing institutions exemplified in calls for justice or democracy on the part of those who have been radically disenfranchized.

Butler is undoubtedly right to draw attention to Bourdieu's tendency to overestimate the accommodation between dominant symbolic codes and corporeal hexis evident, for example, in his essay on gender domination (Bourdieu, 1990). However, there is also an increasing emphasis in his recent work on the potentiality for resistance arising in a fashion similar to Butler's idea of resignification where the opportunities for subversive misappropriation increase with the lengthening of circuits of legitimation in late capitalism (e.g. Bourdieu, 1996: 387). Fundamentally, Butler and Bourdieu do not disagree over understanding the conditions of emergence for subversive behaviour, rather they dispute the conceptualization of the relation between symbolic forms and social context. Bourdieu does not deny the heterodox force of performative resignifications, however, he emphasizes that these are situated within a particular 'field' of power relations which, in turn, is understood in terms of its overarching connections with other fields in the social totality. Butler's assertion that Bourdieu rehabilitates the base/superstructure distinction in order to reduce the symbolic to an epiphenomenon of the social fails to appreciate the refractory force of the concept of the field (Butler, 1997a: 157). The idea of the field enables Bourdieu to produce a differentiated and dynamic model of power relations where each field has its own historicity and logic which may reinforce or conflict with those of other fields. This view, where symbolic power is examined in terms of its connection to other power relations, does not rob symbolic power of its autonomy, or conflate speech with effects. It does, however, produce a more nuanced, and possibly more sceptical, assessment of the changes that can be wrought through resignificatory practices. Bourdieu is critical of the dichotomous logic of domination–resistance which tends to simplify the complex nature of freedom and constraint in capitalist society and suggests instead the term 'regulated liberties' to denote a more complex relation between the dominant and its subjects (Bourdieu, 1991: 102).

A weakness of Butler's primarily symbolic concept of power is that it underestimates the extent to which there can be a systemic recuperation of seemingly radical practices. The emancipatory effects of the emergence of a given subaltern identity have to be considered in the context of the structures of consumerism that have played a part in its creation and which render it susceptible to 'commodification, recuperation, and depoliticization' (Fraser, 1995: 163). The problem with the concept of resignification, and associated terms such as abjection, is that its status as a symbolic mechanism is not sufficient to analyse the 'overdetermined entanglements of discursive and non-discursive social arrangements', of symbolic, political and economic power relations that give rise to the emergence of new identities (Hennessey, 1993: 86). There is no doubt, for example, that the resignification of the term 'queer' has been a powerful catalyst in the emergence of a set of gay identities, however, these transformations are also predicated on a complex set of socio-economic changes associated, on the most general level, with the detraditionalization of social relations in late capitalism. It is not just a case of the resignification of dominant terms by marginal or abject groups because, in a sense, the ability of these groups to collectively institute new forms of identity suggests that their social location is not unambiguously marginal. As historians such as D'Emilio have shown, the emergence of a metropolitan gay identity is predicated on a convergence of social and symbolic relations which tend towards the simultaneous inclusion and exclusion of homosexual groups (D'Emilio, 1984). The economic centrality of the gay consumer – the 'pink pound' – has facilitated the greater visibility of a marginalized sexuality in a way that the notion of resignification does not really capture. This is not to deny the force of Butler's notion of the performative, but it does suggest that an analysis of the transformatory effects of resignification upon entrenched norms requires a contextualization within wider socio-economic relations and an understanding of agency not just as a structural potentiality but as a set of embedded practices.

Psyche and Subject

The second area in which Butler's work on the performative has made a significant contribution is in overcoming the impasse between psychoanalytic and constructivist theories of subject formation. This debate is sufficiently well known to warrant only brief recapitulation. The encounter between the psychoanalytic and constructivist accounts of gender was caught up in the debate over essentialism, focusing on the extent to which a psychic account of identity formation normalized sexual difference by evacuating it of any historical content. This reification is held to arise from Lacan's emphasis on the lack that forms the condition of possibility and impossibility of all speaking subjects, compounded for women by the inevitable assumption of a feminine identity defined in relation to a phallocentric system of signification.[3] Woman's entry into the symbolic is defined in terms of a double negativity or 'masquerade' in which the imposition of patriarchal dominance appears to be an inescapable cost of identity constitution. It is unclear how any position outside of the phallocentric matrix could be maintained, in other words, power is always already patriarchal. Although Lacan states that the symbolic is socially and historically variable, rather than an abstract system of signification, his primarily structural account of sexual differentiation tends towards a form of aculturalism that obfuscates the variable and changeable nature of systems of power. The failure to consider how social power may be composed of other norms and relations which may reinforce or conflict with patriarchy, means that Lacanian psychoanalysis provides no way of explaining the variability of sexual identity, either across cultures or in terms of cross-cutting identifications which exceed the binary frame of heterosexuality (Grosz, 1990; Moore, 1994). The extent to which socio-historical variability is negated is evident, for Butler, where homosexual identity is confined to the pre-social domain of the imaginary thus 'preserving the heterosexism of culture through relegating homosexuality to the unrealizable life of passing fantasy' (1993: 111).

Despite reservations about the extent to which the Lacanian paradigm produces a dehistoricized understanding of sexuality, Butler recognizes the force of the idea of the unconscious. The concept suggests a more compelling view of the instabilities intrinsic to the process of subject formation than a constructivist perspective whose use of concepts such as normalization and internalization tends to be functionalist, e.g. the Foucauldian account of individuals as docile bodies. Butler frames this difference between the psychoanalytic and constructionist accounts of identity in terms of the distinction between the categories of soul and psyche: 'the psyche, which includes the unconscious, is very different from the subject: the psyche is precisely what exceeds the imprisoning effects of the discursive demand to inhabit a coherent identity to become a coherent subject' (1997b: 86).

Some psychoanalytic feminist theorists have attempted to overcome this opposition between the concepts of psyche and subject. Countering claims of its ahistorical nature, Jacqueline Rose has argued that the concept of the unconscious – as indicative of an irreducible discontinuity in psychic life – has political relevance for feminism in that it draws attention to the difficulty that women have in assuming socially defined feminine roles (Rose, 1986: 91). Also rebutting accusations of ahistoricism, Teresa Brennan argues that psychical structures do not exist in isolation and the force with which they manifest themselves at any given time is determined by the social-historical context (Brennan, 1990). There exists a relation of non-exhaustive mutual determination where the content of the psyche is not simply a repository for social determinations, nor, however, do psychical structures have an overriding influence within the social: the psychic exists in an 'as yet to be determined extent' within social relations. This discontinuous relation is manifested in the structure of fantasy which, insofar as it involves the representation of a primordial absence, is linked to a universal structure of desire – a 'foundational' but not ahistorical fantasy (Brennan, 1993: 22). Fantasies necessarily draw upon the social-historical for their specific content, and yet the immanence of the social-historical within the content of fantasy can not be established in any straightforward fashion. The effects of fantasy are not contained within the private sphere of the individual psyche but influence interaction with others in that they are constantly propelled into the social realm. In this way, psychic reality may be sustained, intensified or contradicted by its material context. Thus, as Brennan questions, would the fantasy of woman (as virgin-whore) persist or would it fade into a 'pale myth' if it were not tied to concrete relations which disempower women, which literally 'passify' them.[4]

While conceding the force of the psychoanalytic account of the instability of identity, Butler retains doubts about the extent to which a primarily psychic account of resistance to what Castoriadis has called 'identarian logic' evacuates the social realm of any specificity. The psychic might well be the source of resistance to normalization, but it has little explanatory force in terms of the status and efficacy of this resistance. For Butler, there are difficulties with the way in which psychoanalytic theorists construe the unconscious or the Real (e.g. Žižek) as the invariant source of trauma or point of non-closure for any ideological or symbolic system. Such concepts denote the contingency of any social formation in that they constitute a traumatic kernel which prevents its full institution. However, in as much as these concepts represent a self-identical dynamic that emerges in all social formations, then, the specific historicity or contingency of social systems is undercut:

> the notion of a lack taken from psychoanalysis as that which secures the contingency of *any* and *all* social formations is itself a presocial principle universalised at the cost of every consideration of power, sociality, culture, politics, which regulates the relative closure and openness of social practices. (Butler, 1993: 202)

To what extent can this psychic remainder be understood as a negative source of disruption within the dominant or as a more positive force through which new social identities might be created? Furthermore, what happens to the unruly status of the unconscious when there are unconscious attachments to subjection rather than resistances? As Butler puts it: 'To thwart the injunction to produce a docile body is not the same as dismantling the injunction or changing the terms of subject constitution' (1997b: 88). In other words, can the concept of unconscious disruption adequately explain the variable and innovative nature of change within the socio-political realm?

Butler's response to this failure to conceive of historicity in a more substantive sense is to reverse the causal privilege that the psychic is accorded in respect of the social. Although Brennan attempts to draw out the social and political implications of a psychic account of identity, there is still a sense in which the priority accorded to psychic structures forms the parameters of the social rather than vice versa. The primacy invested in the psychic is evident in Brennan's idea of the 'foundational' fantasy. For Butler, it is not so much a case of pre-social psychic structures propelling themselves into the social, but, in a Foucauldian fashion, it is the introjection of historically variable symbolic norms that is formative of the psyche. Unlike Foucault, however, who underestimates the indeterminacy of the mechanisms of internalization, Butler argues that the internalization of norms is an uneven process whose dynamic is shaped by prevailing social and historical relations. It is this socially determined process of internalization which is constitutive of the split between psychic and social power (1997b: 19). At the same time, the dynamic temporality of the process of internalization means that the psyche is not reducible to the social: 'Just as the subject is derived from conditions of power that precede it, so the psychic operation of the norm is derived, though not mechanically or predictably, from prior social operations' (1997b: 21). Power turns back upon itself producing the domain of the psychic which inheres within the social – evident in the way in which psychic phenomena circumscribe the domain of liveable sociality – but which is never prior to the social and is always vulnerable to historical change.

The force of Butler's sociocentric concept of the psyche is the extent to which it can explain the non-correspondence between hegemonic gender norms and sexuality in terms other than pre-social imaginary identifications which leave the symbolic intact as an immutable law. Thus, for Butler, all forms of symbolic identification – heterosexual and homosexual – are achieved only at the cost of a certain foreclosure or *melancholia*, understood as a refused process of grieving. The relinquishment of the object of desire necessary to the formation of gender identity involves a loss which is never fully avowed by being melancholically incorporated into the ego. Thus, heterosexual identity is based on the abandonment of homosexual attachments which, because they cannot be grieved for, are preserved in the psyche as repudiated identifications. Conversely, rigid forms of homosexual identity can sometimes be based on a rejection of heterosexuality that is to some degree an identification with it, for example, the gay drag queen could be seen as an allegorization of an unavowed loss of the feminine object of desire. For Butler, it is important that this idea of melancholia be understood not as a psychic economy, but as part of the operations of regulatory social power which are contingently organized through certain kinds of foreclosure. Thus, to give expression to that grief is to acknowledge a loss which is denied, and to voice an anger which can result in political acts of resistance, for example the Names Project Quilt commemorating those who have died of AIDS (1997b: 148). In this way, Butler's notion of the performative provides a way of investing psychic terms with a political force without losing sight, as social constructionism often does, of the indeterminacy of subject forms.

By locating socialization in the system of signification that far exceeds the meta-cultural dynamic of Oedipus, Butler offers an explanation of how social roles may be historically variable and culturally specific. The necessarily social-historical character of language permits the creation of the new in and through language – an impossibility if language were a completely determined code or the symbolic an apparently incontestable order. Indeed, this aspect of language as a magma of infinite significations and referrals is the condition of possibility of any identity fixation since it can only emerge as such against the background of instability and non-identity. It is by positing the essential instability of historical significations that Butler's thought discloses the potential to disrupt and challenge patriarchal systems of meaning. At the same time, however, the instability and variation within gender identity is not construed as pure contingency. As Stuart Hall has pointed out, this is a weakness of certain types of poststructural thought which overemphasize the open-endedness of identity at the expense of a consideration of its overdetermination, that 'some stories have a much longer structuration, a *longue durée*, almost an historical inertia' (Hall, 1997: 32). Thus, Butler limits the contingency of the social by showing how its inherence within psychic constraints can lead to an attachment to subjection and to an unwillingness to acknowledge the possibility of change. In this way, Butler's original reworking of the relation between the psychic and the social bypasses the dichotomy of fixity and contingency that hampers debates on identity and pushes a feminist understanding of gender identity on to a new terrain.

Agency and Creativity

Although Butler's reformulation of the relation between psyche and social represents an important development in the feminist understanding of gender identity, there is a sense in which, by focusing on that relation, the concept of agency remains a predominantly negative one. The subject's relation to the socio-symbolic is conceived, by and large, in terms of negativity or constraint which, as we have seen, results in a tendency to valorize the act of resignification per se. This primarily negative account of agency as displacement fails to draw out fully, however, the ways in which the symbolic realm is composed of conflicting values and resources which may be actively, and sometimes creatively, appropriated by actors to institute new value systems and new forms of collective identity. The construal of the socio-symbolic order as a uniform realm of constraint disregards the innovative and dynamic nature of action by confining it to the relatively narrow idea of resistance. Furthermore, by locating the source of change in the permanent disjunction between the psyche and social, Butler's model runs the risk of dehistoricizing the idea of performative agency. Insofar as she fails to develop a more active or positive account of agency, Butler could be said to be vulnerable to her own criticism of the concept of the unconscious: resignification becomes a self-identical principle which forecloses an analysis of the variable nature of social action and change. Arising from the negative formulation of agency as displacement is a second difficulty, namely that the performative results in a primarily individualistic notion of political practice where important questions are left unaddressed, such as the nature of the relation between the private and the public and how a primarily sexualized politics can have an effect on wider collective values. I will finish by expanding briefly on these two points.

The creativity of action is a recurrent if somewhat submerged theme in the work of continental social theorists and philosophers such as Paul Ricoeur, Cornelius Castoriadis, Michel de Certeau and Alain Touraine. By emphasizing the creative dimensions of action, these authors highlight, in different ways, how even the most normative forms of behaviour presuppose imaginative elements. In Ricoeur's terms, social reproduction rests upon a dialectic of innovation and sedimentation. From this perspective, for example, Castoriadis argues that Lacanian psychoanalysis has a central weakness in that it cannot conceive of the psyche as radical imagination, that is, as the ability to create the new *ex nihilo*: 'the emergence of representations or as representative flux not subject to determinacy' (Castoriadis, 1987: 274).[5] The extent to which the constitutive role of the imagination is overlooked is evident in Lacan's account of the mirror stage which, in Castoriadis's view, reduces the plenitude of the imaginary to the flatness of the specular structure. The imaginary is illusory to the extent that it conceals or sutures a fundamental lack in the subject which, in the mirror stage, is connected to the anatomical underdevelopment of the infant and which, subsequently, is connected to the impossibility of acquiring stable identity within the symbolic realm. Castoriadis criticizes this notion of the imaginary because its specular logic is unable to explain why it is that the infant is first impelled to identify, invest and recognize itself in the mirror. In other words, prior to the specular moment of reflection, the mirror itself must be invested with desire:

> The imaginary does not come from the image in the mirror or from the gaze of the other. Instead, the 'mirror' itself and its possibility, and the other as mirror, are the works of the imaginary, which is creation *ex nihilo*. (Castoriadis, 1987: 3)

The anterior investment of the mirror signals the work of the radical imaginary which is able to invest, create and represent *ex nihilo*, it is an originary capacity of figuration.

Castoriadis's concept of the radical imagination is not without its difficulties, particularly with regard to his occasional insistence on the radical heterogeneity that exists between psyche and society (Whitebook, 1996). However, of interest is the way in which he extends the idea of radical imagination to the concept of the social imaginary in order to explain the self-production of society in terms of innovation and the capacity to create new socio-symbolic forms. An understanding of the creative dimensions of action or agency need not necessarily denote a celebratory populism, evident in types of cultural studies or feminist standpoint theory (McNay, 1996: 66). Action is not purely creative, even the most obviously innovative practice presupposes an incorporation of the tendencies of the social world in the form of routine and pre-reflexive forms of behaviour suggested, for example, in Bourdieu's idea of habitus. Nor, however, is agency purely rational or normatively oriented; as Joas points out: 'action that is appropriate to the situation and conforms to norms cannot simply be deduced from norms themselves, but often requires that the actor devise a new and unfamiliar path of action' (Joas, 1996: 233). Creativity is needed not only in order to realize norms and values in concrete practices; the existence of values also presupposes a creative process by which values are fashioned and transmitted.[6]

Lacanian psychoanalysis misses this imaginative and active aspect of social action because of the emphasis it places on the repressive inscription of the individual which is a condition of entry into the socio-symbolic order: 'these standpoints fail to accord due recognition to the active dimensions of subjecthood; to the point that ideological and social fields are rewritten and changed within the indeterminacy of subjectivity' (Elliott, 1992: 243). Although Butler attempts to overcome Lacan's predominantly repressive account of the symbolic by reframing it in social terms, she retains an element of its negativity in her notion of agency as primarily a strategy of displacement of constraining symbolic norms, rather than, in more active terms, as an appropriation of cultural resources arising from the broader struggle 'for the social control of historicity' (Touraine, 1977: 31). This model of agency as displacement tends to fetishize the marginal and celebrates, in an unqualified fashion, the notion of non-identity. The spontaneous and fluid politics of the performative is implicitly aligned with the amorphous, rather than being regarded as a product of the shifting power relations between groups of social actors. This is evident in Butler's explanation of gender as melancholia which, although it provides a compelling explanation of the anger or desire that may underlie various forms of social protest, leaves unaddressed the mechanisms through which these psychic reserves are channelled into collective forms of activity. This would necessarily involve looking beyond the interface between psyche and social to consider the dynamics internal to civil society and how these relate to institutional and non-institutional politics. As it stands, the account of agency implied in the performative arises from the non-identity between psyche and social. However, given that this non-identity is the condition of possibility of all identity, it cannot really explain the process of active appropriation that is required to explain certain types of action that result in the emergence of new social forms.

In sum, an important implication of conceptualizing the creative dimensions of action is that it raises the issue of social change at a collective level. That is, the question of how creative or innovative action detaches itself from its original conditions of enactment and may give rise to a set of new values which become resources for further action. Such a notion is suggested in Touraine's work on the self-production of society understood not as a simple act of creation but as a complex process involving value clashes between groups, changes in consciousness, social protests and repression based on force (e.g. Touraine, 1977). It is this collective dimension that is missing from Butler's account of performative resignification whose underpinnings in a theory of psychic dislocation confine its explanatory force to the private realm of individual action. The examples she cites of performative resignification imply a collective dimension, however, because of her unwillingness to stray beyond a primarily linguistic model of identity formation, issues relating to value conflict, how new forms of collective identity emerge and how they may or may not relate to wider institutional change are foreclosed. Butler's discussion of the affirmative revaluation of the category of woman, for example, doesn't address the extent to which this change might be predicated on some of the complex transformations in women's economic and social status documented, say, by Sylvia Walby in her work on the restructuring of gender relations (Butler, 1997a: 158; Walby, 1997). The notion of the performative is certainly capable of accommodating these questions, but the relation between the psyche and the social needs to be elaborated more fully if the analysis of change within identity formations is not to be confined to an individualistic paradigm. This tendency of the politics of the performative to leave unexamined how symbolic changes may catalyse or hinder change within wider social relations leaves it caught within a public–private dichotomy or what Jonathan Dollimore calls a politics of the bedroom (Dollimore, 1991: 321). In short, while it provides an ontological account of the psychic conditions that permit resistance on an individual level, it fails to explore fully how the active appropriation and reshaping of values and resources by actors may result in changes, at a collective level, to socio-symbolic definitions of identity.

Conclusion

I have argued that Judith Butler's work on the performative construction of the subject has made an important contribution to an understanding of gender identity as durable but not immutable in two respects. First, by expanding on Foucault's remark that the autonomous subject emerges from constraint, Butler has outlined a non-voluntarist conception of agency that breaks out of dualisms of domination and resistance which sometimes hamper feminist thought. Second, Butler's account of the inherence of the psychic in the social, introduces a fuller understanding of the ambiguities of subject formation to a constructivist perspective without losing the emphasis on the social and historical specificity of identity. The criticisms I have raised relate to this issue of historical specificity in that, in various ways, Butler needs to explain in more detail how symbolic norms relate to other social and political structures through which gender identities are also fashioned. These criticisms are not intended as indications of insurmountable flaws in Butler's thought, but rather are intended to be complementary to her project. Indeed, I hope that the method of immanent reading deployed here, of reading with Butler in order to highlight the strengths of her thought, makes this clear and also demonstrates the extent to which her work has sketched out important new areas for feminist debate.

Notes

1. In the light of this criticism, it is somewhat ironic that the idea of the performative has been criticized for being too voluntarist, a charge that Butler has convincingly refuted (Butler, 1994: 33).

2. Butler herself acknowledges this in a recent article in *New Left Review* (Butler, 1998).

3. The phallus is a symbolic, not a literal term, it is that to which value accrues. Yet anatomical differences come to acquire significance insofar as the actual penis comes to figure in the representation of lack marking symbolic castration. The penis of the little boy lends itself to an approximation to or symbolization of the phallus. The problem, however, is that the penis is not the phallus and, therefore, the boy struggles to have the phallus. The little girl, however, does not possess the penis which means that she has no means to represent her lack. Thus, while both the position of the boy and girl to the phallus is problematic, the girl's position is more problematic because it is assigned a negative relation to the phallus (see Grosz, 1990).

4. Brennan illustrates this discontinuity using the work of Sarah Koffman who shows how the complaint amongst Freud's female patients that their mothers did not give them enough milk did not actually correspond to reality. Rather it involved the projection of feelings of frustration arising from the structurally inaccessible nature of desire on to the finite, external figure of the mother/wet-nurse. Whilst demonstrating that there is no one-to-one correspondence between fantasy and reality, Brennan argues that Koffman's work also illustrates that fantasies inevitably involve a process of projection into social reality: 'psychoanalysis is a theory of the derivation of certain fantasies and (inescapably) a theory of how fantasies go *out*, over there. Into the social, onto people and things who are thereby credited or confused with, or constructed by imaginary attributes' (Brennan, 1990: 131).

5. Freudian psychoanalysis partially recognizes the psyche as radical imagination or as the capacity to make representations *ex nihilo*. Although it accords a central role to dreams, fantasy, etc., it fails to fully take account of the constitutive nature of the radical imagination in the formation of the psyche. Understood as a process of originary phantasmatization, the radical imagination pre-exists and presides over every organization of the drives even the most primitive ones (Castoriadis, 1987: 286–7).

6. My remarks in this article on the implications of the thought of Castoriadis, Bourdieu and Ricoeur for feminist theory are developed in more detail in my forthcoming *Gender Reconfigured*.

References

Adams, Parveen (1990) 'A Note on the Distinction between Sexual Division and Sexual Differences', in P. Adams and E. Cowie (eds) *The Woman in Question*. London: Verso.

Alexander, Jeremy (1994) *Fine de Siècle Social Theory: Relativism, Reduction and the Problem of Reason*. London: Verso.

Benhabib, Selya (1995) 'Subjectivity, Historiography and Politics', in S. Benhabib et al. (eds) *Feminist Contentions: A Philosophical Exchange*. London: Routledge.

Bourdieu, Pierre (1990) 'La Domination masculine', *Actes de la Recherche en Sciences Sociales* 84: 2–31.

Bourdieu, Pierre (1991) *Language and Symbolic Power*. Cambridge: Polity Press.

Bourdieu, Pierre (1992) *An Invitation to Reflexive Sociology*. Cambridge: Polity Press.

Bourdieu, Pierre (1996) *The State Nobility: Elite Schools in the Field of Power*. Cambridge: Polity Press.

Brennan, Teresa (1990) 'An Impasse in Psychoanalysis and Feminism', in S. Gunew (ed.) *A Reader in Feminist Knowledge*. London: Routledge.

Brennan, Teresa (1993) *History after Lacan*. London: Routledge.

Butler, Judith (1993) *Bodies that Matter: On the Discursive Limits of Sex*. London: Routledge.

Butler, Judith (1994) 'Gender as Performance: An Interview with Judith Butler', *Radical Philosophy* 67: 32–9.

Butler, Judith (1997a) *Excitable Speech: A Politics of the Performative*. London: Routledge.

Butler, Judith (1997b) *The Psychic Life of Power: Theories in Subjection*. Stanford: Stanford University Press.

Butler, Judith (1998) 'Marxism and the Merely Cultural', *New Left Review* 227: 33–44.

Castoriadis, Cornelius (1987) *The Imaginary Institution of Society*. Cambridge: Polity Press.

D'Emilio, John (1984) 'Capitalism and Gay Identity', in A. Snitow, C. Stansell and S. Thompson (eds) *Powers of Desire: The Politics of Sexuality*. London: Virago.

Dollimore, Jonathan (1991) *Sexual Dissidence: Augustine to Wilde, Freud to Foucault*. Oxford: Clarendon Press.

Elliott, Anthony (1992) *Social Theory and Psychoanalysis in Transition: Self and Society from Freud to Kristeva*. Oxford: Blackwell.

Foucault, Michel (1988) 'An Aesthetics of Existence' in L. Kritzman (ed.) *Politics, Philosophy, Culture: Interviews and Other Writings 1977–1984*. London: Routledge.

Fraser, Nancy (1995) 'False Antitheses', 'Pragmatism, Feminism, and the Linguistic Turn', in S. Benhabib, J. Butler, D. Cornell and N. Fraser (eds) *Feminist Contentions: A Philosophical Exchange*. London: Routledge.

Gilmore, Leigh (1994) *Autobiographics: A Feminist Theory of Women's Self Representation*. London: Cornell University Press.

Grosz, Elizabeth (1990) *Jacques Lacan: A Feminist Introduction*. London: Routledge.

Hall, Stuart (1997) 'Interview on Culture and Power', *Radical Philosophy* 86: 24–41.

Hennessey, Rosemary (1993) *Materialist Feminism and the Politics of Feminism*. London: Routledge.

Holloway, Wendy (1984) 'Gender Difference and the Production of Subjectivity', in J. Henriques, W. Hollway, C. Urwin, C. Benn and V. Walkerdine (eds) *Changing the Subject: Psychology, Social Regulation and Subjectivity*. London: Methuen.

Joas, Hans (1996) *The Creativity of Action*. Cambridge: Polity Press.

Lefort, Claude (1986) *The Political Forms of Modern Society: Bureaucracy, Democracy, Totalitarianism*. Cambridge: Polity Press.

McNay, Lois (1996) 'Michel de Certeau and the Ambivalent Everyday', *Social Semiotics* 6: 61–82.

McNay, Lois (1998) 'Foucault and Agonstic Democracy', in A. Carter and G. Stokes (eds) *Liberal Democracy and its Critics*. Cambridge: Polity Press.

McNay, Lois (1999) 'Gender, Habitus and the Field: Pierre Bourdieu and the Limits of Reflexivity', *Theory, Culture & Society* 16(1): 95–117.

McNay, Lois (forthcoming) *Gender Reconfigured: Feminism and Social Theory*. Cambridge: Polity Press.

Moore, Henrietta (1994) *A Passion for Difference: Essays in Anthropology and Gender*. Cambridge: Polity Press.

Rose, Jacqueline (1986) *Sexuality in the Field of Vision*. London: Verso.

Touraine, Alain (1977) *The Voice and the Eye: An Analysis of Social Movements*. Cambridge: Cambridge University Press.

Walby, Sylvia (1997) *Gender Transformations*. London: Routledge.

Whitebook, Joel (1996) 'Intersubjectivity and the Monadic Core of the Psyche: Habermas and Castoriadis on the Unconscious', in M. Passerin d'Entreves and S. Benhabib (eds) *Habermas and the Unfinished Project of Modernity: Critical Essays on the Philosophical Discourse of Modernity*. Cambridge: Polity Press.

Winship, Janice (1985) 'A Girl Needs to Get "Street-Wise"', *Feminist Review* 21: 25–46.

Lois McNay is a lecturer in politics and fellow of Somerville College, Oxford. She is the author of *Foucault and Feminism: Power, Gender and the Self* (Cambridge: Polity Press, 1992), *Foucault: A Critical Introduction* (Cambridge: Polity Press, 1994) and *Gender Reconfigured: Feminism and Social Theory* (Cambridge: Polity Press, forthcoming).

Performativity, Parody, Politics

Moya Lloyd

We're born naked and the rest is drag. (Ru Paul)

THE WORK of Judith Butler has been enormously influential in posing a challenge to the assumptions underpinning the politics of identity, particularly in the context of feminist and gay and lesbian liberation movements. My aim in this article is to explore some of the key themes of Butler's writing in an attempt to clarify three particular areas of ambiguity: the relation between performance and performativity, the revision in Butler's arguments from *Gender Trouble* to *Bodies that Matter*, and the politics enabled by performativity. Underlying this is a concern with the writings of so-called adherents of Butler's. I am especially interested in the transformations effected in Butler's argument by these adherents, at least one of which is to recentre a humanist subject as the agent of performativity. This, in turn, suggests a politics where queer is good, queerer is better, but queerest is best of all. As a preliminary, I begin with the question of subjectivity.

Thinking about Subjectivity

'Gender' is a core concept of much feminist enquiry. It is taken to be an ineluctable feature of all human identity; a means of marking and defining differently 'sexed' beings. From the day we are born we are interpellated as gendered beings, and we continue to be gendered throughout our lives in a variety of ways. Moreover, we understand ourselves as gendered beings. Filling in forms, reacting to wolf whistles in the street: in a multiplicity of ways gender impinges upon and encodes us. But what does 'gender' mean? Is it something we acquire? Or is it, as Judith Butler suggests, something we do?

▪ *Theory, Culture & Society* 1999 (SAGE, London, Thousand Oaks and New Delhi), Vol. 16(2): 195–213
[0263-2764(199904)16:2;195–213;008261]

Most feminist accounts of gender rely upon a spatial and substantialist conception of identity. First, most assume that it is possible to define the boundaries that demarcate one gender from another (the 'spatial' dimension). Take, for example, the definition offered by Jane Flax in *Thinking Fragments*: 'Through gender relations two types of person are created: males and females, each posited as an exclusionary category. One can only be one gender, rarely the other or both' (1990: 23). Although the content of what is to be male or female may be historically and culturally variable, what is invariable is the opposition between male and female. To be female is not to be male. Gender, in this sense, is understood in constative terms. It signals 'what we are': subjects of a discernible and given set of characteristics. Moreover, these are characteristics not shared by the Other. Rather, masculinity assumes analytically the existence of femininity. Indeed, femininity might be regarded as the very condition of possibility for the perpetuation of masculinity: the Other which must be legislated against. In the context of gender, however, masculine and feminine are also bound together in heterologic. Male assumes female; female assumes male.

This account of gender as a set of characteristics also involves a second dimension: the substantialist. Here the emphasis is on what is often referred to as the metaphysics of substance: the idea of an internal essence or presence that precedes 'social and linguistic coding' (Poovey, 1992: 241). In the context of gender, it is assumed that there is a *something* which is regarded as fundamental to female identity prior to engendering (the acquisition of feminine characteristics): a maternal nature, a specific mode of reasoning, natural passivity, a specific erotic nature, a developmental trajectory. Together, these two elements (the spatial and the substantial) produce accounts of identity that are essentially descriptivist; that is, that permit of analysis and political articulation only through the enumeration of *relevant* features of identity (Butler, 1992; Norval, 1994: 117, 121). Such ontologies of gender establish, therefore, what counts as 'intelligible sex', determining the kinds of identity that are permitted to exist and those that are not (Butler, 1990b: 148). By setting out boundaries and markers around specific identities gender, understood in oppositional and substantial terms, becomes another (literal and figurative) mode of containment. It produces another version of those disciplinary and normalizing strategies discussed by Foucault; establishing, to echo Canguilhem, categories of the normal and the pathological. Gender norms operate to regulate and police the acceptable and the licit.

In the place of this conception of gender identity, Judith Butler proposes the idea of gender performativity: gender not as an expression of what one is, but gender as something that one does: 'the stylized repetition of acts through time'. The emphasis shifts from the spatial to the temporal comprehended as 'a gendered corporealization of time' (1990b: 141). Space does not disappear but is reconstituted: gone is metaphorical space – the continents of subjectivity habitable only by authentic substantive identities – and in its place is social space: the symbolic realm in which subjects interpellate and hail other subjects, in which the performative enactment of gender occurs.

Butler's theory of gender performativity echoes both Austin and Derrida in proposing that the performative 'enacts or produces that which it names' (1993b: 23). She differs from Austin, however, in rejecting the idea that there is an autonomous agent that authors performative utterances. Instead, she takes from Derrida the idea that intentionality is always limited by the iterability of the sign. Repetition is central to performativity. This means that performative utterances are not singular events but, rather, the effects of 'citational doubling' (Derrida, 1991: 103). Performativity, for Butler, thus operates through the 'reiterative power of discourse to produce the phenomena that it regulates and constrains' (1993b: 2). It is not in a single act of constitution or invention that the subject is brought into being, but through re-citation and repetition. This, as we will see below, has an important bearing on the capacity of parodic recitation to produce certain transgressive effects. In addition, Butler endorses Lacan's contention that there is no possibility of recovering or recollecting previous acts – no chance of identical re-enactment. Recitation and repetition, although always already different from prior acts and significations remain reiterative of the norms that produce the regulatory sexual regimes within which gender is imbricated. As a consequence, Butler eschews the very possibility of stable gender identities:

> In the place of an original identification which serves as a determining cause, gender identity might be reconceived as a personal/cultural history of received meanings subject to a set of imitative practices which refer laterally to other imitations and which, jointly, construct the illusion of a primary and interior gendered self or parody the mechanism of that construction. (1990b: 138)

The gendered self has no ontological status apart from the acts which compose it; only 'bodily gestures, movements and styles constitute the illusion of an abiding gendered self' (Butler, 1990b: 139, 140). 'Straight' or 'queer' comprehended in these terms are not fixed categories: they do not identify or represent particular groups of subjects. One 'is' never straight or queer, merely in a condition of 'doing' straightness or queerness (Luckhurst, 1995). There is, thus, no single modality of embodiment that stands for straight-ness or queer-ness. Rather there is openness, fluidity, flux; an endless possibility of de-determination and re-citation (with 're' understood both as repetition and as a different citation).

The purpose of Butler's analysis is to challenge what Janice Raymond has called 'hetero-reality'): 'the ideology that woman is for man' (Raymond, 1986: 11); an ideology – or set of discursive practices – that has been instrumental in constructing a phantasmatic, but severely regulated, notion of compulsory heterosexuality. The discursive constitution of heterosexuality articulates a specific relationship between sex, gender and desire where gender follows from sex, and desire follows from gender. This relationship occludes, however, the panoply of 'gender discontinuities' that actually exist, wherein 'gender does not necessarily follow from sex, and desire, or sexuality generally, does not seem to follow from gender' (Butler, 1990b: 135–6). The revelation of these so-called 'gender discontinuities' exposes heterosexuality as a regulative fiction that produces stable gendered identity as a truth effect of discourse. In order to more fully highlight the imitative quality of gender identity, Butler turns to the example of drag.

Drag, Butler avers, is a cultural practice that parodies the belief in an original/primary gender identity. In drag three distinct 'contingent dimensions of significant corporeality' are discernible, and are played upon: anatomical sex (contingent maleness), gender performance (the feminine figure displayed in the impersonation), and gender identity (heterosexuality versus homosexuality). Through the production of a coherent picture of 'woman', drag discloses the '*imitative structure of gender itself*' (Butler, 1990b: 137). By disclosing that there is no original to imitate, drag denaturalizes, divulging the culturally fabricated nature of gender. It reveals all gender as only ever parody. Thus, Butler claims, the recitation of 'heterosexual constructs in non-heterosexual frames brings into relief the utterly constructed status of the heterosexual original', exposing 'gay to straight *not* as a copy to the original, but, rather, as copy is to copy' (1990b: 31). There is no original from which gay, lesbian, transvestite subjects deviate; the original is itself a mythical figuration. In this regard, all gender enactment comprises a failure to 'become "real" and to embody "the natural"' (Butler, 1990b: 146). At this stage, parody is seen as inherently subversive: 'parodic proliferation', Butler asserts, 'deprives hegemonic culture and its critics of the claim to naturalized or essentialist gender identities' (1990b: 100). As Gail Hawkes observes in her appraisal of Butler in the context of dressing-up:[1]

> If 'drag' is the verbal shorthand for the performative use of gendered dress codes to subvert the hegemonic twinning of gender and sexuality, then we can speak, in this sense, of dress as performance, of women 'dragging up as women'. Or of men 'dragging up as men'.... Dressing-up as performance allows rereading of all dressing-up as playful ... [where] the readings of the male/masculine/heterosexual, female/butch/lesbian, male/camp/homosexual, are not reversed but deliberately scrambled. (1995: 269)

As dressing-up proliferates (lipstick lesbians, butch cowboys, etc.), it inaugurates a game of 'guess the sexuality(ies)' (Hawkes, 1995: 269; see Martin, 1992: 107), where all gendered meanings are queered. But does it? In what senses are drag and gender parody ipso facto transgressive activities? Is gender proliferation politically subversive of compulsory heterosexuality? In exploring these questions I want to turn my attention away, momentarily, from Butler to an example of how she has been read.

Performativity and Performance

In a recent piece, Elspeth Probyn refers to the 'current celebration and appropriation' of Butler's argument in which:

> . . . it is said that *we can have whatever type of gender we want*, and that there are as many genders as there are people, and that we wear our genders as drag – in short, the sort of feel-good gender discourse at large . . . (1995: 79, my emphasis)

The imputation here is that subjects can decide for themselves what gender they want to be. It suggests a subject who can act at will. This type of argument is exemplified in the article 'All Hyped Up and No Place to Go', an attempt to apply Butler's ideas to the concept of space (Bell et al., 1994). In this Bell et al. explore two illustrations of what they perceive as the denaturalization of heterosexual space: the gay skinhead and the lipstick lesbian. Both cases are seen to exemplify a hyperbolic mimicking of heterosexuality (hypermasculinity versus hyperfemininity) that simultaneously re-encodes and decodes or denaturalizes hetero-space. As I demonstrate, however, the argument that Bell et al. make reinstates the voluntarist subject that Butler disavows (1993b: x). This happens because they overlook the problematic relationship between the intention(s) behind, and the understanding(s) of, any purportedly 'parodic' action. That they do this is partly the result of the ambiguity of Butler's own account of the distinction between performance and performativity in *Gender Trouble*.[2] In order to make my argument I will concentrate on the example of the gay skinhead.

In the early 1990s the skinhead look became 'fashionable in gay London', becoming, for Bell et al. 'one form of gay "uniform"' (1994: 34). It was not simply a style of dress, the authors argue, it represented a 'way of life' (1994: 35) and, moreover, a politically affirmative one: 'the gay skinhead can be seen as a progressive identity' (1994: 35). The argument hinges on two claims: first, citing Joseph Bristow, they argue that: '[t]his type of gay identity . . . consciously inhabits a publicly acceptable one which is, in fact, its enemy' (in Bell et al., 1994: 36). In other words, the gay skinhead challenges, through parody ('passing for straight'), the idea that all 'straight' (i.e. masculine) men are straight. Second, this parody is read as transgressive of heterosexual space: '[t]his visibility means that through mutually-constituting exchange of glances on the street, gay skinheads create a queer space in a heterosexual world, which is in itself empowering' (Bell et al., 1994: 37). While these claims may have some credence in (selected) 'queer' circles, it is unclear why this identity should be construed as progressive. Indeed, terms such as 'progressive', 'transgressive' and 'subversive' are simply conflated by the authors. But this is not the real difficulty with the view that parody is political. The problem is that Bell et al. reinstate the voluntarist subject that Butler jettisons. Reverting to a more Austinian account of performativity (while claiming legitimacy from Butler), they make the authorial moment determinant: the degree of transgression of a 'style of the flesh' depends, they aver, upon 'the author's intentions' (Bell et al., 1994: 34). Disregarding the difficulties of this reading of Butler, emphasizing intentions to the exclusion of other factors (such as context) has serious implications (Kirkby, 1995; Walker, 1995).

Bell et al. claim that gay skinheads inhabit a publicly acceptable identity. But in what sense? Which publics regard this identity as acceptable? Citing the marches through London in support of consensual gay sadomasochism in response to the Spanner trial, Bell et al. deny any affiliation with neo-Nazism and racism, declaring that the 'queer march is not a march of fake fascists taking place in a straight space' (1994: 38). Only by ignoring the fact that the skinhead style has an historical present that involves (inter alia) racial violence can the authors understand this stylization in such politically positive terms. The focus on the gay skinhead as a parody of straight hypermasculinity occludes black people in general, but gay black men in particular. As Walker notes, it 'excludes black men from the [white male] ga(y)ze, the queer space created on the street amongst those "in the know", by not acknowledging that it could be dangerous for a black gay man to initiate construction of that space' (1995: 73). The judgement of Bell et al. relies upon decontextualizing the skinhead; on representing him as ipso facto transgressive. Consequently, the material and symbolic structures within which he is embedded are overlooked. Signs, though not necessarily fixed, are not free-floating. Bell et al. can only make their claim because they elide any distinction between performance and performativity: a problem entailed by Butler's own vacillations on this point over time. This raises two questions: can performance and performativity be analytically separated? And, does drag necessarily work disruptively?

Butler contends (throughout her work) that the practices that produce gendered subjects are also the sites where critical agency is possible. Gender is simultaneously a mechanism of constraint (a set of norms which define us as normal/abnormal) and a locus for productive activity. This doubled relation draws on three sets of claims, the first Lacanian: that failure to embody the ideal is inevitable, that subjects are unable to achieve a stable gendered identity. The second Derridean: that the repetition central to the maintenance and constitution of gender is always repetition with a difference (or a *différance*). The last Foucauldian, that this repetition creates the space for transformation.[3] Gender performativity may be inevitable but gender identity is always open and incomplete. Or, as Hawkes puts it: compliance with internalized codes (in her case, dress codes) 'is at one and the same time unconscious and profoundly managed' (1995: 262). In *Gender Trouble*, Butler observes that the option is not 'whether to repeat, but how to repeat or, indeed, to repeat and, through a radical proliferation of gender, *to displace* the very norms that enable the repetition itself' (1990b: 148, see also 141). It is in the interstices between the impossibility of identical recitation and necessary reiteration, in the 'failure to repeat, a deformity, or a parodic repetition' (1990b: 141), that critical feminist practice and the opportunity for 'gender transformation' becomes possible. The task is:

> ... to locate strategies of subversive repetition ... to affirm the local possibilities of intervention through participating in precisely those practices of repetition that constitute identity and, therefore, present the immanent possibility of contesting them. (1990b: 147)

It is in this context that Butler asks: 'what kind of gender *performance* will enact and reveal the *performativity* of gender itself in a way that destabilizes the naturalized categories of identity and desire' (1990b: 139, emphasis added)? The question is how? What is it that differentiates a performance from the performativity of gender? The example used to illustrate this relation is that of drag which, as noted, operates through a disjunction, and rewriting, of the connections between sex, gender identity and gender performance. As a practice, drag suggests that constituted subjects can 'act out' fictional gender roles. In the context of theatre or film where men play women or women play men there would appear to be no problem. Butler is not principally concerned with theatre or film, however. In developing her account of performativity, Butler abandons Austin's distinction between pure speech acts and parasitic speech acts. Here the former refer to utterances issued in 'ordinary circumstances' (Austin, 1962: 22) while the latter pertain to theatrical or poetic uses of the same words. Instead, Butler endorses Derrida's contention that both ordinary speech acts and theatrical performances are underpinned by the same citational practices (Butler, 1995: 134–5). This means that an easy separation between a performance and the performative is difficult to uphold since both reiterate the same conventions. So, if performativity produces that which it names, what is it that prevents a performance operating performatively? Is the comment Butler makes in *Bodies that Matter*, that drag is 'an example of performativity' (1993b: 230), recognition of this?

Butler outlines her distinction between performance and performativity in 'Critically Queer' (1993a, reprinted with revisions in *Bodies that Matter*). A performance is a 'bounded "act"' that is differentiated from performativity on the grounds that performativity: '*consists in a reiteration of norms which precede, constrain, and exceed the performer and in that sense cannot be taken as the fabrication of the performer's "will" or "choice"*' (1993a: 24, original emphasis). Performatively, there is no subject that precedes or enacts the repetition of norms. The subject is the effect of their compulsory repetition. This 'subject-effect', as Spivak calls her/him, is nothing more than the 'effect of an effect' (1988: 204). 'There is no "one" who takes on a gender norm' (Butler, 1993a: 23) as Bell et al. surmise. The 'one' is produced through the reiteration of the discursive norms that precede, and are in excess of, her/him. This repetition denies (rather than confirms) voluntarism. Even though performativity may acquire 'act-like status', it is always a recitation of conventions (however dissimulated).

Gender, performatively construed, has thus a linear, albeit bumpy and uneven, trajectory and historicity that is occluded through necessary repetition.

But where does that leave performance? Performance is defined by Butler as a 'bounded "act"'. What does this mean? In what sense is the 'act' bounded? Performance is characterized, by her, as a form of 'theatricality' (seeming to blur the Derridean idea that everything is in some sense always already theatrical). By this, she means, that a performance is theatrical in the sense of miming or hyperbolizing existing signifiers. This is not theatre as self-creation nor self-display, nor as pure invention. It is the performance of certain signs, certain outward codifiers. It is a process of *re*-signification and not signification *ab initio*. For Patton: performance 'involves deployment of signs which have already attained meaning and/or standard usage within the legitimated discourse and crystallized practices of a "social", understood as a place of contestation' (1995: 182). This intimates that performance also undermines the idea of voluntarism since the subject of drag is taking up and reciting the terms that always already constitute gendered identity. If this is so, it does not explain why or how the act is bounded. Indeed, it suggests that, paradoxically, a performance is itself performative. That is, its conventions too exceed, constrain and precede the performer. One way out of this, intimated by Butler, might be to say that the performance is an expression of the 'will' or 'choice' of the performer. Thus, a performance may draw on the conventions of gender but the performer decides which gender s/he wishes to act out (a position close to that of Bell et al.). This implies that there is a performer preceding the performance, an impersonator prior to the impersonation. Given the caveat that there are no constative gender identities only performative ones, to argue that a performance represents choices made by an autonomous actor does not clarify the issue since the impersonator can only ever be generated through the very impersonation. Since all gender is always already imitative, the problem is compounded. One implication is that drag may indeed constitute the gender of its practitioner. If a performance is now no longer a distinct act independent of performativity, but rather a still taken from the continuous reel of gender performativity, is it possible to distinguish a series of one-off acts from ones that constitute someone performatively? When, that is, is dressing-up 'theatrical' and when is it constitutive of gender identity? If all instances of doing gender are treated equally as instances of subjectification, which they must be if we reject the idea that we *are* straight or gay, there is little in this view, analytically, to distinguish between a performance and the performative.

An alternative way to read performance is to regard it in terms of hyperbole or excess (Butler in Osborne and Segal, 1994: 38). As Fuss puts it: 'to be excessively excessive, to flaunt one's performance as performance, is to unmask all identity as drag' (1995: 81 n). Drawing on Irigaray's distinction between 'mimicry' (parody) and 'masquerade' (passing or imitation) this implies, for Fuss, that a performance cannot be read as parodic if it is not excessive. In this respect, the gay skinhead who passes as straight is not unmasking the constitutivity of straight identity since there is nothing hyperbolic in his performance. But is such a distinction sufficient? What represents evidence of excess: a specific walk? particular clothes? a voice pitched too high or too low? Performance as hyperbole suggests that it is the degree of excess that determines political effectiveness and subversion. This has implications for drag which, as the gay skinhead example demonstrates, does not have to be excessive or parodic at all. While drag may be transgressive in that it breaches certain norms of behaviour, it is not clear either that this is sufficient to expose the fiction of gender nor to subvert the heterosexual matrix. There is a remaining difficulty: why should anyone want to parody a parody?

The only way that Butler can account for the investment subjects make in parodic practices is to return to psychoanalysis. In *Gender Trouble* she explicitly rejects expressive theories of gender; that is the view that performances are expressions or exteriorizations of interior truths about the self. In *Bodies that Matter*, however, Butler endorses another form of psychoanalysis, one premised on a more fluid relation between the psyche and gender (understood in relation to identification) in which 'the opacity of the unconscious sets limits to the exteriorization of the psyche' (1993a: 24). In particular, she claims that the unconscious plays a constitutive role in the fabrication of identifications. There is, therefore, no possibility of the subject ever being able to fully control or manipulate their gender performances or identifications. Drag is not, therefore, the expression of the performer's will. If anything, Butler notes, '*what is "performed" works to conceal, if not to disavow, what remains opaque, unconscious, un-performable*' (Butler, 1993a: 24, original emphasis). Explored as an instance of Freudian melancholia, drag should be understood in terms of supposed disidentifications which are really disavowed identifications (ones both made and rejected in the unconscious). It is thus reinterpreted as an attempt to 'negotiate cross-gender identification' (Butler, 1993a: 25) understood as a doubled attachment to, yet repudiation of, femininity. What drag symbolizes, for Butler, is that all gender identities are themselves a mélange of such disavowals and identifications. How gender appears (or what is performed) can only be comprehended, therefore, in relation to what gender signifies (here understood to include that which is 'barred' from the signifier and from the realm of 'corporeal legibility' [1993b: 234]).

The acknowledgement of a process of unconscious identification is patently absent from those writings, drawing on Butler, that reinstate the voluntarist subject. It is the concept of psychic excess, as disruptive of intentions, that undermines the plans and intentions of the volitional subject and that guarantees the failure – at some level – of heterosexual ideals (Butler, 1991: 24). More significantly, though, the notion of politics implied by performance alters. The latitude for conscious, critical or self-reflective politics shrinks as the sphere of the unconscious (comprehended as loss, lack, etc.) encroaches. Whether this amalgamation of psychoanalytic and discursive elements is ultimately plausible is open to question. Its immediate effect, of course, is to shift the terms of the debate. The question now becomes: what distinguishes (if indeed anything can) a parodic performance based upon disavowed identification from a parodic performance emanating from a critical strategy of transgression? Where Butler differs from the advocates of 'feel-good' gender discourses, is in recognizing that individuated subjects presently operate within the constraints of normative heterosexuality; that, as such, all gender bears traces of the script of that normative system. This raises another question: do the revisions in Butler's work reinforce her earlier surmises about the transgressive potential of drag or do they undermine that very notion?

Transgression and/or Recuperation?

To illustrate some of the knotty problems linked to the political effectiveness of parody I want to use examples from two recent feminist crime novels where the key protagonists engage in drag:

> Before I went out I checked in the full length mirror on the closet door. The ankle of one stocking picked up the light and flashed its diamond triangle at me. I pulled off the [leather biker's] jacket and lifted myself up on my toes and twirled. High heels make you do that sort of thing. . . . I was a girl. . . . I wondered if I was going to cause any heart attacks among friends shocked *to see me in drag*. (Emma Victor in *She Came Too Late*, by Mary Wings, 1986: 90, my emphasis)

> I've chosen a fashionable gray wool dress and gray leather boots with pointed toes.
>
> Kip comes into the bedroom between patients. She looks at me as if I'm insane.
>
> 'Why are you dressed like that?'
>
> '*I felt like being in drag*' (Lauren Laurano in *Everything You Have is Mine*, by Sandra Scoppettone, 1992: 189, my emphasis)

Drag, in these two instances refers to lesbian women passing as heterosexual (using the armoury of femininity most typically associated with 'straight' women,[4] that is, wearing high heels and make-up) in order to enter undetected certain environments or spaces scripted as heterosexual.[5] In neither case is drag used to destabilize heterosexual norms; quite the contrary. For these instances of drag to be effective they have to pass as 'real'; otherwise the lives of the two private detectives will be threatened. What counts is that these performances cannot be read or recognized as performances. They must evoke belief. Rather than the denaturalization of gender norms, the performances of Laurano and Victor operate to re-idealize heterosexual norms through the (re)iteration of the conventions of hetero-femininity. In the contexts in which their performances occur, there is no contestation of heterosexual hegemony, no gender trouble. Instead, familiar, already encoded, signs (actions, gestures, forms of dress) are simply mobilized to achieve a specific result. To those who do not know them, Laurano and Victor are legible only as heterosexual. They are interpellated as heterosexual; their indifferent, unquantifiable bodies are turned into marked and intelligible ones. This, however, does not detract from the fact that, at some level, they are lesbians 'acting' straight.

In *Gender Trouble*, commenting on Kristeva, Butler writes that:

> If subversion is possible, it will be a subversion that emerges from within the terms of the law, through the possibilities that emerge when the law turns against itself and *spawns unexpected permutations of itself*. The culturally constructed body will then be liberated, neither to its 'natural' past, nor to its original pleasures, but to *an open future of cultural possibilities*. (1990b: 93, emphasis added)

In other words, the disruption of naturalized assumptions concerning sex/gender will be effected by the proliferation or 'unexpected permutations' of gendered identities. It is this proliferation that will confound binary sexual categories 'exposing [their] ... fundamental unnaturalness' (Butler, 1990b: 149). This sentiment recalls Barthes's utopian claim that once the binaries constitutive of sex(uality) dissolve: 'meaning and sex become the object of a free play, at the heart of which the (polysemant) forms and the (sensual) practices, liberated from the binary prison, will achieve a state of infinite expansion' (1977: 133). However, Butler substantially revises her position in *Bodies that Matter*. Here she claims that:

> The critical promise of drag does not have to do with the proliferation of genders, as if a sheer increase in numbers would do the job, but rather with the exposure or the failure of heterosexual regimes ever fully to legislate or contain their own ideals. Hence it is not that drag *opposes* heterosexuality, or that the proliferation of drag will bring down heterosexuality; on the contrary, drag tends to be the allegorization of heterosexuality ... (1993b: 237)

No longer is it the sheer permutation of gender identities through drag that counts. Now it is what that permutation attests to: the impossibility of normative heterosexuality containing its own ideals; its 'inefficacy'. Subversion is, consequently, a question 'of *working the weakness in the norms*' (Butler, 1993b: 237). This is important. The idea, common to some readings of *Gender Trouble*, that dressing-up *tout court* will lead to a proliferation of genders and, therefore, to gender transformation is downplayed in *Bodies that Matter*. The norms which form the matter of recitation 'taken not as commands to be obeyed, but as imperatives to be "cited", twisted, queered, brought into relief as heterosexual imperatives' are not necessarily 'subverted in the process' (1993b: 237). They may simply be re-idealized as the above fictional examples illustrated.[6]

The mutable world of gender in fiction is, however, far removed from the heteronormative world of, for example *Paris is Burning*[7] where the theatre of the drag balls is a comparative safe haven (in relation to their daily environments) for the transvestites who participate. As the plight of Venus Xtravaganza demonstrates all too starkly, when her ability to pass as a light-skinned woman (to actualize an idealized version of white femininity) in the world outside the ball fails, s/he dies a violent death.[8] Her death is, as Butler construes it, 'performed by a symbolic that would eradicate those phenomena that require an opening up of the possibilities for the resignification of sex' (1993b: 131). Although heterosexuality may constitute a form of imitation of an unattainable, phantasmatic ideal, a '*panicked* imitation of its own naturalized idealization' (Butler, 1991: 23), the penalties attached to failure in the contexts of transvestism are far more grave than in the instance of failed heterosexuality. Transvestism does not necessarily result in death but it portends few possibilities for living at ease in a heterosexual world. In contrast to a permissive perspective on the transgressive effects of parody in *Gender Trouble*, Butler develops a more circumspect account of these practices in *Bodies that Matter*. Drag is shown up as neither necessarily transgressive nor destabilizing. While this more nuanced reading overcomes the problem of assuming that the mere proliferation of genders can threaten the heterosexual matrix, it raises other issues. Is it possible to discriminate between a parodic performance that consolidates the heterosexual matrix and one that threatens the normative hold of heterosexuality? Can one ascertain, in some way, the effectiveness of any drag performance?

One of the difficulties in discriminating between the effects of parodic practice is analytical. Butler contends that all performances are imbricated in hegemonic power relations even as they contest them. This means that there is no possibility of pure opposition to a regime such as compulsory heterosexuality, since all types of sexual behaviour are positioned within this regime: homosexuality takes its meaning (in part or in full) from its constitutive relation with heterosexuality. Parodic performances operate from within the system, not from a position outside. This helps to explain how it is that transgressive practices may be recuperated or domesticated by dominant discourses: '[b]y working in the context of ... traditional categories, the simulacrum may seek to destabilize; but in practice, the categories are simply stretched and reproduced' (Kirkby, 1995: 93; see Butler, 1993b: 125).[9] Since performance operates through the deployment of signs with already standardized meanings, recuperation is ever a real possibility. But even if this is so, and I would want to concede this point, it does not evacuate the need to distinguish between parodic political activity that reinforces the heterosexual matrix and that which threatens to subvert it.

In 'Critically Queer', Butler is adamant that the only thing that renders a performance subversive is that it: 'is the kind of effect that *resists calculation*' (1993a: 29).[10] In relation to the effects of discourse, she proclaims, that they are not bounded by acts of legislation, the utterance of specific statements, nor by specific events. By contrast, 'the reach of their signifiability' cannot be controlled by their utterer. Resituating performances in particular contexts thus cannot help to gauge their force, for the very demarcation of a context is itself an attempt to prefigure the result. The whole point, for Butler, is that subversive actions always signify in unexpected ways and with unintended effects. It is simply impossible to plot the range or reach of all the forms of subversion emanating from specific discourses, acts, practices. Clearly at one level, her point has a certain validity. There is no way to outline all the possible effects of any action. A particular instance of parody may provoke simultaneous yet contradictory responses being seen as both transgressive and recuperable at the same time. The reach of an utterance may not be contained by the wishes, intentions or desires of its author. The earlier gay skinhead example is a case in point. The deployment of certain signs by gay (white) men may be read by others, particularly black gay others, in an entirely different way to that intended. To claim that pure intentions can be read off an act, ignores questions about 'when, where and to whom gendered performances are either "passable" for straight or readable as queer' (Walker, 1995: 71).

Even if we accept that there are incalculable effects to all (or most) statements or activities, this does not mean that we need to concede that there are no calculable effects. Without this possibility, political intervention may be construed as either totally meaningless (why bother?) or entirely spontaneous (it just happens). Critical reflection upon past, present, or future practices is essential to the exploitation of the gaps within hegemonic norms that allow for potential transformation of social relations. At least one dimension of that critique is generated by an attention to context. This enables us to measure, to some degree, the efficacy of past practices but it also provides us with a (historically sedimented) resource base from which to draw ideas and practices about suitable political tactics for specific contexts. Even though there is no guarantee of efficacy, there is a likelihood that certain parodic practices will be more efficacious in certain contexts than in others. This is illustrated, contrary perhaps to her own intentions, by one of Butler's own (earlier) examples: the case of 'the neighbourhood gay restaurant [that] puts out a sign explaining "she's overworked and needs a rest"'. Butler comments:

> This very gay appropriation of the feminine works to multiply possible sites of application of the term, to reveal the arbitrary relation between the signifier and the signified, and to destabilize and mobilize the sign. Is this a 'colonizing' appropriation of the feminine? My sense is no. That accusation assumes that the feminine belongs to women, an assumption surely suspect. (1990b: 122–3)

The point of this reading is to demonstrate how this usage of the pronoun 'she' is simultaneously a denaturalization of the link between 'she' and the 'feminine' as an attribute of womanliness and a redeployment which interrogates the legitimacy accorded to this unitary relationship. Butler's interpretation relies upon specific contextual knowledge: that the restaurant in question is a gay restaurant and that the author of the sign is not being sarcastic about the gay cook – that 'he' is not using the feminine pronoun to inscribe homosexuality as inherently effeminate (*contra* 'real' masculinity which is not). Only then might we (other readers) recognize this as parody. Not knowing this might lead us to regard the sign as confirmation that a woman's place is in the kitchen. The problem about Butler's interpretation (in the light of her own later) pronouncements is precisely that it limits the possible readings of this sign in order to demonstrate the radical destabilization of signifiers. While this may have the desired effect on specific users of the restaurant, a feminist reader may simply conclude that the sign-writer is a sexist pig. While Butler is right to claim that there are few or no ready-made meanings that can be inferred from signs, and while the very possibility that 'we' may read the above sign differently to 'her' suggests that we cannot contain entirely the possible consequences of our political interventions, she is mistaken in my view in abandoning (in her later work) any attention to context. To reiterate my point: the potential effects of any action may be more numerous than we may imagine or plan for; their effects may not be open to curtailment in advance. This does not undermine, however, the need for planned political action. In the above instance it is not the sign per se that compels us to renegotiate our reading practices (Butler in Osborne and Segal, 1994: 38) but rather the sign in its historical present.

The question is not just about what parodic intervention signifies but also where, when and to whom it signifies in the ways that it does. Parody may be transgressive from the perspective of the specific linear history of practices that constitute a particular individuated subject (exposing the fact that their doing of gender is always contingent). This does not guarantee, however, that it is parodic when seen in the context of others. It does not, that is, forefront sufficiently the lateral relations between bodies and subjectivities within determinate historical contexts. Osborne and Segal make a similar point when they note that 'transgressive reinscriptions' operate most effectively within 'critical subcultures' (1994: 38). It is within communities predisposed towards the dissolution of stable gender norms that parodic performances are likely to have the greatest effect, precisely because it is these communities that have least to lose from the denaturalization of heterosexuality. This centres specific people in specific places at specific times. They too, however, downplay the effect of these performances in a wider context; say, when they are reiterated in the dominant culture. Where for Butler identifying, in advance, who will be affected by parody is deemed to constitute an illegitimate attempt to prescribe its results, the absence of any account of context turns politics into an entirely haphazard endeavour. It implies that when parody is at its best, the actions themselves, and the radical responses and appropriations it inspires, may lead to the performative production of new groups; that is, groups which do not exist prior to these (re-)citational practices. It leaves open the question of parody at its worst: what are its effects?

Conclusion

My aim in this article was to explore a set of issues which are critical to Butler's project: the connections between performance and performativity; the theoretical shifts in her work after *Gender Trouble*; and the question of how to understand the political effects of performativity. In addition, I wanted to consider some of the ways in which Butler's work has been taken up. My purpose was to better understand one of the most vital ways of dealing with 'identity' in recent times. As an explanation of gender identity, Butler's argument has much to recommend it: it avoids unnecessary universalization; it explains how gender comprehended discursively is lived on a day-to-day basis not as the effect of determinism but as the reiterative effect of an historically specific ensemble of practices, gestures and ideas. Moreover, through the very idea of (re)iteration, Butler explores how change may be engendered where 'the demand to resignify and repeat the very terms which constitute the "we" [e.g. women or lesbian] cannot be summarily refused, but neither can they be followed in strict obedience' (Butler, 1993b: 124). The idea that occasional gaps open up within contemporary culture where norms (both dominant and annihilating) can be mimed, reworked, resignified and, of course, reincorporated is suggestive. There are, however, a number of difficulties with this project.

First, as I demonstrated above, Butler's work has been appropriated to endorse a hyper-voluntarist gender politics where it is assumed that we can meddle at will with our gender identities, changing them as we choose. This view is predicated on the ambiguity in Butler's work concerning the connections between performance and performativity. Butler's idea of performance is read as instituting a politics of subversion. The difficulty is that it is hard to see what precisely renders a performance discrete from the performative context of gender since both rely upon recitation of the same norms and conventions. Given Butler's repudiation of the notion of the autonomous agent as the originator of performances, the idea that a performance is the expression of free choice is rejected. Similarly, the idea that performance is hyperbolic display of ordinary performative effects is contested on the grounds of measuring what counts as excess (and here context is surely important). The lack of clarity about how a performance is to be understood leads to a paradoxical position. Since the performative produces that which it names, and since gender is understood in performative terms as the effect of the intersection of discourses and practices of gender, and since these discourses and practices also underpin performances, it suggests that a performance is itself performative. The distinction seems to be of little help. Indeed it raises more questions than it answers. This ambiguity also raises a second set of questions about the kinds of politics ensuing from the idea of gender as performative.

In terms of political productiveness, the focus of the discussion concerned the contextualization of parodic performances. As the fictional examples showed, drag in itself is not subversive. It only works as such on particular occasions in determinate locales. One of the weaknesses of the concept of performativity as an explanation of gender is that it is comprehensible primarily as an account of individuation: the historicity of a particular subject's construction as a gendered being. As a consequence, it is easy to over-emphasize the discontinuities in gender performance; to present them as indicative of disruptive behaviour. What is occluded, as a consequence, is the space within which performance occurs, the others involved in or implicated by the production, and how they receive and interpret what they see. The possibility for continual resignification immanent to performativity hides the fact that not all resignifications are pertinent or efficacious politically; indeed they are highly contingent. Only some performances in some contexts can impel categorial rethinking. Butler's decision to abandon her more contextually sensitive account of parody in *Gender Trouble* for a concept of subversion as resisting all calculation confuses, rather than clarifies, the issue. Accepting that there will be unplanned effects of any discourse or practice does not mean that there is no point in planning political tactics. Moreover, the very fact that certain activities come to have an authority as modes of political intervention prompts not only their recitation in the present but may also enhance their recognition and efficacy. In arguing that every political action generates incalculable effects, Butler over-emphasizes the unplanned effects of activity at the cost of the planned.

Notes

I owe a debt of gratitude to several people: first to the anonymous reviewers who offered useful suggestions for improving the piece. Second, to those friends and colleagues who have not only read earlier versions of this article but have had to put up with my endless questions as I tussled with Butler's fascinating but often opaque writings. These include: Anna Cutler, Iain MacKenzie, Alan Finlayson, Kimberly Hutchings and Andrew Thacker (who also has the misfortune to have lived with this article and these discussions on a daily basis). In addition, many thanks to all who participated in the intellectually (and socially) invigorating workshop on sexuality in Oslo organized through the ECPR. Especial thanks, in this context, to Terrell Carver and Véronique Mottier for all their hard work.

1. Dressing-up can only be read as one facet of gender; it is neither coextensive nor synonymous with it.

2. For a different reading of the relationship between performance and performativity see Schrift (1995).

3. I am not at all convinced that these elements can be combined without producing tension in Butler's theory. In particular, Butler never clearly distinguishes between a failure to repeat (the Lacanian), a difference produced simply by repetition (the Derridean) and a practice of transgression (the Foucauldian). I explore the tension between the politics of negativity and that of positivity in greater detail in my forthcoming book, *A Feminist Politics of Difference*.

4. This interpretation relies upon a particular construction of lesbianism as eschewing specific kinds of dress which might be seen as inappropriate –

inauthentic? – modes of self-expression and of heterosexuality as coded through high heels and make-up, arguably a highly satirical version of straight femininity. Emma learns 'her' heterosexuality via imitation: 'I fluffed my hair, a lesson from Patricia.' Further her movements are also imitative: 'I lifted my heels, turned on my toes, shoulders back, and ass in. I pranced into the room' (Wings, 1986: 98, 94).

5. Emma Victor is attending a function at the house of a murder victim – a space coded as heterosexual, while Lauren Laurano is out on a blind date with a suspected murderer who picks his victims through the virtual heterosexual space of an Internet mailing list.

6. In fiction, the options for unsettling expectations about gender are plentiful as the following précis of *Gaudi Afternoon* by Barbara Wilson evidences: 'Frankie, the "wife", is really a male–female transsexual; Ben, the "husband", is a radical feminist bulldagger; April, her New Age cultural feminist "girl"friend, an Earth Mother who dislikes children, is a male–female transsexual but Ben doesn't know it; April's "friend" is her gay closet cross-dressing stepbrother with whom she shares "Shame Issues" . . .' (Munt, 1994: 143–4).

7. This is the film by Jennie Livingstone that documents the highly stylized drag balls that occur every year in Harlem, New York. At these balls, 'men' dress up as women (and as various 'types' of white male) in order to compete for various prizes. This film is discussed by Butler in *Bodies that Matter*.

8. Whether from the violence of racism when s/he is recognized as Hispanic and not white, or from the violence of homophobia when s/he is recognized as a biological male is unclear. On race in *Paris is Burning* see hooks (1992).

9. The context for Kirkby's remark is the self-transformation of Michael Jackson of which he is critical. The notion that there is either an authentic black identity or indeed a natural identity for black people is challenged by Kobena Mercer (1994).

10. Indeed in 'Critically Queer' she talks only about the incalculability of subversive actions. This is remedied, partially in *Bodies that Matter*, where she concedes that certain actions are planned, although her overall argument remains the same.

Bibliography

Austin, J.L. (1962) *How to Do Things with Words*, 2nd edn. Oxford: Oxford University Press.

Barthes, Roland (1977) *Roland Barthes by Roland Barthes*. Basingstoke: Macmillan.

Bell, David, Jon Binnie, Julia Cream and Gill Valentine (1994) 'All Hyped Up and No Place to Go', *Gender, Place and Culture: A Journal of Feminist Geography* 1(1): 31–47.

Bordo, Susan (1994) *Unbearable Weight: Feminism, Western Culture and the Body*. Berkeley: University of California Press.

Butler, Judith (1990a) 'Gender Trouble: Feminist Theory, and Psychoanalytic Discourse, pp. 324–40 in Linda Nicholson (ed.) *Feminism/Postmodernism*. London: Routledge.

Butler, Judith (1990b) *Gender Trouble: Feminism and the Subversion of Identity*. London: Routledge.

Butler, Judith (1991) 'Imitation and Gender Insubordination', pp. 13–31 in Diana Fuss (ed.) *Inside/Out: Lesbian Theories, Gay Theories*. London: Routledge.

Butler, Judith (1992) 'Contingent Foundations: Feminism and the Question of "Postmodernism"', pp. 3–21 in J. Butler and J.W. Scott (eds) *Feminists Theorize the Political*. London: Routledge.

Butler, Judith (1993a) 'Critically Queer', *GLQ: A Journal of Lesbian and Gay Studies* 1: 17–32.

Butler, Judith (1993b) *Bodies that Matter: On the Discursive Limits of 'Sex'*. London: Routledge.

Butler, Judith (1995) 'For a Careful Reading', pp. 127–43 in Seyla Benhabib, Judith Butler, Drucilla Cornell and Nancy Fraser (eds) *Feminist Contentions: A Philosophical Exchange*, with an introduction by Linda Nicholson. London: Routledge.

Derrida, Jacques (1991) 'Signature Event Context', pp. 82–111 in Peggy Kamuf (ed.) *Between the Blinds: A Derrida Reader*. Hemel Hempstead: Harvester Wheatsheaf.

Flax, Jane (1990) *Thinking Fragments: Psychoanalysis, Feminism and Postmodernism in the Contemporary West*. Berkeley: University of California Press.

Fuss, Diana (1995) *Identification Papers*. London: Routledge.

Hawkes, Gail (1995) 'Dressing-Up – Cross Dressing and Sexual Dissonance', *Journal of Gender Studies* 4(3): 261–70.

hooks, bell (1992) 'Is Paris Burning?', pp. 145–56 in bell hooks, *Black Looks: Race and Representation*. Boston: South End Press.

Kirkby, Andrew (1995) 'Straight Talk on the PomoHomo Question', *Gender, Place and Culture: A Journal of Feminist Geography* 2(1): 89–95.

Lloyd, Moya (forthcoming) *A Feminist Politics of Difference*. London: Sage.

Luckhurst, Roger (1995) 'Queer Theory (and Oscar Wilde): Review Essay', *Journal of Gender Studies* 4(3): 333–40.

Martin, Biddy (1992) 'Sexual Practice and Changing Lesbian Identities', pp. 93–119 in Michele Barrett and Anne Phillips (eds) *Destabilising Theory: Contemporary Feminist Debates*. Cambridge: Polity.

Mercer, Kobena (1994) *Welcome to the Jungle: New Positions in Black Cultural Studies*. London: Routledge.

Munt, Sally (1994) *Murder by the Book: Feminism and the Crime Novel*. London: Routledge.

Norval, Aletta (1994) 'Social Ambiguity and the Crisis of Apartheid', pp. 115–37 in Ernesto Laclau (ed.) *The Making of Political Identities*. London: Verso.

Osborne, Peter and Lynne Segal (1994) 'Gender as Performance: An Interview with Judith Butler', *Radical Philosophy* 67: 32–9.

Patton, Cindy (1995) 'Performativity and Spatial Distinction: The End of AIDS Epidemiology', pp. 173–96 in Andrew Parker and Eve Kosofsky Sedgwick (eds) *Performativity and Performance*. London: Routledge.

Poovey, Mary (1992) 'The Abortion Question and the Death of Man', pp. 239–56 in Judith Butler and Joan W. Scott (eds) *Feminists Theorize the Political*. London: Routledge.

Probyn, Elspeth (1995) 'Lesbians in Space: Gender, Sex and the Structure of Missing', *Gender, Place and Culture: A Journal of Feminist Geography* 2(1): 77–84.

Raymond, Janice (1986) *A Passion for Friends: Towards a Philosophy of Female Affection*. Boston: Beacon Press.

Scoppettone, Sandra (1992) *Everything You Have is Mine*. London: Virago.

Schrift, Alan D. (1995) 'Reconfiguring the Subject as a Process of Self: Following Foucault's Nietzschean Trajectory to Butler, Laclau/Mouffe, and Beyond', *New Formations* 25(Summer): 28–39.

Spivak, Gayatri (1988) 'Subaltern Studies: Deconstructing Historiography', pp. 197–221 in Gayatri Spivak, *In Other Worlds: Essays in Cultural Politics*. New York and London: Routledge.

Walker, Lisa (1995) 'More than Just Skin-Deep: Fem(me)ininity and the Subversion of Identity', *Gender, Place and Culture: A Journal of Feminist Geography* 2(1): 71–6.

Wings, Mary (1986) *She Came Too Late*. London: Women's Press.

Moya Lloyd is lecturer in Political Theory at the Queen's University of Belfast. She has written articles on Foucault and feminism and on the politics of the body. She is co-editor (with Andrew Thacker) of *The Impact of Michel Foucault on the Social Sciences and Humanities* (Macmillan, 1997) and is working on a book entitled *A Feminist Politics of Difference* (Sage).

Beyond Food/Sex
Eating and an Ethics of Existence

Elspeth Probyn

> Appetite is nothing but the very essence of man. (Spinoza, *The Ethics*, in Balibar, 1998: 82)

What's Eating Us?

IT SEEMS like a strange time to be arguing that the primacy of sex may be passing. After all, the world has watched in horror and mostly disbelief as Bill's concept of sexuality was disclosed. In fact, my horror was caused less by the Monicagate ensemble than by the idea that this article would be totally out of sync with the times. But as commentators (perhaps especially outside the US) constantly complained about being bored with sex, and as the sex–non-sex definitions were aired, it became legitimate to wonder whether this scandal constituted the last gasp of the reign of sex. (It also led me to wonder if oral sex wasn't sex, was it eating?) Possible epistemological ruptures aside, in this article, and under the rubric of the question that Foucault (1997: 303) takes from Kant ('*Was ist die Aufklärung?*' ['What is Enlightenment?']), I want to ask 'What's eating us now?' As you will recall, this is to question 'who we are in the present'; to engage with passion in 'stalking the elusive singularity of the present' (Rabinow, 1997: xviii). In my own small quest to figure the present, I try to follow the line of sex as it intersects with that of food. My argument takes from research that I have been conducting in Australia on the role that food now occupies in re-articulating national identity. More generally, I am interested in thinking about a new ethics of existence, one which is theoretically indebted to Foucault and his work on the dietetic regimen, or as Deleuze puts it, the alimentary-sexual regime (1986: 102). Along with others, I want to try to push at our ways of thinking sexuality in order to get beyond the impasse that threatens studies of sexuality. Simply put, I will argue that thinking sex through food is compelling for the ways that it focuses our attention on the

▪ *Theory, Culture & Society* 1999 (SAGE, London, Thousand Oaks and New Delhi), Vol. 16(2): 215–228
[0263-2764(199904)16:2;215–228;008262]

interrelation of various corporeal dimensions: that constituting oneself as an ethical subject involves conjugating the forces of sex along with those of food, exercise, sleeping, writing and thinking.

Like a rhizomatic line that always turns into something else, the vector of food soon leads into other areas, and along the way I have been struck by the ways in which the boundaries between food and sex are currently being blurred. As others have argued, food has a propensity for hazing the frontiers of categories. For instance, Georg Simmel argues that food encapsulates the paradox of absolute individuality and complete universality: 'Of everything that people have in common, the most common is that they must eat and drink. It is precisely this which is, oddly enough, the most egoistic, and the most unconditionally and most immediately linked to each individual' (1994: 346). Food here is both what we all share and forms the absolute limit to any commonality. Simmel writes that 'what the individual eats, no one else can eat under any circumstance' (1994: 346). By this rather strange statement, Simmel gestures to what we might call the brute physicality of food: as the morsel is going into my mouth, pricking up my tongue and taste buds, and then sliding down on its route to digestion and finally defecation, you cannot be anything more than a witness. In the face of this fundamental alienation of one from the other, it is only 'the shared meal [that] lifts an event of physiological primitivity and inescapable commonality into the sphere of social interaction' (Simmel, 1994: 346).

As that which both viscerally segregates us and radically brings us together, without doubt food is a hugely powerful system of values, regulations and beliefs; in short a system of representation that hides its nature in appeals to immediacy, and non-mediation. One of the difficulties that faces any investigation of food is its enormity, and the ways in which it spills into every aspect of life. As it lends itself to easy metaphor, the chances are that any sociological specificity will be lost. Mary Douglas quite rightly warned against the propensity to privilege an overly cultural or symbolic reading of food, stating that 'Food is not only a metaphor or vehicle of communication; a meal is a physical event' (in Symons, 1994: 339). In a similar fashion, Arjun Appadurai argues that 'Food may generally possess a special semiotic force because of certain universal properties.... But this special force must always remain tacit until it is animated by particular cultural concepts and mobilized by particular social contexts' (1981: 509). Appadurai qualifies the rush to celebrate food's innate universal qualities by arguing that 'the cultural notion that food has an inherently homogenizing capacity ... is itself converted from a metonymic hazard into a metaphoric convenience in the contexts where sharing, equality, solidarity, and communality are, within limits, perceived as desirable results' (1981: 507).

The problems that arise from either 'a metonymic hazard' or a 'metaphoric convenience' are especially troubling if one wants to use food to think through different relations of sociality. To name but a few, food is imbricated in nation-building, the reproduction of the family, constitutes a major site of the division of labour, and is central in the production of geo-political inequalities. But if food statements commonly contain a metonymic connection ('you are what you eat'), the peculiarities of what and how you are eating and the connections to who or what you are soon get lost. As Appadurai reminds us, food seems to possess inherent tropic qualities. Simply put, food moves about all the time. It constantly shifts registers: from the sacred to the everyday, from metaphor to materiality, it is the most common and elusive of matters. This is, of course, not 'natural' to food, and as Roland Barthes has argued 'food has a constant tendency to transform itself into situation' (1979: 171). For as he states, food is always 'bound to values of power', revealing the fact that 'a representation of contemporary existence is implied in the consciousness we have of the function of food' (1971: 171).

I will now turn to several sites that highlight the scrambling of sex, gender and food. I use these somewhat idiosyncratic examples to sketch out the possibilities that food may offer in rethinking the limits of sex deployed as the sole or privileged object within the theorization of identity. I should be clear that this is not a polemic against those theories (queer and feminist) that have centred on sex, and which I have myself used. Rather, it is my wish to *extend* the reach of sexuality by looking first at the way that sex now spills on to food, and, second, at accounts of food that compel us to think in terms of another ethics of living. While I realize the enormity of the term, here I take Foucault's fairly simple if demanding line on ethics in order to concentrate on modes of living already in existence, 'to learn from and strengthen these, not to discover or "invent" others' (Rabinow, 1997: xxvii). If 'ethics' cannot be reified as an object, but rather it is always a mode of relating to oneself and to others, then the task of thinking ethics will necessarily be a doubled one. On the one hand, it enjoins us to seek out the singularities marking our present, and on the other hand to engage with them as they mark us. The promise of thinking food/sex is that it requires attention to what Foucault calls 'attitude': 'a way of thinking and feeling; a way too of acting and behaving that at one and the same time marks a relation of belonging and presents itself as task' (in Rabinow, 1997: xxxi). The question I put to myself, then, is in what ways might food and sex come to constitute the outlines of another way of thinking and feeling, one that is fuelled by what the novelist Antoine Laurent calls 'sympathy': 'Sympathy for where she is, for who she's with, and for what's feasible at any time or place. For the ingredients themselves, the people she's cooking for, all play a part' (1989: 24). In this sense, sympathy highlights an ethical practice, not a passive acceptance of life. In what follows, I will first sketch out certain overdetermined ways of constituting food/sex, and then focus on the ethical possibilities that food and sex offer when practised with care, restraint and good timing.

Food Chic

To start, come with me to Sydney in order to experience the sights and smells. It is a hazy summer evening in the fashionable enclave of Potts Point, and around the corner from the flesh spots of King's Cross things were getting hot and sticky at the Paramount restaurant. The buzz spilled on to the pavement as a veritable who's who of Australian power-queers sipped a concoction called 'passion pops'. In terms of the Sydney Gay and Lesbian Mardi Gras, 'Eat our Words', a queer fiction and food fest, was the hottest ticket and sold out in minutes. The event had gay and lesbian writers squashed in like mere membranes of a *mille-feuille*, digestive fodder in between the sumptuous courses. The real star of the night was Christine Manfield who, along with her partner Margie Harris, owns the Paramount. The mistress of ceremonies introduced her as 'the dominatrix of the kitchen', 'sex on a plate', and described one of Manfield's famous dishes, 'Creaming Cock' which compels the eater to go down on large *tuile* cones with apple-ginger custard and Tokay caramel. In turn, Manfield said grace, telling us 'to eat the words that you are given and if you want to go down, go ahead'. The *pièce de resistance* was not a cigar but Manfield's signature dish, the 'slice of pride', a beautiful pink and white ice cream triangle which in true commensal fashion we were to share.

Let me turn now from the restaurant to television. In one of the weirder series, two large women regale with tales of derring-do among the landed gentry of Scotland, ham it up with the members of a girls' school lacrosse team, flirt with boy scouts, and play at being Annie Oakley on the moors as they shoot small birds. In between titbits about cooking testicles in Benghazi (in cream of course), or musings about their 'kitchenalia fetish', one of the ladies plunges her beringed fingers complete with long red nails into a bowl of raw mince and egg, the other passes scathing remarks about vegetarians, microwave ovens and supermarket bought chicken, the conversation is peppered with remarks about 'real faggots' (meatballs), instructions to wrap your meatloaf in bacon so it looks like a Union Jack, and we learn that 'pan Asian' is really Australian. This is all lubricated with asides about 'slap-up meals', 'toothsome meat', and odd refrains of songs: 'The playing fields of Eton have made us frightfully brave' croons the one, as the other declines Latin verbs.

The programme is the phenomenally successful BBC cooking show *Two Fat Ladies*, starring the decidedly upper-class Clarissa Dickson Wright who apparently owes her girth to a destroyed thyroid brought about by an excess of gin, and the worldly and at times rather 'pukka' Jennifer Paterson; she of the long red nails to be found at the end of an episode clutching cigarette and gin and tonic. Talking to others, it wasn't surprising to find that many found this show decidedly queer. Certainly, Jennifer's arch comments belie a Cowardesque inclination (her immediate advice to the young female producer was 'to find yourself a nice poof'). And the easy banter of the two ladies is evidence of a female homosociality, which may also be a mellowed version of the edgy homoerotism rampant in private girls' schools. If the Ladies were good on their first series, in the second they get down and have a great time with each other. Perhaps being centrefolds in the British gay mag, *Attitude* (November, 1997) has given them the cue to show off that they are as queer as a bent sixpence in a rich fruit loaf (lavished with cream no doubt). While the interviewer, Nick Taylor had them pegged ('Eccentric, shameless and unmarried? They're clearly lesbians'), they will only admit to being vegetarian-phobic, and very *fond* of men. But as they drool over the young boys from King's College Cambridge, remarking on the fact that the white ruffles around the singers' necks make them look like deliciously edible little lamb chops, it is their pronounced taste for all forms of flesh that tantalizes.

In their latest cookbook, *Two Fat Ladies Full Throttle*, we're told that 'the whole of the USA seemed to have developed Fatladymania' (Paterson and Dickson Wright, 1998: 7). Given the fact that Clarissa 'holds the home of the hamburger responsible for everything that's wrong with the modern world – including fast food, political correctness and plastic surgery', they may be deluding themselves about their status in the States. However, certainly in Britain they move with the powerful, and dine with the Blairs. In short, they inhabit the world where, as a recent columnist writes, 'Chefs are the new rock 'n' roll stars, cookbooks are the new pornography'. Wendy Harmer concludes that 'When the difference between a boring Saturday night alone and an evening of mind-blowing erotic adventure is a backlit picture of a chargrilled eggplant ... you've got it made' (1998: 29). In the boudoir, the kitchen, or more likely in a trendy restaurant, it seems that food has become more exciting than sex. As a case in point, the *Sydney Morning Herald* recently instructed that we should 'Forget sex sells – these days food sells. Replace the motor show dolly birds with a plate of stuffed squid draped over the car bonnet and see what happens' (9 February 1998). The article focuses on the new smart restaurant in Sydney, 'MC Garage' which offers 'extravagant petrol heads a sportscar as a side with their octopus ... snapper and mussel stew with saffron, tomato and rouille'. Apparently, replacing girlies with sexy and expensive food has resulted in a doubling of the sales of MGs which start at $45,000. Food also seems to sell queer mags. The Australian gay glossy *Blue* recently published a display of the popular Manfield doing 'rude food'. According to a breathless newspaper report, this featured an s/m scene with two models in meringue, raspberry sauce, nipple rings, and 'plenty of black leather'. In actual fact, the scenes were pretty tame with a rather sweet looking Manfield in black lurex and spikes. While one can only agree with Manfield's motto that 'Life's too short for bad food, bad sex or no sex at all' (in Karpinski, 1998: 88), her recipes and food are, in fact, a lot sexier than the photos.

This is hardly surprising given that the food pages of newspapers have replaced the personals as the site of titillation and innuendo. For example, one newspaper recently outed vegetables with the headline of 'Look What's Crawled Out of the Crisper: Glam Veg' (*Sydney Morning Herald*, 4 November 1997). Citing k.d. lang, the article describes vegetarians as 'sort of, well, glamorous. Emerging chrysalis-like from their earth-brown shirts, the new vegetarians match sauvignon blanc with their asparagus ... and get terribly upset if the chef hasn't double-peeled their broad beans' (Dupleix, *Sydney Morning Herald*, 1 November 1997). As vegetables oust lesbian chic, food writers have become political philosophers, telling us why eating seasonal food will save the world. Food writer, Jill Dupleix, turns sexologist, and alongside a scrumptious recipe for oysters, comforts us with a thought that could have been lifted from any number of sexual manuals. She comments that in matters of sex, 'Just remember ... that your mood is even more important than your food. If you are feeling warm, relaxed, happy and loved, then cheese on toast and a nice cup of tea are going to work just as well' (1994: 100). Following the cue of the Californian doyenne of food as philosophy, Alice Waters, restaurateurs and critics alike now are on a crusade: 'For me food is a totally painless way of awakening people and sharpening their senses' (Waters, 1982: xi).

So what *is* this food fetishism all about? Could it be simply that food is now replacing sex as the ground of identities, be they gendered, national, postcolonial, collective or individual? If this is so, what happens to the purchase of all those theories – feminist, gay, lesbian, queer, psychoanalytic, etc. – that have privileged sex in one way or another as either constituting the very truth of ourselves; or those that have invested in endlessly deconstructing that supposed truth? While it is tempting to categorically proclaim that sex is dead, long live the cook as queen, this is not only hasty but would, I think, miss the insights that the current popular cultural food scene provides. While there are numerous analytic lines that flow from food, here I want to consider whether in the celebration of food as sex and sex as food we can see some of the limitations of dominant theoretical uses of sex. For instance, certain examples of food porn forcefully reveal the limits of thinking in terms of transgression, be it about food or sex.

Bluntly put, the conflation of food/sex may be simply convenient (the use of easy metaphors), or sloppy (the type of inversion that makes meat equal masculinity). Either way, these appropriations of food miss their mark. For surely sexuality, like food, is only of interest insofar as it allows us to see new connections between individuals, collectivities: to ask what sex and food allow and disallow. Whether it be food or sex, or a doubled reconfiguration of both, what matters is how they enable precise connections to be thought and enacted. In Deleuze and Guattari's words, 'What regulates the obligatory, necessary, or permitted interminglings of bodies is above all an alimentary regime and a sexual regime' (1991: 90). In turn, I also want to question what types of ethical bodies the intermingling of sex and food might produce.

This is at the heart of Foucault's argument in the second volume of *The History of Sexuality*, where he is interested not in sex per se but rather in the conception of corporeal ethics that the Greeks practised. As a way of defining 'the uses of pleasure ... in terms of a certain way of caring for one's body', diet, or the notion of the regimen was central (Foucault, 1986: 97). Foucault argues that regimen was dietetic not therapeutic, thus signalling an important difference between a Greek conception of ethics and sex, and how the ensuing history of Western thought and practice would deal with sex. Thus, 'diet', what, how, when and where one eats 'characterised the way in which one managed one's existence . . . a mode of problematisation of behavior. . . . Regimen was a whole art of living' (1986: 98). If one were interested in generalizations of history, one could say that sex became the object of what Foucault describes as the Christian motif of 'knowing oneself', whereas food and diet continued as the way in which one cared for oneself.

The Moral of the Flesh

Of course, things are not quite so clear cut. The long tradition within anthropology reminds us that food has also functioned as a privileged way by which we know and categorize the other. For instance, the preoccupation with cannibalism within anthropology reveals much about the colonial imagination as well as the constitution of the discipline (Hulme, 1998).[1] 'Eating the other' is both a metaphor for imperial violence, and the point where knowing the self and caring for the self merge, where food and sex intersect (Derrida, 1991; hooks, 1993). Either way we are faced with the elemental fact of the flesh. In a bare manner, flesh confuses the limits of what we are and what we eat, what or who we want; flesh encapsulates the quandary of whether the body in question is edible, fuckable, or both. As Derrida so famously states, it is 'a question no longer of knowing if it is 'good' to eat the other or if the other is 'good' to eat. . . . One eats him regardless and lets himself be eaten by him' (1991: 114).[2] Breast or thigh, dark or white meat, or a sweaty sexy entanglement of limbs? Angela Carter's early feminist critique of the function of sex in Sade mines the possibilities as well as the limits of flesh. As she writes, 'The word "fleisch", in German, provokes me to an involuntary shudder. In the English language, we make a fine distinction between flesh, which is usually alive and typically, human; and meat, which is dead, inert, animal and intended for consumption' (1979: 137). Her musings set off others: in French, '*la chair*' evokes the delicious intermingling of species as well as the variety of human form. '*La chair*' equally refers to animal, human and vegetable flesh, but also always brings to mind the image of a woman '*bien en chair*', rounded, voluptuous, or again in the superbly evocative French adjective, '*plantureuse*' – copious, lavish, buxom, fertile, of an ample *poitrine*. In French one dives into the expansiveness of flesh, describing penetration as '*entrer dans les chairs*', and firm young flesh is seemingly of necessity exemplified in the dictionary as '*aimer la chair fraîche*', for indeed how could anyone not *aimer entrer dans les chairs fraîches,* not wish to enter into young firm flesh.

Carter uses the semiotic slides between body/flesh/meat to give a compelling critique of Sade, and by extension of certain modern understandings of sexuality. She draws out the ways that a mechanics of transgression based solely in the inversion of body and meat is at the core of Sade's work. Against either celebration or simple condemnation, Carter shows how his mania for sexual transgression as inversion was fundamentally uninteresting. Her argument constitutes an early warning against an overvalorization of sex as transgressive when she proposes that Sade provides a model of sex that in the end is devoid of complication. For all his physical exertion, sex is rigidly compartmentalized and serves to confine the leakages between categories. 'Sade is a great puritan and will disinfect of sensuality anything he can lay his hands on; therefore he writes about sexual relations in terms of butchery and meat' (1979: 138).

In Carter's argument, sexual pleasure through transgression maintains a sovereign position for the transgressor and serves only to reinforce the inward-looking, isolated and alienated subject. It is the very principle of containment, with sex as 'nothing but a private and individual shock of the nerves'. As such, 'sexual pleasure is not experienced *as* experience; it does not modify the subject' (1979: 144). When sex is a cerebral, knowing act of transgression, 'where desire is a function of the act rather than the act a function of desire, desire loses its troubling otherness' (1979: 145). It becomes a way of reterritorializing the subject rather than sending it into lines of flight. In other words, this model of transgression fundamentally reterritorializes the body in sex. Instead of being the fusion of bodies that confuses their limits, sex as meat becomes the principle to reintegrate.

In a wonderful line, Carter writes that the bed is 'as public as the dinner table and governed by the same rules of formal confrontation' (1979: 146). Carter's reading of Sade clarifies for me why I find much of the current food-porn boring. Call me the Sheila Jeffreys of food-sex, but representations of sex combined with food are not per se transgressive (although of course that would not be the complaint that anti-porn campaigners would use). In a recent example of transgression as inversion, Linda Jaivin's bestselling novel and soon to be film, *Eat Me*, uses food to disguise the ways sex is rendered as the very principle of normalization. In the opening story, one of the heroines, Ava, is in the supermarket stuffing different kinds of fruit up her cunt. To be more precise, figs, strawberries, grapes, and a kiwi fruit before the store detective stops her and is ordered to eat her out. He then fucks her with a banana. She then fucks him with a Lebanese cucumber. The store closes, and as they leave it turns out that this is a regular routine: 'See you next week, honey pot? asked Adam. 'Usual time, usual place?' 'You bet, sweet pea', answers Ava (1995: 1–7).

What emerges from Jaivin's novel is the sense that sex on its own is no longer terribly interesting. And to be fair, she is not alone in this regard. Indeed the issue of 'sex on its own' is implicitly raised by 'the ampersand problem' of sexual politics, a problem that queer was supposed to fix by its expansive inclusiveness, but may have instead aggravated. While Jaivin's account is fundamentally about heterosex, she seeks to queer it by hyphenating sex and food. But surely the queerness of sex is not to be found in merely adding on another bit; does it not lie in the way in which it compels other combinations, sends lines out to seemingly distant realms and brings other worlds into dizzying proximity. When queer becomes content merely to *be* sex, is it possible that it may actually hinder our capacities to make connections? Posed as the answer, we need to question whether sex can really explain everything.

The Repressive Hypothesis of Meat

Within certain cultures of eating it seems that sex can explain everything. When it comes to *not* eating meat, it also seems that the repressive hypothesis is well and truly alive. If we no longer say 'no' to sex, in some articulations of eating, 'no' is the way to go. Carole Adams is the guru of such thought, and takes a radical feminist anti-porn line into the realm of eating, equating s/m and butchery in a sort of weird return to Sade. In her book, *The Sexual Politics of Meat*, women and animals are the 'voiceless' victims of patriarchy. She reiterates endlessly that 'Eating animals acts as a mirror and representation of patriarchal values' (1990: 187). In fact it doesn't seem to matter whether it is animal or woman that is the object of consumption because 'Meat eating is the re-inscription of male power at every meal' (1990: 187). This yields a direct equation of the terms meat and men, which then can be inverted at will: 'The killed and slaughtered animal yields ... imagery of ferociousness, territorial imperative, armed hunting, aggressive behavior, the vitality and virility of meat eating' (1990: 189).

Strangely enough Adams' unreconstructed rad-fem analysis of sexual politics is similarly structured to the wannabe 'bad girl' Jaivin's orgy of heterosex dished with fruit and veg. To use Carter's phrase, in neither does the combination of food and sex fulfil the capacity of the flesh for the 'fusion to confuse'. In Jaivin's story, it is clear that she 'knows' what sex is, and the addition of vegetables and fruit merely serves to enforce this knowingness. And in a congruent fashion, Adams wants to police the troubling fusion of flesh eating flesh. In her rage against meat-eaters and, worse, those 'bad' vegetarians who eat fish, we hear not ethics but the maintenance of strict predetermined boundaries.[3]

In these scenarios, the importation of food into sex tends to close down the troubling possibilities of sex – as well as those of food. I would suggest that these examples show up some of the limits of sex, or at least the limited possibilities of an ampersand model of sex, whereby addition doesn't alter the other term. As Foucault argued throughout his work, the point was to lose oneself, to have oneself rearranged through sex or thought or writing. We are however increasingly faced with the question of whether sex can rearrange us when it is transformed into an object, the measure of inclusion and exclusion.

It is perhaps inevitable that human practices will take on the force of stratification, and then require other actions to free them up. In Deleuze and Guattari's argument, lines of flight will always be reterritorialized, and then require a change in attitude in order to open them up again. An example of both the stultifying weight of concepts as well as the positivity of freeing them can be heard in Maria Angel and Zoë Sofia's wonderful reading of Peter Greenaway's film, *The Cook, the Thief, His Wife and Her Lover*. You will recall that Greenaway fuses food and sex, using the figure of the cannibal to carry his contempt for the lower middle-class rich. Angel and Sofia concentrate on the excess of his representation in order to elaborate a feminist rethinking of the ethics of eating and sex. Arguing against the limitations of the phallus, they instead plunder the surplus generated around anal and oral eroticisms which produce 'an extraordinary mobility and confusion of organs and spaces and the things that go in and out of them' (1996: 479). This produces the politics of food and sex as complex, ambiguous, not to say downright messy.

Following these considerations, I want to now turn to ways of putting the doubledness of sex and food to work: to use their enfolding as both analytic vectors and as sites of ethical becoming. From the various food-sex sites I have touched upon, it seems to me that those that work, those that send off new lines and beg new connections, are the ones motivated by what makes cooking, eating and sex all potent. For instance, the 'Eat Our Words' event (which I described earlier) produced unexpected connections. Following one speaker, and in the smoke break outside between courses, I listened as a group of young gay men struggled to think about the violence that their mothers had experienced in the confines of the suburban homes and kitchens of their youth. The women present reacted to these thoughts with encouragement and some restraint: none of us pointed out that the boys were stumbling on well-trodden feminist ground. In small ways, the connection of food and sex made possible other vectors, considerations of conduct not usually associated with 'queer pride'. In a spontaneous way, it provoked reflection on questions that are all too often separated out from those of sexuality per se. Of course, one cannot lay too much hope or weight on what was, after all, an event for the affluent. However placed within a network that includes charity dinners in aid of people living with AIDS, and the poor, and volunteer organizations that coordinate individuals who cook for home-ridden HIV sufferers, it is important to remember that this practical caring for strangers, friends and lovers coexists with the wilder manifestations of queer life. Here it does not make sense to say that food is more important than sex, or vice versa.

In fact, it brings home the practical, embedded and corporeal nature of thinking ethics, or an ethno-poetics of food and sex. My wager is that through food we may begin to formulate an ethics of living that works against the logics of categorization that now dominate much of the politics of identity. To return to my question of 'what's eating us', I want to be clear that food cannot simply supersede sex. Rather it is a way of retraining the ethical and political impulse that propelled much of queer theorization: the wish to make connections between our sexualities and our lives; the imperative not to be subsumed within sex. Thus for me food offers a way of returning to questions about pleasure within restraint, sympathy understood as a means of respecting the situatedness of identity. It also returns our attention to the forces that regulate our everyday lives: in short to a very practical figuring of an everyday ethics of living.

One of my favourite mistresses of the 'alimentary-sexual' as a guide for life is Alice B. Toklas. Beyond her *renom* for a piquant version of brownies, *Alice B. Toklas' Cookbook* embodies a sort of caring, translated as practical advice. In her eminently sensible way, Toklas tells us that 'the only way to learn to cook is to cook' (1995: 37). Along with being very good, her recipes are suggestive of a certain conduct; we glimpse through them the intermingling of bodies, nations, memories, war and love. As she roams over decades and constantly eddies around the love of Gertrude Stein, her book is completely informed by, and instructive of the role of restraint. Her golden rule is 'Respect for the inherent quality and flavour of each ingredient' (1995: 4). In culinary terms, as in others, this comes from considering seriously the qualities of each element before they are combined: 'This restraint, *le juste milieu* . . . the golden mean, is what makes . . . not only good cooks but good critics of food' (1995: 5). Of course, one can object that she and Stein were the products of a certain time and class, when good cooks had maids, and good critics like Stein had independent means, not to mention the company of the adoring Toklas. Nevertheless, her desire to train the palate reverberates with the wider themes I have been discussing. To extend Deleuze and Guattari's point, this is to recognize that while alimentary and sexual regimes regulate the 'interminglings of bodies in a society', how we practice *le juste milieu*, alimentary or sexual, is what allows for more ethical arrangements of bodies.

Thinking of the limits and possibilities provoked by this, in conclusion I want to draw on another representation of the sexual alimentary that flays food and sex into their composite dimensions, and then recombines them in suggestive ways. As many will remember, Dorothy Allison's wonderful short story 'A Lesbian Appetite' opens with an homage to biscuits, buttermilk, beans, pork fat, bacon and greens. With a scrumptious list of meals, she remembers her girlfriends by what they ate together. Later she will describe both the girls and the meals, but first she writes of the 'one lover who didn't want to eat at all. We didn't last long. The sex was good, but I couldn't think what to do with her when the sex was finished. We drank spring water together and fought a lot' (1988: 151–2).

Reflecting on this experience, Allison refuses to conflate sex and food. Rather, she uses food to trace out one direction, which then intersects with the tracing provided by sex. Yet another line is clearly and distinctly drawn as she tells of her childhood worry and shame that they were not getting enough vitamin D. A teacher instructs her that 'the children of the poor have a lack of brain tissue simply because they don't get the necessary vitamins at the right age' (1988: 156). The child is horrified by the image 'of my cousins, big-headed, watery-eyed, and stupid': 'We will drink milk, steal it if we must' (1988: 156). Like salt on an eggplant, with these images Allison draws out the meaning of food within poverty, and gives us a profound understanding of the connections between food, family, pride, shame and love.

In Allison's story, women are hungry for other women, for real Southern barbecue, coleslaw and hush puppies, for sex, for chocolate, for remembering (1988: 163). While 'A Lesbian Appetite' strikes me as a great deal more erotic than some of the current food-porn, it is also a deeply pedagogic tale of the ethics, the modes of living that food and sex can forge.

Her text strangely echoes or embodies Foucault's argument. If, as he argued, 'homosexuality . . . is an historic occasion to re-open affective and relational virtualities' (1984: 207), in Allison's tale affective and relational possibilities are embodied in the slow caress given to each detail, each ingredient, the sense of timing and movement so essential to eating, cooking, loving and being. Lest one think that this is only possible in an avowedly lesbian text, this exploration of timing and touch is also what makes the *Two Fat Ladies* so suggestive: food here is something to be felt, touched ('get those hands in there'), enquired after (who has grown it and can we go play with it on the hoof), cared for and ultimately eaten with appreciation. In short, food is the opportunity to explore the tangible links between what we eat, who we think we are, how and with whom we have sex, and what we are becoming. In short, what we have here are descriptions of the lines that can be wound between food, sex, bodies: an ethics of connection and disconnection between the various assemblages we inhabit.

To end, let me be clear that if I have argued that certain representations of food and sex belie the limits of sex as the sole optic through which to elaborate an ethics of existence, it should also be clear that I am not advocating the wholesale replacement of sex by food. On the contrary, what I have tried to suggest is that thinking *through* food to sex may make us 'infinitely more susceptible to pleasure'. Pleasure and ethics, sex and food are all about breaking up the strict moralities which constrain us. Just as 'food' must break open into production, preparation, exploitation, consumption, reading, writing, play and work, so too should sex fall apart. In articulating an alternative ethics of social connection between all those aspects that have been too summarily subsumed by sex, we need to proceed with respect for the inherent qualities of each element. Guided by the question of what is eating us, and the exigency of reflecting on our manners of living, this may also remind us of the necessity of enacting *le juste milieu*, a care for the self and for others guided by pleasure and restraint, in theory and in practice. It is an alimentary matter of common sense that delicacy and restraint make for good cooking; they are equally essential for an alternative ethics of existence.

Notes

The arguments presented here are further developed in my forthcoming book, *Visceral Citizens: Essays on Eating, Sex and Ethics*. My thanks for research assistance to Gill Dempsy, Michelle Imison and Megan Jones, and to the ARC for funding the project.

1. For a fascinating discussion of the range of uses of the cannibal, see the anthology, *Cannibalism and the Colonial World*, (Barker et al., 1998).
2. Elsewhere I take up Derrida's argument more fully in the context of the concept of citizenship, and Balibar's (1991) compelling analysis of equality (Probyn, forthcoming).

3. Of course, Adams is hardly representative of the more developed arguments on 'ethical eating'. As David Bell and Gill Valentine put it, 'Being a citizen of the world also means, for some people, eating only your share, and eating only what is ethical.' The push to 'green cuisine' is 'an important countercultural response to being in the world' (1997: 188). In Lisa Heldke's argument, this entails thinking of our relations with food as 'participatory', that 'acting in the world is a communal, relational activity – that we are in correspondence with, and are also responsive and responsible to, others in the world' (1992: 310). However, the confusion over sex and food reappears in Wendall Barry's summation that, 'Like industrial sex, industrial eating has become a degraded, poor, and paltry thing.' It follows for him that the contemporary eater is 'passive and uncritical – in short, a victim' (1992: 375).

References

Adams, Carole (1990) *The Sexual Politics of Meat: A Feminist Vegetarian Critical Theory*. New York: Continuum.

Allison, Dorothy (1988) 'A Lesbian Appetite', in *Trash*. Ithaca, NY: Firebrand.

Angel, Maria and Zoë Sofia (1996) 'Cooking Up: Intestinal Economies and the Aesthetics of Specular Orality', *Cultural Studies* 10(3): 464–82.

Appadurai, Arjun (1981) 'Gastro-Politics in Hindu South Asia', *American Ethnologist* 8: 494–511.

Balibar, Etienne (1991) 'The Subject Citizen', in Eduardo Cadava, Peter Connor and Jean-Luc Nancy (eds) *Who Comes After the Subject*. London and New York: Routledge.

Balibar, Etienne (1998) *Spinoza and Ethics*, trans. by Peter Snowdon. London: Verso.

Barker, Francis, Peter Hulme and Margaret Iverson (eds) (1998) *Cannibalism and the Colonial World*. Cambridge: Cambridge University Press.

Barry, Wendall (1992) 'The Pleasures of Eating', in Deane W. Curtin and Lisa M. Heldke (eds) *Cooking, Eating, Thinking: Transformative Philosophies of Food*. Bloomington: Indiana University Press.

Barthes, Roland (1979) 'Toward a Psychosociology of Contemporary Food Consumption', in R. Forster and O. Ranum (eds) *Food and Drink in Historical Selections from Annales*, vol. 5. Baltimore, MD: Johns Hopkins University Press. (Orig. 1961.)

Bell, David and Gill Valentine (1997) *Consuming Geographies: We Are Where We Eat*. London and New York: Routledge.

Carter, Angela (1979) 'Speculative Finale: The Function of Flesh', in her *The Sadeian Women: An Exercise in Cultural History*. London: Virago.

Deleuze, Gilles (1986) *Foucault*. Paris: Editions de Minuit.

Deleuze, Gilles (1994) 'Désir et plaisir', *Le Magazine Littéraire* 325 (October): 59–65.

Deleuze, Gilles and Félix Guattari (1991) *A Thousand Plateaus*, translated by Brian Massumi. Minneapolis: University of Minnesota Press.

Derrida, Jacques (1991) '"Eating Well", or the Calculation of the Subject: An Interview with Jacques Derrida', by Jean-Luc Nancy, in Eduardo Cadava, Peter Connor and Jean-Luc Nancy (eds) *Who Comes After the Subject*. London and New York: Routledge.

Dupleix, Jill (1994) *New Food: From the New Basics to the New Classics*. Port Melbourne: William Heinemann Australia.

Foucault, Michel (1984) 'Friendship as a Way of Life', trans. by John Johnston, in Sylvère Lotringer (ed.) *Foucault Live*. New York: Semiotext(e).

Foucault, Michel (1986) *The Use of Pleasure: The History of Sexuality, vol. 2*, trans. by Robert Hurley. New York: Vintage.

Foucault, Michel (1997) 'What is Enlightenment?', in Michel Foucault, *Ethics, Subjectivity and Truth*, ed. by Paul Rabinow. New York: The New Press.

Harmer, Wendy (1998) 'Rock 'n' Rollingpins', *HQ Magazine* March/April: 26–9.

Heldke, Lisa M. (1992) 'Food Politics, Political Food', in Deane W. Curtin and Lisa M. Heldke (eds) *Cooking, Eating, Thinking: Transformative Philosophies of Food*. Bloomington: Indiana University Press.

hooks, bell (1993) 'Eating the Other: Desire and Resistance', in b. hooks *Black Looks: Race and Representation*. Boston, MA: South End Press.

Hulme, Peter (1998) 'Introduction: The Cannibal Scene', in Francis Barker, Peter Hulme and Margaret Iverson (eds) *Cannibalism and the Colonial World*. Cambridge University Press.

Jaivin, Linda (1995) *Eat Me*. Melbourne: The Text Publishing Company.

Karpinski, Barbara (1998) 'Top Tart: Cream Queen Christine Manfield is Sydney's Mistress of the Kitchen', *Blue* Feb.: 84–8.

Laurent, Antoine (1989) *Cuisine Novella*. London: Paladin Books.

Paterson, Jennifer and Clarissa Dickson Wright (1998) *Two Fat Ladies Full Throttle*. London: Ebury Press.

Probyn, Elspeth (forthcoming) *Visceral: Sex, Eating & Ethics*. London: Sage.

Rabinow, Paul (1997) 'Introduction: The History of Systems of Thought', in Paul Rabinow (ed.) *Michel Foucault: Ethics, Subjectivity and Truth*. New York: The New Press.

Simmel, Georg (1994) 'The Sociology of the Meal', trans. by M. Symons, *Food and Foodways* 5(4): 345–50.

Symons, Michael (1994) 'Simmel's Gastronomic Sociology: An Overlooked Essay', *Food & Foodways* 5(4): 333–51.

Toklas, Alice B. (1995) *The Alice B. Toklas Cookbook*. Kent Town, SA: Wakefield Press. (Orig. pub. 1954.)

Two Fat Ladies: A Gastronomical Adventure (1997) An Optomen Production for BBC.

Waters, Alice (1982) *Chez Panisse Menu Cookbook*. New York: Random House.

Elspeth Probyn is Associate Professor and Head of the Department of Gender Studies at the University of Sydney. Her publications include *Sexing the Self: Gendered Positions in Cultural Studies* (Routledge, 1993), *Outside Belongings* (Routledge, 1996), and *Sexy Bodies: The Strange Carnalities of Feminism* (co-edited with Elizabeth Grosz, Routledge, 1995). Her forthcoming book is titled *Visceral: Sex, Eating & Ethics* (Sage), and she is completing a co-edited anthology on the politics of shame.

Playing it Again

Citation, Reiteration or Circularity?

Jan Campbell and Janet Harbord

THE IMPACT of Judith Butler's work on an expansive if somewhat curious range of academic subjects is undoubtedly great. Perhaps equally curious if less extensive is the impact of her work on psychoanalytic clinical practice; or, more accurately and to paraphrase Butler, the interest shown by some practitioners suggests at least a possible dialogue between clinical and speculative approaches to issues of gender identity. The question of why the influence of her work has been so pervasive raises general speculation about what makes some theories mobile while others remain grounded. It seems that the notion of movement and fluidity is part of the force of Butler's work, keeping definition on the move. It can also be said that this work has been timely. Butler's notion of the citation of the body has reconfigured and moved forward debates on sexuality and gender, debates which had, arguably, by the end of the 1980s, become caught in one of two mires: either the sociological separation of sex from gender, which polarized sexuality as the potentially radical force and gender as socially prescribed role, or the critical impasse of the sexual difference debates. In *Gender Trouble* (1990), the theory of gender as performative was elaborated using Austin's linguistic account of an effect produced in the announcement of its presence or naming. Tracing this effect into the arena of sex/gender identity, gender, Butler argues, is produced or brought into being as it is 'announced' in and through the stylized rituals and repetitions of everyday life. These practices retroactively, and over time, create a (gender) identity effect. What is most challenging about Butler's account is that the theatricality of the performative process applies not only to the scenarios of drag, the most 'obvious' sites of cross-gender identifications, but the theatrical acts of mimesis circle back to the centre, to insist that all gender identification is constituted through the imitative process. Femininity and masculinity are

■ *Theory, Culture & Society* 1999 (SAGE, London, Thousand Oaks and New Delhi), Vol. 16(2): 229–239
[0263-2764(199904)16:2;229–239;008263]

but imitations of an imitation with no original. Thus, heterosexuality is pushed from its pedestal of providing the origin of sexual roles.

In subsequent work Butler has pursued the connections between psychoanalysis and performativity, and performativity and melancholia, to rewrite the resolution of the oedipal complex. Identification is not as Freud suggested the process, or not the singular process, that delimits our desires and defines the bounds of the ego. Invoking the more Kleinian notion that the mourning of loss is the recognition of separation and difference, Butler focuses on mourning as one of the constitutive processes of ego formation. Conversely, the inability to grieve for the objects of love which our culture compels us to renounce, according to Butler, produces a 'culture of gender melancholy in which masculinity and femininity emerge as the traces of an ungrieved and ungrievable love'. Thus, the trajectory from performativity to melancholia takes us through a tour of psychoanalytic sites that lead to a conclusion of sorts. Not that homosexuality is inverted within the hierarchy, appearing as the healthy side of the binary after all, but that articulating a coherent gender identity, whether assumed by gay or straight subjects, comes at a cost.

But to skip ahead in this way misses the highlights of the tour, and the complexity of the arguments presented. A disavowed homosexuality is explained by Butler via a return to Freud's essay 'Mourning and Melancholia'. Here, Freud describes melancholic identity as an identification that is disavowed and therefore incorporated lastingly as an unresolved other to the self. For Butler a taboo against homosexuality *precedes* the incest taboo. It is not the oedipal prohibition of the mother as love object that is primary, but an identificatory love of the same-sex parent that is forbidden: the homosexual cathexis. Because of this prohibition the lost object of love, which is the mother for the girl and the father for the boy, become incorporated as a melancholic other. The girl takes on the identificatory aspects of her mother in her melancholic denial that she has lost her. Similarly for the boy with the father. The more extreme the heterosexual identification the greater the degree of melancholia. The resolution to the oedipal complex thus leads to an identification with the same-sexed parent, where the child in effect becomes the lost loved one (the mother or father) by incorporating and preserving the loss within the self.

This is a compelling argument for the construction of gender identity, where gender identification and the ensuing effects of 'identity' are a result of the prohibition and internalization of the homosexual aim and object. Butler's account of melancholia is close to a Kleinian exposition of ambivalence within the object relation, although within her analysis it would be overt heterosexuality rather than homosexuality that would constitute the more defensive, split position. Homosexuality in Butler's account expresses a much more acknowledged gender ambivalence than heterosexuality. This is because a homosexual disposition, rather than a heterosexual, displays all the maturity, separation and loss associated with the mourning of the depressive position. Heterosexuality, rather than homosexuality, is placed within the more unmediated melancholic space where loss remains unacknowledged and therefore incorporated. For the homosexual, because the love object is *acknowledged* as lost, it can be found and located again in relation to the external world. Within this re-reading, rigid heterosexuality is then a more defensive position than homosexuality, ruled not just by melancholia, but also by paranoia and hate. The importance of this account, if it is pushed to its extremity, is the reversal of a normative psychoanalytical account of sex/gender 'development', represented most explicitly by the object-relations model, where homosexuality, and in particular female homosexuality, is viewed as vulnerable to the psychosis of a merging maternal body. Butler in this sense can be seen to reverse Kristeva's conceptualization of the female homosexual relation as abject and outside of the paternal symbolic.

While Butler effectively reconfigures Freud's text on mourning and melancholia, and in so doing rewrites the oedipal structure itself, her re-reading of Lacan, and particularly the symbolic law, produces less of a shift of frameworks than a disruption of the paradigm from within. Perhaps the most effective challenge that she makes to the Lacanian symbolic is to deploy a Foucauldian notion of the productive possibilities of power to counter the rigid prohibitions of the law. Key to this argument is the thesis that in order to be intelligible, the law compels certain repetitions, the remaking of (gender) identity as an ongoing series of repetitious acts that become sedimented as the linear effects of identity. Yet at the same time, in being dependent on repetitious acts of renewal, the law produces possibilities of alternative or even transgressive practices and performances. Butler reads the subversion of the law, through say homosexual transgression, as much a product of the law as its more repressive counterpart – normative heterosexuality. Thus, the law or incest taboo is not just juridical, it is also generative. This effectively historicizes the Lacanian symbolic by subjecting it to the forces of change. It adds a contingency that allows for both the sexual difference that the law repressively institutes, as well as the more generative transgressive desires it produces. Desires produced by the law also threaten its singularity and immutability.

But how far does the juridical law actually become displaced through Butler's more performative reading? In *Gender Trouble*, gender identity is described as a 'stylised repetition of acts'. The end of this book is upbeat; the task Butler reminds us is 'not whether to repeat but how to repeat, or indeed to repeat and, through a radical proliferation of gender, *to displace*, the very gender norms that enable the repetition itself'. This is an ending to which Butler has made a return. Optimists, or readers who do not want to struggle with the density of Butler's prose, have inadvertently understood the performativity of gender as a somewhat simple and willed act of cross-dressing. If we don't like or want to be one identity we can perform and act another. But as Butler makes increasingly clear in her next book, *Bodies that Matter*, performativity is not a singular 'act', with some free agency of choice or subjectivity lying behind it (Butler, 1993). Indeed, 'agency' is only to be located in the circumstance of activities, caught up in different historical forms of repetition.

The question of agency is one that has troubled Foucault's account of power, and in *Bodies that Matter* the question is given a fuller treatment. Using a Derridean notion of citational practice, together with Foucault's notion of a material law (that both produces and prohibits bodies), Butler re-emphasizes a more cautious and conservative limit to her performativity thesis. As a process performativity acts us, and cannot be seen in terms of willed resistance or transgression of the law. Like Foucault's notion that power constructs that which it then sanctions, performativity is a material activity constructing us. We cannot displace the law by any notion of a voluntary subject. For Butler performativity is a citation of power effects that makes the subject's opposition to power (and the law) completely complicit with it. This does not mean that there is *no* agency, simply that it cannot occupy an external position:

> Although this constitutive constraint does not foreclose the possibility of agency, it does locate agency as a reiterative or rearticulatory practice, immanent to power, and not a relation of external opposition to power. (Butler, 1993: 15)

What is seemingly offered here is a theory of deconstruction that can break down oppositions between the prohibitions of language, sanctioned by the law, and the excluded matter of bodies, a theory that moves beyond the linguistic monism of Lacan to articulate a discursive and material practice of sexuality. But how far can Butler actually go in reiterating discursive structures of power differently, if change and difference in the symbolic is always so reversibly collapsed into its normative and prohibitive counterpart?

The brilliance and the frustrating difficulty with Butler's work is that she at times seems to be saying so little and at others so much. This is perhaps an effect of the discursive style developed in and through her work which in many ways performs the condition that is described. The style of her text is itself repetitive and interrogative, repeatedly circling back and moving over ground once again, or constructing in an interrogative form concise challenges to theoretical paradigms which are not explicitly answered. In such a way her text enacts a repetition of dominant theories, such as those of Freud and Lacan, but reiterates them differently, moving into the gaps and ellipses that repetition allows. Thus her work offers a reworking of dominant paradigms that at moments may appear simply as repetition, heavily weighted with a kind of debt to the critics and traditions of poststructuralism that seem to act as a break or obstacle to her more radical theorizations. This, of course, can be seen as a strength or weakness depending on where you situate yourself, not just in terms of poststructuralist thinking, but also individual preferences for Lacan, Foucault, Irigaray and Derrida.

The criticism of how much of a challenge performativity can effect, however, may be developed as a more substantial challenge in relation to the question of the symbolic, its status, fixity and reach. Can the symbolic move, is it in history and therefore open to the force of temporality and thus change? If Butler's theory only accounts for a singular dominant symbolic, where does this leave the abjected subjects of the bodies that precisely do not matter within this realm? This is a contentious issue that has never found any one resolution within feminism, but which also has pressing implications for the discourses both of 'race' and sexuality. While some forms of feminism have found the Lacanian symbolic a compelling account of the compulsory apparatus of heterosexuality, others have regarded it as a critical impasse which denies historical forces of change. In addition, beyond providing an account of the reproduction of femininity and masculinity, the symbolic fails to explicate the exceptions to that normative trajectory, for example lesbian and gay subjectivity. Butler's critical import has been to suggest a reconfiguration and questionable usefulness of the symbolic from the inside, as it were, in a theory of the process of resignification. However, beyond accounting for the normative, the symbolic continues to present a problem of historical accountability for the femme, femininity and indeed 'race'.

It is worth briefly exploring three different readings of the symbolic in order to mark out the difference and blindness of each. The first is the Lacanian account itself, presenting the immovable 'rock' of the Lacanian real as a cornerstone of identity but which is out of sight. The symbolic is then the *fait accompli* of the phallic law to which women are subject, simultaneously represented and erased *as subjects*. The second is the argument for an alternative symbolic that exists in relation to the dominant, perhaps best exemplified by Irigaray's work. Irigaray does not argue for a re-deployment of an oedipal symbolic, but articulates the difficulty and the need to represent the abjected feminine within language as something other than the excluded; her definition is a female symbolic (Irigaray, 1993). The third reading is Butler's account in which it is not possible to represent other narratives within the symbolic; one can merely stretch and reconfigure the terms of the law through reiteration. Crudely, these three accounts can be seen to be in dialogue with each other, and in a sense, to mark the shifts and breaks between positions over recent years.

However, Butler's theory of citation puts certain constraints on the possibilities of a reworking of the symbolic. For, while it is possible to follow the logic of her argument through the cross-signification of gender across the body in terms of drag kings and queens, it leaves the feminine, either lesbian or straight, as uncitable. If the feminine is already signified as masquerade within the dominant, how can this subject position become doubly so? Butler's response would perhaps be that cross-gender citation produces effects within and across the whole domain of the symbolic, so for example, the citation of femininity by men in drag serves to denaturalize all femininity, and by implication, masculinity. However, it could equally be argued that the effects of citation are highly ambivalent and could produce the reverse effects of naturalizing a dominant femininity while returning such citation as drag to the status of an unintelligible abject. In a sense, Butler's argument, in support of Foucault's productive power, chooses to place a critical emphasis not on the force of repression but on the instability of the process of reiteration. But the forces, of both exclusion and reiteration, are but different sides of the same coin. Therefore, both repression and instability constitute the *process* of identity trans/formation as movement, a process which refuses fixity. Pursuing this reading of Butler, there is reason to be optimistic about the possibility of change.

The argument for an effective performativity is perhaps more convincing in relation to the phallus where the relocation of 'power' across the body provides a distinct challenge to the existing normative structure. And if the only way 'abject' bodies can have an impact on the existing phallic structure is through a reiteration of a male imaginary and symbolic, this is surely an indication of the asymmetrical nature of the project and its critical limits. In 'The Lesbian Phallus' and 'Phantasmatic Identification', in *Bodies that Matter*, Butler follows Lacan's argument and turns it round by suggesting that if the phallus as symbol can be detached from the imaginary and the bodily part (the penis), then it is infinitely transferable (an argument that has some affinity with De Lauretis's theory of the phallus as fetish). By implication it can symbolize multiple bodily parts. The lesbian phallus therefore works by displacing the privileged phallus, and symbolizing other body parts: instead of the penis/phallus the lesbian phallus can represent, for example, the breast or the clitoris. Butler rescues lesbian sexuality from its abject position by transporting the lesbian body into a realm of patriarchal language and signifiers. This is then a question of naming. Butler doesn't change language, she changes its referent. Crossing over between having and being the phallus, and between castration anxiety and penis envy, the lesbian phallus can signify both masculine and feminine sex and in effect can remove the distinction between them. Such an imaginary blurs the question of heterosexual difference based on distinct 'masculine' and 'feminine' morphologies.

In deconstructing the Lacanian opposition of being/having the phallus, Butler also reconfigures yet another cornerstone of the Freudian oedipal scenario whereby the distinction between wanting to be and wanting to have is seen to structure the formation of desire. In 'Phantasmatic Identification', Butler explains that identifications are imaginary, but not opposed to desire. Recalling her thinking on melancholia, identifications are melancholic disavowed desires. There is then no actual distinction between identification and desire. This breaks down the fundamental oedipal division between the imaginary and the symbolic. Drawing on the work of Laplanche and Pontalis, Butler rewrites identification as a phantasmatic staging of the event rather than the occasion of an event or act, thus allowing a greater degree of fluidity in terms of the positioning of the subject. The notion of the phantasmatic is important here, for it is a staging of a number of fantasies that converge at one site which refuses the coherence of the law of prohibition. If the symbolic is the normative dimension of the constitution of the sexed subject within language, then the subject only attains this coherence as the result of excluding and abjecting the possibilities of the phantasmatic. The taking up of positions, as either desiring to have (the phallus) or to be (the phallus), is far more precarious than the Freudian and Lacanian accounts would suggest.

While Butler's point here is the need to recognize that which is excluded in the process of forming coherent (if unstable) identifications, the end of the essay on phantasmatic identification issues a warning against a humanistic tendency of inclusion. Phantasmatic identification is not a denial of difference, warns Butler, which is after all the legacy of an imperialist past. Rather, it is a recognition of the cost of rigidly occupying exclusionary identities. Yet, the spectre of exclusion raised here is not one which is so easily laid to rest within, or reconciled to, the larger project. For the discourse of 'race' exists at the periphery of the performative, never fully explicated within its terms nor shown to re-articulate the strategy for its own ends. The possibility of race as a performative is raised in a number of essays, perhaps most directly in 'Gender is Burning' and 'Passing, Queering: Nella Larsen's Psychoanalytic Challenge' (Butler, 1993), where the sexualization of racial ideals and the racialization of sexual ideals are addressed. While Butler announces the need for each to be articulated through one another, it is unclear precisely what form this will take. Certainly Larsen's *Passing* demonstrates the imbrication of ethnicity and gender in the process of eroticization, and the strength of the force of regulation that bears upon the desire to pass both as white and as heterosexual. Yet what relationship sexual and racial passing have to one another is undecided from this account. Whether or not the theory of the performative can be mapped onto 'race' is an area that requires further elucidation.

It is worth outlining briefly here one of the most stimulating theorizations of race as a performative offered by Homi Bhabha's account of mimicry and the colonized subject (Bhabha, 1994). Where the masquerade describes an unconscious performance of a role, mimicry can describe a more conscious ironic parodying of a part, yet the degree of intentionality and readability is precisely the ambivalence that characterizes the practice. Drawing on Fanon's work, Bhabha argues that mimicry is neither the subversion of the colonial subject nor an identificatory collusion with him, but remains ambiguously along the spectrum between these terms. For mimicry can in the worst instance describe the internalization of abjection projected onto the colonized subject, and at best ironize through reiteration the terms of the imperial conquest, the demand to be both like and different from the dominant subject. Like Butler's account of the narcissism of the phallic subject, mimicry reveals the contours of desire and paranoia that operate through the relation between the dominant and the dominated. But for Bhabha, what mimicry importantly reveals is the limits to the knowledge of otherness. At the heart of mimicry is an ambivalence; it may signify an identification with the dominant, or mask the language of the other, raising the spectre that this seeming 'identification' may indeed be parody. For what the colonizing subject confronts in these moments of terror is the possibility of an-other, a difference that suggests the potential existence of other symbolics. Bhabha's point that hate and paranoia are defensive positions of the dominant connects with Butler's characterization of the defensive melancholy of normative heterosexuality.

Clearly, this account of mimicry shares affinities with Butler's performative in the recognition that the dependency of the dominant on reiteration and repetition is also potentially the point of instability. Yet, in contrast, Bhabha's account can be read to suggest a difference that cannot be signified at all within the dominant terms and which will always remain a threatening possibility and indecipherable presence at the edges of the dominant discourse. It is interesting that in *Excitable Speech*, Butler returns to this question of difference in relation to Toni Morrison's 1993 Nobel Lecture in Literature (Butler, 1997a). Butler's interest here is in the performativity of language, and more specifically of how to account for the kinds of injury that language performs. In the lecture Morrison presents a parable in which language appears as a 'living thing', a bird in the hands of some young children. The children use the bird as a cruel joke by asking a blind woman to guess whether the bird is alive or dead. The woman's response is to refuse and redirect the question by replying that she does not know, 'but what I do know is that it is in your hands' (Butler, 1997a: 6). In Morrison's interpretation of the metaphor the woman is a writer and the bird is language, a living thing that is susceptible to death. The point of the woman's response is that the attempt to humiliate and capture her within the terms of their joke is turned back on them by calling attention to the instrument through which that act of cruelty is exercised.

For Butler, the parable is rich in interpretive possibilities, but her point here is that the context of speech and the system of language itself are not the only or defining conditions of an utterance. The relation between speech and its effects is inseparable from the body and speech: 'If the speaker addresses his or her body to the one addressed, then it is not merely the body of the speaker that comes into play: it is the body of the addressee as well' (Butler, 1997a: 12). The blind woman's reference to the hands of the children refers the question back to the position from which it is asked. Thus, for Butler, while the discourse of the other may appear to be within the domain of the dominant subject, it also always implicates the conditions of that relation, conditions that are instituted bodily. Butler reads this parable with a broader purview to argue that speech, and naming in particular, constitute or bring into being other subjects as well as performing injuries. It is an argument once again for the necessary recognition that the subordinated subject can create effects within the symbolic. Yet Morrison's parable also gestures to a position that remains exterior, a site of excess; it is from this position of exteriority that the subordinated subject is able to recognize, and effectively denaturalize what is proffered as 'reality'. Blindness may be interpreted not only as a disempowerment, a disability, but also as a different reading of the world, a different language. Such a different language is not therefore essentialist as it retains a relation to the socio-symbolic. But as another more bodily narrative, it provides a different reading of the abject. As Morrison's famous work *Beloved* shows, the abject can exist as a sign excluded and unnamed within a dominant, colonial symbolic, but its historicity also occupies another place elsewhere, that can creatively name and represent the subordinated body (Morrison, 1987).

Interestingly, this returns to the critique that Butler presents against Irigaray and the notion of other symbolics. Irigaray's insistent demand for the representation of female experience as another symbolic is rejected by Butler on the grounds that it invokes an explicitly feminine reality that operates to exclude others, such as black subjects. Yet, there is a sense in which Irigaray's project is closer to Toni Morrison's in her recognition of an exteriority that remains excluded by the terms of the dominant (appearing only as abject). This is not to argue that parallel worlds exist side by side; certainly, as the parable infers, the dominant attempt to colonize and abject difference is a repetitive condition of the law's existence. What both Irigaray's and Morrison's work suggests is that different psychic realities may be incommensurate, in excess of each other.

This is a point that has been raised most poignantly in a debate between Rosi Braidotti and Judith Butler in the journal *differences*, in which the question of the possibility of more than one symbolic is answered differently (Braidotti, 1994). Butler, for instance, questions the separability of the symbolic from the social, daring to ask whether the symbolic is not merely a 'reification of a social formation'. But this radical suggestion does not lead her to envisage a more plural frame to the symbolic. On the contrary, Butler sees the symbolic as an 'ideality of regulatory power', that limits or sets what can be elected or represented. Braidotti, on the other hand, clearly envisages different theories of the symbolic that we can, and are forced to, move between. For her, regulatory power is not confined to the symbolic domain and exists in a dynamic process between relational terms: between the symbolic, imaginary and real (for Lacan), or between the symbolic, imaginary and political (for Irigaray). If we consider Butler's valuable point that the symbolic is a reification of the social, but also that the social must exceed the symbolic, then bodies that matter do not just exist as an excluded sign within a dominant symbolic, they also exist in another narrative or psychic reality elsewhere. Butler brilliantly deconstructs and reiterates the ruling realm of the phallus, but her hesitation in acknowledging any other narratives to the phallogocentric text leaves an analysis of political otherness in terms of race and the feminine largely unaccounted for.

In her most recent book *The Psychic Life of Power*, these unaccounted differences are perhaps more historically represented. Here Butler returns to the question of melancholia, considering it not just as a psychic economy, but as 'the production of the circuitry of melancholia as part of the operation of regulatory power' (Butler, 1997b: 143). Developing her reversal of a Kleinian argument, Butler argues that heterosexuality not homosexuality refuses the depressive position and is thus characterized by all the idealization, aggression and incorporation so reminiscent of paranoid splitting. It is the performative 'acting out' by certain forms of queer activism that can undo such bounded straight melancholia. In this reversal queer identity represents the more healthy and negotiated *performance and mourning* of a depressive position that can acknowledge sameness and difference. But if a certain, rigid masculinity and femininity are seen as constructed, defensive positions ('I will be the gender that I cannot desire or grieve the loss of'), then is homosexuality a similar denial of heterosexual difference and loss? Butler suggests that there might be other 'equally compelling accounts' of the unconscious that do not necessitate the repudiation of heterosexuality. Such plural and blurred unconscious accounts of sexuality do indeed suggest a beyond to the oedipal injunction of sexual difference. Butler's question, 'But why is primary sexual difference the guarantor of loss in our psychic lives?' is a crucial one (Butler, 1997b: 165). And her theorization of melancholia as founding the subject challenges the assumption that the subject is brought into being through the 'straight' injunction of oedipal symbolic law.

What Butler's work offers, then, is a renewed concept of subject formation, predicated not on the primacy of sexual difference but on the narrative of melancholic loss. Following Michel Borsch-Jacobsen's argument that the subject is formed through a mimetic identification *between* ego and object, Butler stresses that it is the primary and social loss of the object that undoes the ego and creates the subject. This melancholic undoing of the ego is an internal disavowal of loss, coupled with rage which becomes deflected away from the social world and internalized, directed back against the ego (as a death wish). In this same way regulatory power and language become psychically internalized and 'turned' back on to the ego, as a lost object that paradoxically and melancholically constructs the subject. However positively this melancholia is worked through, whether by mourning or an externalization and acknowledgement of rage, at the heart of psychic life exists not identity, but ambivalence and loss.

Butler's latest book is a lucid account that interweaves psychoanalysis with Hegel, Foucault, Nietzsche and Althusser, demonstrating how power works through the operation of conscience to construct the subject. This social and psychic theorization of subjectivity displaces the hegemonic primacy of sexual difference, putting in its place an unconscious modality of ambivalence, loss and power. Moving away from the circularity of the phallogocentric text, the trajectory of Butler's work arcs in one direction toward the arena of ethics. Her emphasis on 'working through' the mourning and rage of a melancholic subjectivity seems to suggest that the violent incorporated relation to the other can make way for a more ethical recognition of alterity and difference. Grief undoes the ego, but does not destroy it; survival is not the finding of an identity, but an acknowledgement of what she calls the 'historicity of loss'. Internalization of the social other, then, does not always have to 'take the form of a mercilessly violent conscience' (Butler, 1997b: 195). Perhaps this also suggests that the violent 'turning' and incorporation of power that founds the subject can be at some level negotiated.

References

Bhabha, H. (1994) *The Location of Culture*. London and New York: Routledge.

Braidotti, R. (1994) 'Feminism by any Other Name', an interview with Judith Butler, *differences: A Journal of Feminist Cultural Studies* 6(2–3): 27–63.

Butler, J. (1990) *Gender Trouble: Feminism and the Subversion of Identity*. New York and London: Routledge.

Butler, J. (1993) *Bodies that Matter: On the Discursive Limits of 'Sex'*. New York and London: Routledge.

Butler, J. (1997a) *Excitable Speech: A Politics of the Performative*. New York and London: Routledge.

Butler, J. (1997b) *The Psychic Life of Power: Theories in Subjection*. Stanford, CA: Stanford University Press.

Freud, S. (1917) 'Mourning and Melancholia', in The Standard Edition, Vol. 14.

Irigaray, L. (1993) 'Divine Women', in *Sexes and Genealogies*. New York: Columbia University Press.

Larsen, Nella (1992) 'Passing', pp. 163–276 in C. Larsen (ed.) *An Intimation of Things Distant: The Collected Fiction of Nella Larsen*. New York: Anchor Books.

Morrison, T. (1987) *Beloved*. London: Chatto and Windus.

Jan Campbell teaches at the School of Cultural and Community Studies, at the University of Sussex.

Janet Harbord teaches at the School of English, Culture and Communication, Middlesex University.

Index